Library of
Davidson College

VOID

WORLD FINANCE AND ADJUSTMENT

By the same author

THE INTERNATIONAL MONETARY SYSTEM AND THE LESS DEVELOPED COUNTRIES

THE QUEST FOR ECONOMIC STABILIZATION: The IMF and the Third World (*with Tony Killick, Jennifer Sharpley and Mary Sutton*)

WORLD FINANCE AND ADJUSTMENT

An Agenda for Reform

Graham Bird

St. Martin's Press New York

© Graham Bird 1985

332.04
B618W

All rights reserved. For information, write:
St. Martin's Press, Inc., 175 Fifth Avenue, New York, NY 10010
Printed in Hong Kong
Published in the United Kingdom by The Macmillan Press Ltd.
First published in the United States of America in 1985

ISBN 0–312–89125–3

Library of Congress Cataloging in Publication Data
Bird, Graham R.
World finance and adjustment.
Bibliography: p.
Includes index.
1. International finance. 2. Monetary policy.
3. Balance of payments. I. Title.
HG3881.B538 1985 332'.042 85–2157
ISBN 0–312–89125–3

86-4123

To my family

Contents

List of Tables

Preface and Acknowledgements

My experience is that writing a book is not easy. The contraction of university resources and the related increase in teaching and administrative loads, combined with the expansion of family size, has meant that writing has had to be more and more tightly squeezed in between lectures, meetings, picking up children, dropping off children and a range of other activities. Although all this can make life much more fun, it does exact its toll. If the chapters in this book read at all coherently it must come close to being the eighth wonder of the world!

That the book has been completed reflects the debt I owe to a number of people who helped by providing me with time to write it and by commenting on various sections of it, or providing me with their views. Into the former category come my wife, Heather, my parents-in-law, Hazel and Gordon Gage, and Christine Elliott; into the latter category come Heather Bird, Gerry Helleiner, Nick Hope, Tony Killick, Tony Thirlwall, John Williamson and a number of IMF staff members who might be embarrassed if I mentioned their names. To my children Alan and Anne I owe the debt of making the financial incentive to write the book more relevant, and to my third child, on his way at the time of writing this book, but now arrived and named Simon, I owe the debt of providing me with an effective time-constraint!

I should also acknowledge the forbearance of my students over the years at the University of Surrey and at Tufts University in London, who have acted as guinea pigs for me to try out various ideas. In fact it has been in teaching international finance to them that I have become aware of the need for a book such as this one.

I must also thank Debbie Horwood for typing the chapters so efficiently. She has, fortunately for me, developed the skill of reading my handwriting better than I can. That the book has an index is thanks to Jane Redfearn, who compiled it in record time.

Guildford GRAHAM BIRD

1 Introduction

This is a policy-oriented book on international finance. Rather than attempting to be completely comprehensive, it sets out to provide a succinct treatment of some of the more important issues that have come to dominate discussions of international financial reform. Given the increasingly frequent calls that have been made for a new Bretton Woods conference to reform existing international financial arrangements, it seems appropriate to examine the items that would be on the agenda for such a conference, and this is the book's principal objective.

It is intended to fulfil two basic functions. The first is to act as a complement to the more conventional textbooks, which spend most of their time comprehensively analysing the operation of the international monetary system. By concentrating on the key policy issues this book will, it is hoped, bring such analysis to life. The second is as a text in its own right for those courses where the wish is to avoid excessive amounts of analytical rigour and modelling and concentrate on policy, or where, within the context of a broader course, it is felt desirable to cover some of the international financial issues that nowadays hardly ever seem to be out of the headlines. As such it may also be of some interest to policy-makers.

The book is written in a style that makes the material genuinely available to those with only a sparse background in economics. Indeed non-specialists should be perfectly able to cope with most of it. No mathematical formulations are used and economic jargon is kept to a minimum. However, readers who possess a sound grasp of international monetary analysis will find plenty of opportunities to apply it. To them it should be clear where a particular piece of analysis underlies the discussion in the text, even if this is not spelled out.

The book is not intended to be the sole textbook for a specialist final year undergraduate option in international financial economics, since some issues that should be included in such a text are neglected here, the analysis used is not always fully presented or followed through, and there is not a full set of references to the literature. On the other hand, the book's contents should be directly relevant to such a course as well as to courses in international relations, economic development, monetary economics, and applied economics. This is not a book that students should find difficult to read – an important consideration, given the increasing amounts of knowledge they are expected to assimilate.

The lack of analytical rigour should perhaps be underlined. There are no mathematical models derived and very few diagrams presented, partly because there are already a number of international economics textbooks which go over this material and there seemed little point in duplicating it here, but also because the policy orientation of the book does not easily lend itself to this sort of approach. Often having spent a long time setting up a model and analysing its implications, one then has to recognise that while looking rigorous it is actually of limited assistance in analysing the real world. To have included a formal presentation of all the models that are implicitly drawn upon would have made the book excessively long, and would have robbed it of what are perhaps its principal attractions. Besides, considerable insight into the complexities and excitement of international financial economics can be gained without the need for equations galore.

The layout of the book is as follows. Part I sets the scene. Chapter 2 catalogues the performance of the world economy in the last ten or fifteen years and discusses the various explanations of events that have been put forward. Chapter 3 charts and analyses the evoluation of the international financial system, pointing to the significant changes that have occurred since the end of the 1960s and the disarray that currently exists. Chapter 4 builds on this to present an agenda upon which discussion of reform might be based. The remainder of the book then picks up the items on this agenda.

Part II concentrates on liquidity issues. Chapter 5 looks at the ways in which reserves may be created, discusses the role of gold, dollars, SDRs and multiple reserve assets, and examines the question of the adequacy of international reserves. However, countries can finance expenditure not only by running down their reserves but also by borrowing, and the importance of the short-term capital market has become a central feature of the world economy in the 1970s and 1980s. Chapter 6 analyses this market and discusses in particular the role of the commercial banks in providing balance of payments financing. In addition to the private sector, the chapter discusses the role of the official sector in the shape of the International Monetary

Fund. Although commercial international financial flows are important, the part played by concessionary flows should not be ignored. Chapter 7, therefore, examines the question of foreign aid. Part II concludes with a chapter which investigates a central problem associated with borrowing, namely debt.

Part III moves on to examine international adjustment. Chapter 9 provides a relatively lengthy treatment of the need for and choice of adjustment policy within individual countries. However, it also broadens out this discussion to examine international adjustment in a global context. Of course one of the principal changes in the world monetary system has been the move over from essentially fixed to more flexible exchange rates since 1973. Chapter 10 provides an assessment of the different exchange rate regimes. Again the choice of exchange rate regime must be an important item on any agenda for reform.

Part IV looks at certain aspects of the political economy of international financial reform. Chapter 11 discusses the interests of different countries and country groupings but concentrates in particular on the interests of developing countries, since this has been an important theme in the north-south discussion that has been a feature of the 1970s and 1980s. Chapter 12 examines the role of the principal institutions operating in the international financial sphere. Again to reflect the current debate, the chapter concentrates on the IMF, but also makes references to the World Bank and the commercial banks.

There is no concluding chapter presenting a summary statement of the reforms that 'should' be made. However, there can be little doubt that in the preceding chapters certain preferences show through from time to time. Instead it is part of the exercise that the reader should be allowed to draw her or his own conclusions.

Although the chapters are interrelated, they can all be read as independent units. This is a book that can either be read as a whole or dipped into as inclination dictates. Additional notes at the end of the book elaborate on or qualify certain points raised in the text, but these have been kept to a minimum to avoid interrupting the 'flow' of the chapters and on the suspicion that such notes are usually ignored in any case. Each chapter is also provided with a 'further reading' list (see p. 332). Given the contents of the book and its intended market this would seem to be more useful than providing a long list of references which might look impressive but would probably be of rather limited relevance to the reader. Experience with what can realistically be expected of undergraduates has resulted in these sections being rather brief and therefore far from comprehensive.

One final point needs to be made. Given the unavoidable lag in publication, much of the data in this book and some of the institutional arrangements referred to will be considerably out of date by the time it arrives on the bookshelves. The intervening period may or may not alter the relevance of some of the arguments put forward. Rather than just passively reading the book, readers should actively take it upon themselves to update the empirical and institutional sections and look carefully at what changes have taken place. Fortunately sources are plentiful and fairly easily accessible, and this task should not be too onerous.

Part I
The Background to Reform

2 World Economic Performance: Facts, Theories and Controversies

1. INTRODUCTION

Just when towards the end of the 1960s observers in many parts of the world thought that the problem of maintaining satisfactory economic performance had been largely solved, events during the 1970s changed to such an extent that few people, if any, would now argue that the performance of the world economy has been satisfactory subsequently. Even such a general statement as this raises a myriad of questions. For example, was economic performance in fact so good during the 1950s and 1960s or is our view of those years tinged by undeserved nostalgia? If performance was good, how can we explain it? Can the performance of these years be regarded as the norm from which the seventies and early eighties are an annoying but temporary aberration, or were the fifties and sixties a special case? In what sense has recent global economic performance been unsatisfactory, and what may be done to improve matters? There is sufficient material here to fill many books, let alone pages. We are, therefore, forced to be selective and to ignore many of the relevant issues.

Recognising such constraints, this chapter attempts to provide an overview of the performance of the world economy since the early 1970s. Section 2 sets out the indicators that will be used to assess performance. Section 3 applies these indicators to the post-war period, focusing in particular on the period since 1973. Section 4 provides a number of explanations of the facts observed. Section 5 briefly discusses the world economic outlook, though pointing out how difficult it is to forecast this with any meaningful degree of precision, and then goes on to introduce and review the range of policy options that are, in principle, available to help improve the world's economic performance.

2. INDICATORS FOR ASSESSING ECONOMIC PERFORMANCE

Just as physicians judge the health of patients by examining such indicators as blood pressure and pulse rate, so economists monitor the health of economies by examining a range of economic indicators. Any list of such indicators can be extended in a seemingly endless fashion. Of course the choice of what indicators to include and exclude is very important. Politicians wishing to support their own case and denigrate that of the opposition will be very careful to select those indicators which show them in the best possible light. While in most cases the indicators they publicise may not actually lie – though in some instances, no doubt, the data may be heavily massaged – they are not intended to tell the whole truth.

Even where the selection of indicators is not politically motivated, there is legitimate academic debate over which indicators give the most accurate picture of economic performance. Thus, some economists may stress the importance of domestic credit creation as the prime or indeed almost exclusive criterion by which economic performance may be evaluated. Others will argue that this is far too narrow and needs to be complemented or even replaced by indicators that monitor the performance of the 'real' rather than the 'financial' sector of the economy. They prefer indicators which more closely reflect the ultimate objectives of economic activity.

Reference to objectives provides one way out of the dilemma of selecting indicators, since there is a reasonable degree of consensus over the principal macroeconomic objectives of most societies. These include the avoidance of rapid price inflation, excessive unemployment and stagnation, and the maintenance of balance of payments equilibrium.

However, even this list subtlely reflects changing aspirations. Only relatively few years ago the objectives would have been stated more positively and would have normally stressed the achievement of price *stability, full* employment and economic *growth.* The effect of events on aspirations and thereby on the subsequent evaluation of the events is an intriguing issue not limited in relevance to the sphere of economics.

If agreement can be reached on the objectives, then economic performance can be assessed in terms of the extent to which they are achieved. According to this approach the simultaneous existence of high unemployment, rapid inflation, stagnation, and balance of payments disequilibrium would be evidence of poor economic performance. However, the acceptability of any pronouncements concerning economic performance based on these indicators depends on a number of factors. It depends, first, on whether disutility is a linear function of the deviation of the actual values from desired values; second, on whether each target has equal weight in determining welfare; and third, on whether the indicators are themselves appropriate.

Part of the difficulty in using employment, price, growth, and balance of payments indicators as a way of evaluating economic performance arises from the fact that, for instance, 10 per cent unemployment need not necessarily be exactly twice as undesirable as 5 per cent unemployment, nor 20 per cent inflation twice as bad as 10 per cent inflation. Furthermore, the respective relative social costs of unemployment, inflation, stagnation and payments disequilibria may be such that some economic situations would be preferred to others which ostensibly comprise similar deviations from targets. Rather than pursue these issues, however, let us concentrate on the appropriateness of the performance indicators chosen.

2.1 Full employment: avoiding mass unemployment

Unemployment is considered undesirable for a number of reasons, social and political as well as economic. Perhaps the principal economic argument against unemployment is that potential output is foregone. But there may also be a fiscal cost, as government expenditure in the form of unemployment benefit rises and tax revenue falls. Furthermore, the social repercussions of mass unemployment on health and crime also have an economic cost.

However, the nature of an unemployment problem is not fully captured by using one total figure. It further depends on such factors as the type of unemployment, demand deficient or non-demand deficient; the duration of unemployment; the age, sex, industrial and regional distribution of unemployment; the level of vacancies; and the trend in unemployment and vacancies. Moreover, there is some doubt concerning the precision with which unemployment data actually reveal the extent of spare productive potential. Unemployment data do not necessarily provide an accurate indication of the amount of 'slack' in the economy. The existence of concealed or hidden unemployment through under-utilization of labour or non-registration will tend to understate the amount of slack, whilst the registration of 'unemployables', those only very briefly out of work and those who are fraudulently registered will serve to overstate it.

2.2 Price stability: avoiding rapid inflation

Inflation is regarded as a 'bad thing' for a combination of both domestic and international reasons. However, the case against inflation varies according to whether or not it is anticipated. With unanticipated inflation income and wealth becomes redistributed. Creditors, savers, and generally speaking anyone not fully protected against it will lose out. The precise nature of the redistribution depends on the precise nature of the inflation, but where inflation redistributes income away from profits and towards wages, investment and therefore growth may fall. In any case the uncertainties generated by inflation may deter investment, or encourage speculative investment at the expense of productive investment.

To a significant extent many of the costs disappear in the context of fully anticipated inflation where index linking is used. However, even here some costs exist in the form of the disincentive to hold money, and the resource costs of getting protection against inflation.

Internationally, and particularly where the international monetary mechanism is based on fixed exchange rates, inflation at a rate higher than that of competitors is of concern because of its impact on the balance of payments. Even under more flexible exchange rate regimes excess inflation which results in a depreciation of the currency rather than a fall in international reserves may still be regarded as undesirable, since depreciation itself tends to raise prices. Yet a moderate rate of inflation not exceeding that in competing countries need not be very harmful. Indeed considerations of efficiency in a growing economy may even require a moderate rate of inflation, as price increases are needed to shift resources into expanding sectors and out of contracting sectors where prices are downwardly inflexible.

2.3 Economic growth: avoiding stagnation

Economic growth is considered beneficial, since it reflects an increase in the output of real goods and services. In principle, however, growth is an increase in productive potential which need not be fully realized. Although frequently interpreted as meaning such, economic growth does not necessarily imply an improvement in living standards. Standard of living is a far broader concept than economic growth. Before it may be argued that economic growth and the standard of living are positively associated, more information is required on the way in which growth is measured, in particular whether it is being measured in real or nominal terms, the direction and rate of population change, the distribution of the extra goods and services being produced, changes in the balance of payments, and the effect of economic growth on the environment and the quality of life.

A few examples may serve to illustrate the fact that the concepts of economic growth and an improvement in the standard of living are not equivalent. First, growth is expressed in terms of production. However, the standard of living is normally thought of in terms of consumption. Although a nation may manage to produce more goods and services, net exportation of these implies that it is not consuming the real resource equivalent of the extra goods and services that it is producing. It is quite possible, then, that a country's standard of living will rise at a slower – or in the case of extra net imports faster – rate than that at which the economy is growing.

Second, the standard of living is affected by the amount of leisure that is taken. Where a given level of production is maintained with a lower input of labour, the standard of living may have risen even though growth as conventionally measured has not occurred.

Third, external diseconomies such as air and water pollution, congestion and urban and rural decay, may be positively associated with economic growth. Where the social costs of growth outweigh the social benefits, the inference follows that economic growth – the measurement of which fails to take many of these externalities into account – in fact results in a decline in a nation's standard of living. Furthermore, additional output of non-marketable goods and services may not be picked up in the growth statistics. However, it is not just a matter of certain relevant factors being excluded; some items which contribute to economic growth, such as extra expenditure on security, for instance, may be required to offset an increase in crime or international tension which if uncombated would result in falling living standards.

2.4 Balance of payments equilibrium; avoiding disequilibrium

Balance of payments disequilibria may either take the form of deficits or surpluses. In some respects both of these situations incorporate desirable as well as undesirable aspects. A deficit represents a net transfer of real resources to the deficit country, which in many ways is desirable. Furthermore, by financing a deficit through international borrowing or the depletion of reserves, a country may be able to select and follow a more efficient balance of payments adjustment programme and may be able to avoid unnecessary adjustment in cases where the deficit is only temporary.

On the other hand, financing deficits brings costs in terms of an accumulation of foreign debt or a fall in international reserves. The need to finance deficits may place limitations on a government's freedom to manoevre domestic economic policy in an independent fashion. Such limitations may be implicit or explicit – implicit in the use of restrictive monetary policy in order to achieve competitively high interest rates, or explicit in the imposition of direct policy conditions by those granting financial assistance. In any case the use of international borrowing to finance deficits is undesirable in circumstances where adjustment is necessary. Here borrowing merely postpones adjustment, and the underlying situation may well deteriorate in the meantime. In the long term, balance of payments deficits are not sustainable, and fundamental correction will be required.

In some respects, and especially under a fixed exchange rate system, the avoidance of balance of payments deficits is not really a target at all, but rather a constraint on the realization of other targets. A balance of payments surplus does not represent a constraint in this way since it implies an accumulation of reserves. The benefit of a surplus is the extra freedom of policy action which it allows in the future; the cost is the current real resource opportunity cost.

The preceding analysis reveals that in the context of the individual country the key indicators identified may not always provide a clear and unambiguous guide to the state of the economy. Unemployment may over- or under-estimate true spare labour capacity and may in any case, and to a degree, serve a useful function in a dynamic economy; moderate inflation may also be beneficial; slow growth may serve to protect the standard of living; and a balance of payments deficit may permit adjustment to take place at an optimal rate. To the extent that these indicators are used, they should be used with care.

Furthermore, the static use of employment, price, growth, and balance of payments indicators provides only a limited appreciation of the economic situation. A fuller investigation of the dynamics of the economy is really required. What is going to happen in the future? In order to answer this question other economic variables have to be consulted. Although the temptation to spend time examining the other variables that would give a more rounded view of economic performance is resisted here, we do need to examine another question.

Are the indicators discussed above as useful in assessing the performance of the world economy as they are in assessing that of individual economies? Certainly inflation, employment and growth may be just as useful at a global level. However, the usefulness of the balance of payments indicator is less clear-cut. After all, the world economy is closed and as such there can be no balance of payments problem in the sense of a deficit or a surplus, since over the entire world economy deficits and surpluses cancel each other out. This having been said, the world economy does experience balance of payments problems in terms of both the size and distribution of disequilibria (deficits and surpluses) and the related financing and adjustment difficulties to which these give rise. The performance of the world economy will in turn reflect the degree of efficiency with which these payments problems are handled. Therefore, it is very relevant to examine the global balance of payments situation.

The four indicators discussed so far deal essentially with the *efficiency* of an economy. It is also instructive to examine the issue of *equity*. At the world economy level this means not only comparing living standards across countries but also investigating the distribution of payments disequilibria, of financial flows and of the burden of adjustment. For instance, does most of the pressure to adjust fall on those economies best suited to undertake it or on the poorest countries which find it most difficult to implement and in which living standards are already both absolutely and relatively low?

3. APPLYING THE INDICATORS: JUDGING WORLD ECONOMIC PERFORMANCE

Having accumulated a range of indicators, we must ask what these show us when applied to the world economy over 1973–83? Immediately we attempt to answer this question, we encounter a fundamental problem. On the one hand it is too simplistic to talk broadly about the world economy. Different groups of countries, sub-groups of countries, and individual countries within the sub-groups have different experiences. Yet, on the other hand, if one insists on looking at every single country individually, important similarities, global trends, and global problems will be missed. Undeniably the world economy is interdependent, and an approach which is highly disaggregated will ignore this crucial feature.

In an attempt to deal with this dilemma the tables that follow usually distinguish at least between industrial and developing countries. However, where this relatively low degree of disaggregation is felt to conceal important aspects of economic performance, further disaggregation is used, on the basis of: (1) per capita income (e.g. low, middle or high income), (2) trade structure (oil-exporting, oil-importing, major exporters of manufactures, primary product producers), or (3) geographical location (e.g. Africa, Asia, Europe, North America, Latin America). While it would certainly be possible to find exceptions to most of the generalisations made here, the hope is that the most significant overall trends will be revealed.

3.1 Unemployment

Table 2.1 shows unemployment rates across seven major industrial countries. However, the upward trend in unemployment there shown is probably reasonably indicative of the global trend. Although not too much should be made of comparisons, because of the different ways in which unemployment is measured in different countries, the particularly good performance of Japan stands out throughout the period. Not only is the rate of unemployment generally low, which can to a degree be explained by industrial practices in Japan, but it actually fell between 1981 and 1982 when rising in all six other countries. Germany also has a reasonable record, though by comparison with 1963–72 its performance since the mid-1970s has been poor. Along with Germany, the United Kingdom is noteworthy for the particularly marked rise in unemployment after 1979.

3.2 Inflation

Table 2.2 illustrates how for all groups of countries the rate of inflation accelerated in the first half of the 1970s. For industrial and

TABLE 2.1 *Unemployment in major industrial countries, 1963–83*[1] *(per cent)*

	Average 1963–72	*1973*	*1974*	*1975*	*1976*	*1977*	*1978*	*1979*	*1980*	*1981*	*1982*	*1983*
Canada	4.7	5.5	5.3	6.9	7.1	8.1	8.4	7.5	7.5	7.6	11.0	12.3
United States	4.7	4.9	5.6	8.5	7.7	7.0	6.1	5.8	7.2	7.6	9.7	10.2
Japan	1.2	1.3	1.4	1.9	2.0	2.0	2.2	2.1	2.1	2.2	2.4	2.5
France	1.9	2.6	2.8	4.1	4.4	4.7	5.2	5.9	6.3	7.3	8.6	9.5
Germany, West	0.9	1.1	2.3	4.1	4.0	3.9	3.8	3.3	3.4	4.9	6.8	8.5
Italy[2]	5.4	6.4	5.4	6.3	6.7	7.2	7.2	7.7	7.6	8.4	9.1	9.8
United Kingdom	2.4	2.6	2.6	3.9	4.0	5.8	5.7	5.4	6.5	10.1	11.9	13.2
All seven countries[3]	3.2	3.4	3.8	5.5	5.4	5.4	5.2	5.0	5.7	6.4	8.1	8.8

1. The figures in the table are not comparable among countries, since they are based on the differing labour force definitions and concepts used by the respective national statistical agencies.
2. Figures for 1963 to 1976 have been adjusted to allow for a discountinuity in Italian labour force statistics.
3. National unemployment rates are weighted by labour force in the respective countries.

SOURCE: *World Economic Outlook*, IMF, Washington, 1983.

TABLE 2.2 *Inflation in industrial and developing countries 1963–83*[1] (*changes in consumer prices, per cent*)

	Average	*Change from preceding year*										
	1963–72[2]	*1973*	*1974*	*1975*	*1976*	*1977*	*1978*	*1979*	*1980*	*1981*	*1982*	*1983*
Canada	3.3	7.6	10.9	10.8	7.5	8.0	8.9	9.1	10.2	12.5	10.8	7.4
United States	3.3	6.2	11.0	9.1	5.7	6.5	7.7	11.3	13.5	10.4	6.2	3.0
Japan	5.6	11.8	24.4	11.8	9.3	8.1	3.8	3.6	8.0	4.9	2.6	2.0
France	4.4	7.4	13.6	11.7	9.6	9.4	9.1	10.6	13.5	13.3	11.8	10.0
Germany, West	3.1	7.0	7.0	5.9	4.3	3.7	2.7	4.1	5.5	6.0	5.3	3.5
Italy	4.3	10.8	19.1	16.8	16.8	17.0	12.1	14.8	21.2	18.7	16.3	14.5
United Kingdom	4.9	9.2	15.9	24.3	16.6	15.9	8.3	13.4	18.0	11.9	8.5	6.6
Other industrial countries	4.9	8.7	12.4	12.3	10.5	11.3	8.6	7.8	10.2	10.3	9.7	8.6
All industrial countries	3.9	7.7	13.1	11.0	8.2	8.4	7.2	9.0	11.8	9.9	7.4	5.5
Of which seven larger countries above	3.7	7.6	13.2	10.8	7.8	7.9	6.9	9.2	12.1	9.8	6.9	5.0
European countries	4.4	8.4	12.5	12.7	10.0	10.3	7.6	8.8	11.8	11.0	9.5	8.0
Oil exporting countries, weighted average[3]	8.0	11.3	17.1	18.8	16.8	15.5	9.8	10.9	12.7	12.9	9.8	12.2
Non-oil developing countries, weighted average[3]	9.1[4]	21.9	28.5	27.6	27.3	26.5	23.4	28.8	36.5	36.5	38.3	39.6
By analytical group, weighted averages[3]												
Net oil-exporters	4.1[4]	11.1	20.6	14.6	14.9	22.8	17.7	17.7	24.2	24.3	44.0	55.1

Table 2.2—*continued*

	Average 1963–72[2]	*1973*	*1974*	*1975*	*1976*	*1977*	*1978*	*1979*	*1980*	*1981*	*1982*	*1983*
		Change from preceding year										
Net oil-importers (excluding People's Rep. of China)	10.0[4]	23.8	29.9	30.1	29.7	27.3	24.5	31.0	38.8	38.9	37.3	36.6
Major exporters of manufactures	14.1[4]	21.3	24.9	40.1	55.7	40.6	37.4	44.9	54.1	62.1	62.9	66.6
Low-income countries[5]	6.5[4]	21.9	29.7	13.4	−0.2	10.7	6.8	11.3	15.9	18.2	13.6	11.1
Other net oil importers	8.4[4]	30.4	38.8	27.3	18.8	19.6	18.6	23.9	31.5	19.6	16.3	16.1
By area, weighted averages[3]												
Africa	4.6[4]	9.7	15.0	15.0	14.6	19.4	15.9	19.3	20.1	22.0	15.8	12.8
Asia[5]	6.5[4]	21.5	30.1	13.2	0.5	7.3	5.6	9.8	15.9	14.8	9.9	5.7
Europe	6.1[4]	12.5	17.6	13.7	11.8	15.1	19.7	25.9	37.8	24.3	23.8	20.2
Middle East	4.3[4]	12.7	23.1	21.7	18.6	20.1	21.7	26.0	43.7	35.3	37.6	35.9
Western hemisphere	15.3[4]	32.1	37.5	52.0	66.1	51.2	42.4	49.6	58.3	65.4	78.0	90.2

1. Composites for the country groups are averages of percentage changes for individual countries weighted by the average dollar value of their respective GNPs over the previous three years.
2. Compound annual rate of change.
3. Geometric averages of country indices, weighted by the average US dollar value of GDPs over the previous three years.
4. 1968–72.
5. Excluding People's Republic of China.

Source: *World Economic Outlook*, IMF, Washington, 1983.

oil-exporting countries the rate subsequently declined, but not for non-oil developing countries. The figures for this group of countries are, however, somewhat misleading, for there has been considerable variation amongst them, with the major exporters of manufactures experiencing very rapid rates of inflation and low income countries experiencing quite modest rates. Thus in 1982 the rate of inflation for the former was 51 per cent while for the latter it was 8 per cent. Although for most groups the rate of inflation had fallen by 1982 from the level reached at the beginning of the 1980s, following an increase of over 100 per cent in the price of oil, it was still higher than that of the late 1970s, and frequently more than double the average rate experienced in the decade before 1973.

Although inflation is to do with a changing *absolute* price level, it is perhaps convenient at this point to draw attention to the changing *relative* prices that have occurred during 1973–83. Table 2.3 not only highlights the well known vicissitudes in the price of crude oil but also reveals the large fluctuations that have taken place in the price of other primary commodities, often particularly with respect to the price of manufactured goods. As Section 3.4 will reveal, these changes in relative prices have had a very significant effect on the global balance of payments situation.

3.3 Economic growth

The performance of the world economy in terms of economic growth is reflected by the data in Table 2.4. The industrial countries show a clear pattern. The successful growth performance of the period between 1963 and 1973 was followed by two years of practically zero growth. However, during 1976–79 quite respectable growth rates were again achieved, only to be followed in the 1980s by first a significant and then a further gradual decline in the rate of economic growth. Turning to individual countries, it is yet again the performance of Japan that tends to catch the eye. Apart from 1974 alone, the Japanese growth rate during 1974–82 compares unfavourably only with its own performance during 1963–73.

As far as the other country groups are concerned, the growth performance of the oil-exporting countries follows a similar pattern to that of industrial countries, although the good years tend to have been better and the bad years worse. Interestingly, it is in the non-oil developing countries that the pattern appears to be much less

TABLE 2.3 *World prices of manufactures and primary commodities in US $, 1963–83*[1] *(percentage changes)*

	Average	*Change from preceding year*										
	1963–72[2]	*1973*	*1974*	*1975*	*1976*	*1977*	*1978*	*1979*	*1980*	*1981*	*1982*	*1983*
Manufactures[4]	3.0[3]	17.7	21.8	12.3	—	9.0	14.7	15.3	10.5	−5.1	−2.0	2.0
Oil[4]	3.0	40.0	225.8	5.1	6.3	9.3	0.1	48.7	62.0	10.1	−4.6	−13.5
Non-oil primary commodities[4] (market prices)[5]	2.5	53.2	28.0	−18.2	13.3	20.7	−4.7	16.5	9.7	−14.8	−12.1	5.0
By commodity group:												
Food		54.1	60.0	−21.2	18.5	−3.7	14.1	14.0	34.3	−13.9	−21.0	4.2
Beverages		23.5	19.4	−3.9	91.8	73.2	−27.5	5.8	−12.2	−22.3	2.5	2.3
Agricultural raw materials		79.2	−3.6	−19.7	24.3	3.2	7.6	21.9	4.1	−9.7	−13.7	4.9
Metals		46.9	24.9	−19.4	6.0	7.5	5.4	29.9	10.7	−14.0	−9.2	9.6

1. Based on foreign trade unit values except where indicated.
2. Compound annual rates of change.
3. Figures are rounded to the nearest 0.5 per cent.
4. As represented, respectively, by (a) the United Nations export unit value index for the manufactures of the developed countries; (b) the oil export unit values of the oil exporting countries; and (c) the International Financial Statistics index of market quotations for non-oil primary commodities.
5. Averages of percentage changes of component commodity prices weighted by the US dollar value of exports of each commodity from primary producing countries 1968–70.

SOURCE: *World Economic Outlook*, IMF, Washington, 1983.

TABLE 2.4 *Economic growth: changes in output in industrial and developing countries, 1963–83[1] (per cent)*

	Average 1963–72[2]	Change from preceding year 1973	1974	1975	1976	1977	1978	1979	1980	1981	1982	1983
Canada	5.5	7.6	3.6	1.2	5.5	2.1	3.6	2.9	0.5	3.1	−4.8	1.9
United States	4.0	5.8	−0.6	−1.2	5.4	5.5	5.0	2.8	−0.4	1.9	−1.7	2.4
Japan	10.5	8.8	−1.2	2.4	5.3	5.3	5.1	5.2	4.8	3.8	3.0	2.8
France[3]	5.5	5.4	3.2	0.2	5.2	3.0	3.7	3.4	1.1	0.4	1.6	—
Germany, West	4.5	4.6	0.5	−1.6	5.6	2.8	3.5	4.0	1.8	−0.2	−1.1	0.5
Italy[3]	4.6	7.0	4.1	−3.6	5.9	1.9	2.7	4.9	3.9	0.1	−0.3	−0.1
United Kingdom[3]	2.8	7.2	−1.8	−1.1	3.4	2.4	2.1	3.0	2.1	0.6	0.2	0.6
Other industrial countries	5.0	5.5	3.4	−0.2	3.6	2.4	2.1	3.0	2.1	0.6	0.2	0.6
All industrial countries	4.7	6.1	0.5	−0.6	5.0	4.0	4.1	3.4	1.3	1.2	−0.3	1.6
Of which seven larger countries above	4.7	6.2	0.1	−0.7	5.3	4.3	4.5	3.5	1.1	1.4	−0.4	1.8
European countries	4.4	5.8	2.0	−1.2	4.6	2.6	3.0	3.4	1.5	−0.2	0.2	0.6
Oil exporting countries,[4]	9.0	10.7	8.0	−0.3	12.3	6.1	2.0	3.1	−2.3	−4.3	−4.8	—
Non-oil developing countries,[4, 5] by analytical group												
Net oil-exporters	7.0	8.3	6.5	6.2	6.7	3.5	6.2	7.3	7.3	6.4	0.8	1.1
Net oil-importers[5]	5.8	5.7	5.2	2.7	5.9	5.5	5.2	4.2	3.8	1.7	0.9	2.1
Major exporters of manufactures	8.0	9.5	6.5	1.3	6.7	5.7	4.9	6.4	4.5	−0.2	0.2	0.4

TABLE 2.4—*continued*

	Average	*Change from preceding year*										
	1963–72[2]	*1973*	*1974*	*1975*	*1976*	*1977*	*1978*	*1979*	*1980*	*1981*	*1982*	*1983*
Low-income countries[5]	3.4	2.0	3.0	5.4	4.4	5.2	5.5	−0.1	3.2	4.4	3.0	4.3
Other net oil-importers	5.5	4.7	5.7	4.7	4.9	5.5	5.9	4.7	3.0	2.3	1.9	2.9
By area[4]												
Africa	4.8	3.0	6.6	2.6	4.2	1.8	2.2	2.3	4.4	2.9	1.1	2.3
Asia[5]	4.5	5.0	3.8	4.9	7.5	6.6	7.9	3.3	3.4	5.8	3.7	4.9
Europe	6.0	5.8	4.2	0.8	6.8	5.4	5.4	3.9	1.5	2.2	2.0	1.5
Middle East	7.5	4.9	4.8	8.7	8.4	4.3	7.4	4.3	7.3	4.7	2.7	3.0
Western hemisphere	7.6	8.4	6.9	3.1	5.5	5.0	4.5	6.7	6.0	−0.1	−1.5	−0.2

1. Composites for the country groups are averages of percentage changes for individual countries weighted by the average US dollar value of their respective GNPs over the previous three years.
2. Compound annual rate of change.
3. GDP at market prices.
4. Arithmetic averages of country growth rates weighted by the average US dollar value of GDPs over the previous three years.
5. Excluding People's Republic of China.

SOURCE: *World Economic Outlook*, IMF, Washington, 1983.

pronounced. Even though their rate of growth declined in the period since 1973 as compared with the previous five years, it was greater than that achieved by industrial countries. While the rate was relatively low in 1975 and in the early 1980s as compared with other years, it was rarely below about 4 per cent. However, disaggregation of the NOLDC (non-oil less developed country) group reveals a number of noteworthy features. Not least amongst these is the very sharp fall in the growth rate of the major exporters of manufactures in 1981 and the poor performance of low income countries in 1979. In the case of the latter countries rapid population growth means that even apparently moderate rates of economic growth may be associated with falling GNP per capita.

3.4 Balance of payments equilibrium

Table 2.5 provides a summary of the global current account balance of payments position over the period since 1973. Again a clear pattern emerges. Following the quadrupling in the price of oil in 1973 the current account balance of payments of the oil-exporting countries moved into substantial surplus.

At the same time the industrial countries shifted from surplus into deficit and the NOLDCs' deficit became considerably larger. By 1978 industrial countries had re-established their surplus. Meanwhile, the surplus of the oil-exporting countries had all but disappeared, and the deficit of the NOLDCs had become even larger. Following a further big increase in the price of oil, there was a replay of events with industrial countries again moving into deficit as oil-exporting countries moved into surplus. However, by 1982 the industrial countries were back in surplus while the oil exporters' surplus was rapidly evaporating. The only constant factor throughout the period was the growing deficit in NOLDCs.

While the general picture is clear, Table 2.5 also shows how the details vary. Thus, the balance of payments performance of individual industrial countries is not identical, nor indeed is that of individual countries within the other groupings, not least the oil exporters, where some countries have experienced deficits while the group as a whole has been in surplus.

What emerges from this cursory glance at the statistics is that the world economy has not been performing well since 1973 as compared with its performance in the previous decade. Unemployment is much higher, inflation more rapid, economic growth more restrained and the global balance of payments unstable and in disequilibrium. Furthermore, not only has there been a quantitative deterioration but there has also been a qualitative one in the sense that quite rapid inflation has existed alongside relatively high unemployment. The co-existence of these two phenomena generated a considerable amount of activity amongst economic analysts who had been brought up on the notion of a trade-off between these two variables. Theories had to be re-examined and conventional policy solutions seemed less relevant and helpful.

Of course it is possible to get the concept of a deteriorating global economic performance out of proportion. This partly results from the masochistic tendencies that commentators display in their anxiety to find 'crises' wherever they can. Just as no news is good news, good news is no news and bad news is news! But it also results from the fact that performance is judged against rising expectations. Thus, while many of the world's population may actually be somewhat better off and others no worse off in the 1980s than they were in the 1960s, the intervening years may still be characterised as a failure if things have not improved by as much as was anticipated. However, while the effect that rising expectations has on the way in which performance is evaluated needs to be recognized, it may also be argued that other unsatisfactory aspects of global economic performance have not been captured by the figures so far presented.

3.5 Other indicators

The period since 1973 has been characterized by a number of other major developments in the world economy. First, there has been the evolving north–south debate, with increasing expression of the view that the structure of the world economy and its principal institutions operate primarily for the benefit of industrial countries and disfavour developing economies.

Second, the financial and trading system devised at Bretton Woods has largely broken down and has been replaced by a less ordered and more decentralized 'non-system'. At the same time, rising protectionism has gone hand in hand with the slow growth of world trade. These trends have left many of the international institutions in a somewhat ambiguous situation as their traditional roles have been written out by events and new roles have not been defined. Third, however, the

TABLE 2.5 *Summary of payments balances on current account, 1973–83*[1] *(billions of US dollars)*

	1973	*1974*	*1975*	*1976*	*1977*	*1978*	*1979*	*1980*	*1981*	*1982*	*1983*[2]
Industrial countries	20.3	−10.8	19.8	0.5	−2.2	32.7	−5.6	−40.1	0.6	−1.2	16.0
Canada	—	−1.6	−4.7	−3.9	−4.0	−4.0	−4.3	−1.2	−4.8	1.9	4.0
United States	9.1	7.6	21.2	7.5	−11.3	−11.6	3.1	6.2	9.0	−2.7	−20.0
Japan	0.1	−4.5	−0.4	3.9	11.1	16.8	−8.0	−9.5	6.2	8.2	18.5
France	2.1	−2.8	3.8	−2.4	1.0	8.5	6.9	−2.4	−2.8	−9.4	−2.0
Germany, West	7.0	13.0	7.6	7.7	8.5	13.4	—	−8.3	0.1	9.9	15.0
Italy	−2.2	−7.6	−0.1	−2.6	3.1	7.9	6.4	−9.5	−7.5	−4.9	−0.5
United Kingdom	−1.3	−6.9	−2.6	−0.2	1.9	5.2	2.6	10.9	15.9	10.3	5.5
Other industrial countries	5.5	−8.1	−5.1	−9.6	−12.6	−3.5	−12.3	−26.3	−15.5	−14.4	−4.5
Developing countries											
Oil exporting countries	6.7	68.3	35.4	40.3	30.2	2.2	68.6	114.3	65.0	−2.2	−27.0
Non-oil developing countries[3]	−11.3	−37.0	−46.3	−32.6	−28.9	−41.3	−61.0	−89.0	−107.7	−86.8	−68.0
By analytical group											
Net oil exporters	−2.6	−5.1	−9.9	−7.7	−6.4	−7.9	−8.5	−12.5	−23.5	−15.6	−14.0
Net oil importers[3]	−8.8	−31.9	−36.4	−24.9	−23.6	−32.7	−51.0	−74.1	−86.2	−76.3	−56.5
Major exporters of manufactures	−3.6	−18.8	−19.1	−12.2	−7.9	−9.8	−21.7	−32.5	−37.6	−34.3	−18.5
Low-income countries[3]	−4.1	−7.5	−7.6	−4.3	−3.7	−8.2	−10.4	−14.0	−15.6	−15.6	−15.0
Other net oil importers[4]	−1.1	−5.6	−9.7	−8.3	−12.0	−14.7	−18.9	−27.6	−33.0	−26.4	−23.0

TABLE 2.5—*continued*

	1973	*1974*	*1975*	*1976*	*1977*	*1978*	*1979*	*1980*	*1981*	*1982*	*1983*[2]
By area											
Africa[5]	−1.9	−3.2	−6.6	−6.1	−6.6	−9.4	−9.9	−12.9	−14.0	−13.2	−13.5
Asia[3]	−2.6	−9.9	−8.9	−2.7	−1.7	−6.5	−13.2	−21.9	−24.2	−20.8	−21.0
Europe	0.6	−4.4	−4.9	−4.7	−8.4	−6.7	−9.9	−12.5	−10.5	−7.1	−4.0
Middle East	−2.6	−4.5	−6.9	−5.4	−5.1	−6.2	−8.5	−9.4	−11.1	−12.9	−12.0
Western hemisphere	−4.7	−13.5	−16.3	−11.8	−8.5	−13.3	−21.4	−33.4	−45.4	−34.9	−21.5
Total[6]	15.7	20.5	8.9	8.2	−0.9	−6.4	2.0	−14.8	−42.1	−90.2	−79.0

1. On goods, services, and private transfers.
2. Figures are rounded to the nearest $0.5 billion.
3. The People's Republic of China, which is classified as a low-income country but is also a net oil exporter, is included in the total from 1977 onward but not in the sub-groups.
4. Middle-income countries that, in general, export mainly primary commodities.
5. Excluding South Africa.
6. Reflects errors, omissions, and asymmetries in reported balance of payments statistics on current account, plus balance of listed groups with other countries (mainly the USSR and other non-member countries of Eastern Europe and, for years prior to 1977, the People's Republic of China).

SOURCE: *World Economic Outlook,* IMF, Washington, 1983.

TABLE 2.6 *Long-term and short-term external debt of non-oil developing countries relative to exports and to GDP, 1973–83*[1]
(*per cent*)

	1973	*1974*	*1975*	*1976*	*1977*	*1978*	*1979*	*1980*	*1981*	*1982*	*1983*
Ratio of external debt to exports of goods and services[2]											
All non-oil developing countries	115.4	104.6	122.4	125.5	126.4	130.2	119.2	112.9	124.9	143.3	144.4
By analytical group											
Net oil exporters	154.7	124.9	162.4	169.5	179.3	176.9	144.3	128.4	154.6	179.5	192.2
Net oil importers	109.4	100.9	115.4	117.5	116.8	121.8	114.1	109.5	118.3	135.1	134.3
Major exporters of manufactures	91.7	88.6	103.0	103.3	99.5	101.1	96.9	94.0	100.6	116.2	114.2
Low-income countries	227.9	214.5	226.1	225.1	217.8	226.3	209.8	201.4	231.1	254.1	262.9
Other net oil importers[3]	96.9	84.7	98.3	104.3	111.6	124.8	115.5	110.9	121.9	138.0	136.6
By region											
Africa	71.5	65.4	80.9	94.2	103.1	111.4	100.8	97.4	119.9	147.4	148.6
Asia	92.9	81.0	91.6	84.4	83.3	77.7	70.2	68.2	72.5	80.9	85.4
Europe	102.4	97.1	108.0	114.9	127.4	136.4	125.6	121.6	118.2	129.6	129.7
Middle East	145.4	105.2	131.5	137.5	140.4	142.4	133.8	113.1	112.6	134.3	133.1
Western hemisphere	176.2	163.4	195.8	204.1	194.1	211.5	192.9	178.4	207.4	245.6	242.8
Ratio of external debt to GDP[2]											
All non-oil developing countries	22.4	21.8	23.8	25.7	27.4	28.5	27.5	27.6	31.0	34.7	34.7

TABLE 2.6—*continued*

	1973	*1974*	*1975*	*1976*	*1977*	*1978*	*1979*	*1980*	*1981*	*1982*	*1983*
By analytical group											
Net oil exporters	26.2	25.5	27.7	32.3	38.4	39.3	37.4	34.0	36.1	44.7	43.5
Net oil importers	21.7	21.2	23.0	24.4	25.4	26.6	25.8	26.3	29.7	32.1	32.7
Major exporters of manufactures	20.2	19.6	22.2	22.7	23.9	25.1	24.6	25.1	29.3	33.2	33.8
Low-income countries	20.1	20.1	20.9	24.4	24.9	24.0	24.4	23.6	24.7	26.2	26.5
Other net oil importers[3]	26.2	25.2	26.2	27.7	28.6	31.5	28.8	30.6	34.1	35.8	35.6
By region											
Africa	19.4	19.6	21.6	25.8	28.4	29.4	28.9	28.8	30.6	35.2	35.1
Asia	19.7	18.9	20.4	22.4	23.4	22.3	22.2	23.2	25.2	26.7	27.1
Europe	24.5	23.1	22.8	24.6	25.7	28.6	25.1	29.0	33.1	34.7	34.5
Middle East	36.2	34.0	39.0	42.3	45.4	48.3	56.0	52.6	51.3	50.3	47.4
Western hemisphere	23.0	22.8	25.5	26.4	28.4	30.3	28.8	27.0	31.9	38.2	38.6
Memorandum items											
Ratios (including People's Rep. of China)[2]											
To exports:											
All non-oil developing countries	—		—	—	123.6	127.0	116.1	109.4	119.8	136.5	137.7
Low-income countries	—	—	—	—	169.0	170.0	152.0	137.7	140.0	148.7	155.5

TABLE 2.6—*continued*

	1973	*1974*	*1975*	*1976*	*1977*	*1978*	*1979*	*1980*	*1981*	*1982*	*1983*
To GDP:											
All non-oil developing countries	—	—	—	—	23.9	24.6	23.9	24.1	27.3	30.5	30.5
Low-income countries	—	—	—	—	14.3	13.5	13.4	13.2	14.3	15.1	15.3

1. Excludes data for the People's Republic of China, except where noted.
2. Ratio of year-end debt to exports or GDP for year indicated.
3. Middle-income countries that, in general, export mainly primary commodities.

SOURCES: *World Bank, Debtor Reporting System; and Fund staff estimates and projections.*

new non-system has not proved entirely satisfactory. Not only is it philosophically inconsistent – greater emphasis on free and private financial markets often being accompanied by less emphasis on free and liberal trade – but it has also contributed to creating the debt problems (illustrated in Table 2.6) and the threat of international banking and financial collapse that have caused so much concern in the 1980s.

Even some of the limited but apparently hopeful signs catalogued earlier, in particular the falling rate of inflation, have their worrying aspects. Thus, if the inflation rate drops more rapidly than do nominal interest rates, then the effect is that the real interest rate rises (as shown in Table 2.7) and this in turn has directly adverse implications for borrowers, for world economic growth and trade, and, therefore, indirectly for debtors again. Perhaps a particular, but at the same time more general, worry is the susceptibility of the world economy to the vicious circles that can easily be generated through world economic interdependence. It is the dynamics of the situation that are potentially alarming, since they can easily transform what is a brief recession into a prolonged depression. Thus, falling aggregate demand in one part of the world reduces the demand for goods from other parts of the world. The resulting balance of payments and debt

TABLE 2.7 *Short-term real interest rates in major industrial countries[1] (per cent per annum)*

	1976	*1977*	*1978*	*1979*	*1980*	*1981*	*1982*
Canada	−0.3	0.4	2.2	1.6	1.9	7.4	3.2
United States	−0.2	−0.5	−0.2	1.3	1.9	4.2	4.4
Japan	0.5	0.4	0.4	3.2	7.7	4.9	4.9
France	−1.1	0.1	−1.3	−1.2	0.3	2.9	2.5
Germany, West	0.8	0.7	−0.5	2.5	4.9	7.6	3.9
Italy	−0.2	−3.6	−2.5	2.1	4.0	1.0	1.6
United Kingdom	−3.1	−5.6	−2.2	−1.8	−3.4	0.7	3.1
Average, above countries[2]	−0.3	−0.6	−0.3	1.2	2.4	4.2	4.0
Average, four major European countries[2]	−0.7	−1.3	−1.4	—	0.6	3.7	3.0

1. Approximated by using annual changes in GNP deflators to adjust the respective nominal rates.
2. These composites are averages of individual country rates, weighted for each year in proportion to the US dollar values of the respective GNPs in the preceding year.

SOURCE: *World Economic Outlook*, IMF, Washington, 1983.

problems in these countries then create pressures to pursue deflationary policies which in turn spread back to other countries, via a reduced demand for imports. These countries then respond by increasing protectionist barriers and by deflating their economies, and this further reduces world trade and output.

History will tell whether the world recession of 1980–3, illustrated by the figures in Tables 2.1, 2.3 and 2.5, turns out to be a temporary interlude or the beginning of just such a prolonged depression. From our point of view the interesting observation is that such a threat exists; and the interesting question is what may be done to alleviate the situation and to reduce the likelihood that similar world economic recessions will occur in the future.

But first is it possible to explain the world's economic performance since 1973?

4. EXPLAINING WORLD ECONOMIC PERFORMANCE: CONTENDING THEORIES

As might be anticipated, there is no consensus amongst economists about the causes of the apparently poor performance of the world economy since 1973. Instead there are a range of contending theories. It is impossible to do each of these justice in the short amount of space available, but at least it is possible to mention and comment briefly on some of them.

However to begin with it is important to recognise that the central issue may be posed in a rather different way. The alternative approach emphasizes the particularly good performance of the world economy between 1950 and 1973, with low inflation, high employment, and rapid growth, and seeks to explain this. Were these relatively good years the fruits of a conversion to Keynesian economic policy and the result of efficient governmental economic management? Did they directly reflect the institution-building that was done in the 1940s, with the establishment of the International Monetary Fund (IMF), the International Bank for Reconstruction and Development (World Bank) and the General Agreement on Tariffs and Trade (GATT)? Or were they the result of certain more basic structural changes in the world economy, as patterns of production and trade changed in response to both demand and supply side factors? We choose not to delve into these questions here except to note that experiences in the years since 1973 challenge such simplistic explanations of the pre-1973 years. If Keynesian policies were so effective in the 1950s and 1960s, why did they cease to be effective afterwards? In any case, were Keynesian policies actually pursued in the 1950s and 1960s? Again if the activities of the international institutions account for the economic success of the 1950s and 1960s, why have they failed to prevent subsequent economic deterioration; other factors are clearly at work. However, let us revert more specifically to the period since 1973.

4.1 Business cycles and long waves

One explanation suggests that there are inbuilt cycles in economic activity. These may be of short duration, lasting no more than three or five years, or may be of much longer duration, lasting many decades. Such long waves may well have shorter-term cycles around them. Within this analytical framework the period since 1973 could be characterised as the beginning of a long-wave downturn, and the variations in economic activity throughout the 1970s as representing aspects of the business cycle. While long waves are often taken to reflect the pattern of innovative activity through time, business cycles can reflect the interactions between multiplier and accelerator mechanisms, augmented by lagged, and therefore sometimes procyclical, demand management policy. They may also be associated with variations in investment caused by a changing profit rate, and may therefore share some features with the longer wave cycles, though they can exist independently of them.

An alternative explanation of short-term variations in economic activity stresses the so-called political cycle. On the supposition that demand management policies are effective, it is argued that economic upturns come immediately before elections and downturns after them.

However, can business cycle theory explain global cycles? Why should economic experiences be simultaneously shared across countries? Clearly one potential answer is that they are exposed to similar external shocks, such as a large change in the price of a strategic commodity. Another answer is that through trade the fortunes of different economies become inexorably interrelated, so that variations in the level of aggregate demand in one or a few major trading countries are transmitted to other countries.

For the political cycle to provide an explanation of global

variations in the level of economic activity either one national economy would need to dominate the world economy, or the timing of elections in a number of major industrial countries would need to overlap. Such an explanation cannot be dismissed out of hand, since the acceleration in inflation rates at the beginning of the 1970s did coincide with an unusually high degree of synchronisation in the level of economic activity in OECD countries and the unusually close temporal proximity of elections in a number of them.

Amongst the many difficulties associated with the inbuilt cyclical explanation of observed world economic performance are, first, the rather tenuous empirical support and poorly developed theoretical analysis of long waves, and, second, the fact that business cycle theory has still to explain why the recessions experienced in the 1970s and 1980s have been so unusually severe as compared with the previous twenty years.

4.2 Global monetarism

From amongst the various dimensions of the world's economic performance global monetarism focuses initially on trying to explain inflation. The performance of the other variables is then usually explained largely in terms of policy reactions to rapid inflation. Thus, rising unemployment and falling economic growth are presented as reflecting attempts by governments to reduce the rate of inflation. Given that monetarists argue that changes in the rate of growth of the money supply exert their impact on prices after a long (though variable) lag, it is not surprising to find that the acceleration in inflation during the first half of the 1970s is felt by them to have had its source in events in the late 1960s and early 1970s. This source is argued to be a large increase in the United States' money supply and a related large increase in the dollar component of the world's foreign exchange reserves. Under the fixed exchange rate system that existed until 1973 foreign trade balances and international capital flows exerted a significant impact on domestic money supplies, with the result that monetary excesses in economically important countries could easily affect other countries. Hence a monetarist explanation of global inflation can be offered. Variations in inflation rates across countries can then be explained by differences in productivity, exchange rates, and the size of the non-traded goods sector.

Again it is difficult to be too cursorily dismissive of global monetarism. The data confirms that a large increase in the foreign exchange component of international reserves did predate the rapid acceleration in global inflation in the early 1970s and that falling reserves predated the decline in global inflation in the early 1980s. Yet, as with monetarism in general, correlation must not be confused with causation, and there is legitimate debate amongst economists concerning the impact that a change in the money supply has on other economic variables. While some see money as absolutely central, others see it as accommodating rather than causative and as of only secondary importance.

4.3 Structural trends, profits and productivity

Excess aggregate monetary demand may be caused in two basic ways. The first, and the mechanism on which global monetarism concentrates, is through an overly rapid increase in the money supply. The second is through a decline in the growth of output or productivity. Certainly attempts have been made to explain the problems of particular economies such as the United Kingdom in terms of trends in production and industrial structure. Thus, it has been argued that the size of the 'productive' manufacturing sector has been allowed to shrink, leading to a fall in output, while the size of the 'unproductive' government sector has been allowed to expand, serving to maintain a level of aggregate demand which therefore becomes excessive. However, in order to finance employment in the government sector, extra taxes are imposed on workers and firms in the productive sector. Workers respond to increased taxes by demanding compensatory wage increases. Inflation further accelerates and profits fall. With falling profits employment in the productive sector contracts and there is then pressure on governments to neutralize the resulting unemployment by increasing public expenditure, which sets off the whole process again.

If the rate of profit falls, as it will where a declining share of profits in national income is combined with a constant capital-output ratio,[1] there will be less incentive for entrepreneurs to invest and the rate of growth of productivity will fall. Falling productivity can both raise the rate of inflation, if its effect is to raise unit labour costs, and increase the level of unemployment if it reduces the demand for labour. Evidence drawn from the late 1960s and early 1970s does indeed suggest that a slow-down in productivity growth, particularly in sectors where growth had previously been relatively rapid, was unaccompanied by an equivalent slow-down in the growth of many wages, with the result that unit labour costs rose in a number of industrial countries. Yet to explain macroeconomic performance in terms of declining productivity growth is only a partial answer. One also needs to come up with a satisfactory explanation of the decline in productivity growth.

If prices are determined by some mark-up over full costs, rising unit costs will lead to rising prices. But if prices rise by less than money wages, real wages will rise and employers will be encouraged to economise on labour. Under such a productivity-oriented cost push framework it becomes quite possible simultaneously to explain rising inflation, rising unemployment, falling profits, and falling investment. In as much as falling investment leads to further falls in productivity growth, the mechanism becomes dynamically destabilizing. But again the fact that a consistent explanation may be offered in these terms does not necessarily mean that this is what happened.

4.4 Changing terms of trade

While the explanations contained in both 4.1 and 4.3 emphasize increases in absolute prices, there is another explanation which instead focuses on the changing relative prices of primary products and manufactured goods catalogued in Section 3.2. Instability in commodity prices is seen as being the principal determinant of world economic instability, inflation and recession.

Under this explanation the sharp rise in primary product prices in the early 1970s is largely attributed to falling output, particularly food output, and stockpiling. From this starting point the story runs as follows. Primary products are inputs into manufacturing, and the increase in primary product prices therefore represented an increase in costs to manufacturers. Assuming that the prices of manufactures are cost-determined, the increase in commodity prices was then reflected in an increase in prices of manufactured goods. As a result, the movement in the terms of trade in favour of primary products was only temporary, as therefore was any incentive to increase their supply. Faced with cost inflation, primary product importing countries responded by deflating aggregate demand, and this had the effect of reducing the demand for commodity imports. Export earnings in producing countries fell, therefore, even though their commodity terms of trade had initially improved. Equilibrium was approached not primarily by changes in relative prices but rather by income changes which reduced the demand for primary products. But the fall in aggregate demand overshot the level required for the restoration of equilibrium and the terms of trade moved against commodity producers. However, even though falling commodity prices had the effect of increasing real income in consuming countries, thereby expanding the demand for both primary and manufactured goods, this effect was overpowered by the fact that effective demand for manufactured goods emanating from primary product producing countries fell. Industrial recession was therefore exacerbated.

This explanation of world economic performance has a number of interesting and novel features. Not least among them is the suggestion that once an equilibrium combination of terms of trade and industrial growth is disturbed, it is quite possible, and indeed likely, that the system will not quickly move to a new equilibrium but rather start off on a potentially highly unstable path with continuing cycles in both growth and the terms of trade, during which either an increase or a fall in the price of manufactures relative to primary commodities is accompanied by a slow-down in the growth of the world economy. At this somewhat superficial level the explanation has the appeal of being able to explain any observed relation between the terms of trade and economic growth and is certainly consistent with the performance of the world economy in the 1970s and the 1980s. However, it contrasts very sharply with other theories – in particular global monetarism – since, although it emphasizes the role of effective demand as influenced by changes in the terms of trade, it displays a marked neglect of monetary variables.

4.5 Changing patterns of world production and trade

A rather different explanation of world economic developments still emphasizes the changing structure and pattern of world production and trade, but in particular stresses the emergence of the Newly Industrialising Countries (NICs) and the adjustment problems to which this has given rise. Again this explanation cannot be completely discounted. Undeniably some traditional industries in industrial countries have suffered from new competition, with the result that output and employment have fallen. However, it is difficult to generalize this into an explanation of changing global macroeconomic performance. Indeed to some extent the success of the NICs should have expansionary as well as contractionary repercussions, as their economic growth encourages growth in the demand for the goods in which they do not specialize. Put simply, the actual impact of the NICs on the world economy can easily be exaggerated; it is difficult to see how the emergence of NICs could have had such a dramatic impact on such a wide range of economic variables in such a wide range of countries over such a relatively short space of time.

4.6 Changing oil prices

Rather than looking at the terms of trade between primary products and manufactured goods, as the explanation contained in Section 4.4 does, another approach focuses more exclusively on oil prices. One aspect of the appeal of the oil price explanation of world economic performance since 1973 is that it provides just such a simple and apparently all-embracing story. In its most extreme version the story runs as follows. In 1973–4 OPEC (Organization of Petroleum Exporting Countries) administered a four-fold increase in the price of crude oil. At the global level this had two principal effects. The first was to cause cost inflation, as the cost of oil and oil-related inputs increased. The second was to deflate the global level of aggregate demand, both directly by transferring income from oil-importing countries with relatively high propensities to spend to oil-exporting countries with lower propensities to spend, and indirectly by inducing governments in oil-importing countries to pursue demand deflationary policies in order to reduce their domestic rates of inflation.[2]

However the story does not end there. The oil-price rise is also used to explain the massive balance of payments disequilibria experienced, the switch in the recycling of international finance away from the IMF and towards the private international banks and by implication the related debt problems that subsequently developed, and the increasing tensions between north and south as the economic performance of many southern countries deteriorated and northern countries turned to demand deflation and protectionism as ways of dealing with their oil-induced inflation and balance of payments deficits, thus limiting the scope for developing countries to improve their own economic situation. Furthermore, it is argued that the reluctance by workers to accept the fact that with slow productivity growth the oil-price rise had the effect of reducing the equilibrium real wage has resulted in rising unemployment, not least because profits and investment fell.

Differences in the details of the effects on individual countries are explained in terms of a range of factors, including reliance on imported oil, the price elasticity of demand for oil and the implied scope for switching to alternative energy sources or for conserving energy, the pattern of production and trade, the distribution of international capital flows, the domestic mobility of resources and the scope for macro and micro adjustment to the rise in oil prices, and the policies of government with respect to the taxation of oil, macroeconomic management, microeconomic efficiency and the exchange rate.

Thus, for example, a country heavily reliant on oil, selling exports to countries pursuing deflationary policies, with an inflexible economic and social system, and unattractive to commercial lenders, would be expected to have been more adversely affected by the rise in the price of oil than another country able to switch out of oil, with growing export markets, and able to attract international loans. Of course on the basis of the characteristics listed above it might have been expected that the precise details of the impact of the oil price rise on industrial economies would differ. Some would experience a more marked increase in inflation, others a more marked rise in unemployment and so on.

As compelling as this story is, it has to be contrasted with the monetarist view at the other extreme of the range, which argues that in explaining the events of the 1970s and 1980s the oil price rise is largely irrelevant. The essence of this argument is that the rise in the price of oil in 1973–4 was a symptom of excess global monetary demand rather than a cause of subsequent events; it was a basically once for all change in relative prices. While of course the absolute global price *level* did rise, there was no general and persistent tendency for it to continue to rise as a result of the increase in the price of oil.

This view argues that there is nothing special about oil, pointing to the fact that commodity prices in general rose strongly during the early 1970s. At the end of the 1970s an attempt by OPEC to adminster a further increase in the price of oil was followed by a period when oil prices began to fall, since at this time demand conditions were less condusive and other commodity prices were not rising. Of course it is unnecessary to accept either one of these extreme views in their entirety. For instance, one can argue that while the rise in the price of oil reflected, or was permitted by, market forces, it still had a considerable impact in its own right on the economic events that followed.

Unfortunately a superficial examination of the statistical evidence does not provide a ready answer to the question of how much emphasis to place on oil prices as a cause of world macro performance, nor indeed do the rather more rigorous econometric studies that have been undertaken, conflicting conclusions have frequently been drawn in them. While it is surely difficult to imagine that oil prices have been irrelevant, the joint phenomenon of falling oil prices and deepening recession in the early 1980s also suggests that the price of oil cannot provide a complete explanation.

4.7 The conduct of economic policy

An additional factor at work, as briefly mentioned in previous sections, is governments' conduct of demand management policy. An explanation based on this suggests that countries, or more precisely their governments, are themselves to blame for their own economic traumas, inasmuch as they have either *caused* the problems by pursuing inappropriate policies, or have *exacerbated* problems initiated by other factors. Thus, it is argued that inflation in the first half of the 1970s was caused by over-expansionary monetary policy and that recession in the early 1980s was caused by contractionary fiscal policy. Note that the former explanation of inflation differs somewhat from the global monetarist explanation discussed earlier, since the latter places the principal blame for monetary expansion not so much on all individual governments but on the United States in particular.

However, an explanation that emphasizes economic policy in individual countries can still clearly explain global phenomena if enough large and important countries pursue similar policies. Thus, if contractionary demand policies and increasing protectionism feature in a number of OECD countries, rising interest rates and falling rates of growth of world trade are to be expected. These in turn would be expected to create additional problems for those countries heavily in debt, and anxious to expand their exports to the rest of the world in order to strengthen their balance of payments. The result is that the global effects are likely to be greater than the sum of the individual country effects as a vicious interactive circle of deflation becomes entrenched.

TABLE 2.8 *Central government fiscal balances and impulses in major industrial countries, 1978–83*[1] *(in per cent of GNP)*

	1978	*1979*	*1980*	*1981*	*1982*	*1983*
Fiscal balance						
(+*surplus*, −*deficit*)						
Canada[2]	−4.6	−3.6	−3.5	−2.4	−6.0	−6.8
United States	−2.0	−1.2	−2.4	−2.5	−4.3	−6.3
Japan[3]	−6.4	−6.3	−6.0	−6.2	−5.8	−5.3
France[4]	−1.4	−1.1	−1.4	−2.7	−2.8	−3.0
Germany, West	−2.1	−1.8	−1.7	−2.2	−2.6	−2.6
Italy[5]	−14.6	−11.1	−10.9	−12.9	−15.1	−14.8
United Kingdom	−5.1	−5.3	−4.9	−4.1	−2.8	−2.7
All countries above	−3.6	−3.0	−3.5	−3.8	−4.8	−5.6
All countries above except United States	−5.0	−4.5	−4.4	−4.8	−5.1	−5.1
Fiscal impulse[6]						
(+*expansionary*, −*contractionary*)						
Canada[2]	1.2	−0.7	−0.4	−1.0	1.2	0.2
United States	—	−0.8	0.4	—	0.5	1.7
Japan[3]	1.1	0.2	−0.2	0.2	−0.6	−0.6
France[4]	0.1	−0.3	—	0.8	−0.2	−0.4
Germany, West	0.3	0.1	−0.4	−0.6	−1.0	−0.6
Italy[5]	5.3	−3.1	—	0.6	0.7	−1.7
United Kingdom	2.8	0.3	−2.2	−2.8	−1.7	−0.3
All countries above	0.7	−0.5	−0.1	−0.2	−0.1	0.4
All countries above except United States	1.4	−0.3	−0.4	−0.3	−0.5	−0.6

1. Composites for the country groups are weighted averages of the individual national ratios for each year, with weights proportionate to the US dollar value of the respective GNPs in the previous year.
2. Data for Canada are on a national income accounts basis.
3. Data for Japan cover the consolidated operations of the general account, certain special accounts, social security transactions, and disbursements of the Fiscal Investment and Loan Program (FILP) except those to financial institutions. Japanese data other than FILP transactions are based on national income accounts.
4. Data for France do not include social security transactions.
5. Data for Italy refer to the 'state sector' and cover the transactions of the state budget as well as those of several autonomous entities operating at the state level, but do not include transactions of social security institutions.
6. As measured by the difference between the 'cyclically neutral' fiscal balance and the unadjusted fiscal balance. For further information on the derivation of these figures, see *World Economic Outlook,* 1983, Appendix A2, pp 110–11.

SOURCE: *World Economic Outlook,* IMF, Washington, 1983.

Library of
Davidson College

Two factors lend some credence to this explanation of world economic performance, particularly in the 1980s. First, as Table 2.8 shows, fiscal policy in a significant number of industrial countries did indeed inject a contractionary impulse; and superficially at least the evidence seems to suggest that the recession was most marked in those economies where fiscal policy was most contractionary. Second, the price the oil, rises in which had been blamed by some for the recession that followed 1973, began to fall, and this on its own might have been expected to have had an otherwise reflationary effect on global aggregate demand. Indeed the falling price of oil in the early 1980s seems to lend some support to the view that it is a symptom of other factors (in this case falling global aggregate demand) rather than a cause. An additional factor in this general explanation is that after mid-1981 OECD countries as a group encouraged the IMF to push those countries turning to it for financial assistance towards adjustment programmes of a rather more demand deflationary type than had been the case immediately beforehand. At the same time many of them became more reluctant to provide financial assistance to developing countries through channels such as the International Development Association (IDA), and this in turn tended to have small deflationary effect on the world economy, since recipient countries were as a result less able to afford imports.

4.8 The breakdown of the Bretton Woods system and the move to flexible exchange rates

It has been suggested by some observers that part of the reason why individual governments were more prepared to pursue expansionary policies in the early 1970s than before was the move over to flexible exchange rates, which removed the constraint that had previously been imposed by the fact that deficits led to reserve losses. Furthermore, there is the argument that variations in exchange rates have been excessive and that this has led to destabilizing short-term capital flows, and has created uncertainty, which had had an adverse effect on trade and employment. To the extent that there has been exchange rate misalignment, this has created inappropriate price signals, and resources have therefore been inefficiently allocated throughout the world – the impact of North Sea oil on the sterling exchange rate and thereby on the competitiveness of UK industry is often quoted as an example. It is also suggested, however, that the move over to flexible rates has been used as an excuse by some governments not to allow international reserves to expand, and this in turn has had an adverse effect on world trade, output and employment. More generally the breakdown of the old Bretton Woods system has been superseded by a period in which there has been no 'system' as such and no central management of international financial affairs, and this state of affairs has been used to explain the recession, debt crises, and the threat of international banking collapse.

While there may be some truth in these arguments, considerable care needs to be exercised in interpreting them. A few counter comments will suffice here. First, there is the problem of timing. In fact the world moved on to flexible exchange rates at the end of the boom in the early 1970s and just before the recession of the mid-1970s. In many ways the adoption of flexible rates was a *response* to economic instability rather than a cause of it – though there may of course be a two-way affect between exchange rates and instability. Second, the Bretton Woods system broke down because of certain fundamental deficiencies in operation. It would certainly have been too inflexible to deal with the events of the 1970s. Third, the lack of central management that has characterised the period since 1973 allowed the private sector to make a significant contribution to the recycling difficulties that followed on the oil-price rise in 1973. Had the private international banks not performed this role, there would almost certainly have been a much deeper recession during the mid to late 1970s than there was. Thus, while the nature of the international financial system is far from irrelevant in discussing the world's economic performance, it is too simplistic to assume that it provides the complete explanation.

4.9 Composite explanations

The explanation of global economic performance since 1973 is made more complex, though probably also more accurate, by the fact that the hypotheses presented above are not mutually exclusive in all respects – though in certain specific cases they are. It is quite possible to come up with an explanation which draws selectively on a combination of the various hypotheses. As already noted, for instance, it is not necessary to argue that the determination of oil prices is completely administered and independent of market forces in order to argue that the changing price of oil has had a significant impact on the world economy. Furthermore, to believe, for instance, that the conduct of demand management policy has exerted an important impact does not mean that secular trends in production and trade or other changes on the supply side resulting from changes in the growth of productivity have to be regarded as unimportant.

The picture is further complicated by the fact that different explanations may have been more important at some times than at others, more relevant in some countries than in others, and better equipped to account for changes in some variables than in others. Indeed there is a strong commonsense attraction to the view that no one hypothesis has a monopoly of the truth and that world macroeconomic performance is in fact the outcome of an interaction between many forces which may sometimes be mostly pulling in a similar directly and at other times in different and even opposite directions. The snag is that such an explanation runs the risk of becoming no explanation at all, and it certainly makes it much more difficult to formulate policy, since this is best facilitated where a clearly defined causal relation has been identified.

5. GENERAL POLICY OPTIONS AND THE FRAMEWORK FOR POLICY IMPLEMENTATION

A prior question when discussing policy is whether it is necessary to adopt a particular policy at all. The answer depends on whether objectives are likely to be achieved if things are left as they are, and if not, whether it is possible to come closer to realizing them via a positive approach to economic policy.

The basic objective in the case of the global economy is growth and development with stability. However, this simple statement conceals the very many aspects of global economic performance discussed above which entail avoiding mass unemployment, rapid inflation, recession, payments disequilibria, debt crises, international financial crises, and an unacceptable degree of inequity between countries. Although attempting to forecast the behaviour of the world economy is a particularly hazardous exercise, even the most optimistic projections see little chance of a major change in the world's economic performance during the 1980s. Unemployment seems likely to remain historically high, inflation high by the standards of the 1950s and 1960s even though low by those of the 1970s, the growth of output low, and payments disequilibria large. Furthermore, problems of international indebtedness remain yet to be fundamentally solved, as does the whole question of the most appropriate mechanism for moving finance around the world, and the correct balance between international financing and adjustment. A positive policy approach cannot then be ruled out on the basis that it is not needed.

With regard to the effectiveness of policy, there are indeed variables on which it is difficult to exert a direct impact, at least in the short term. It is, for instance, difficult to influence global population size or the price of crude oil. Looking more broadly at supply side variables, policy-makers in market economies have shown themselves to have only a very limited influence over these. In any case the contribution of such factors as education, and therefore the quality of the work force, and capital formation to economic growth is not well defined nor the process of technical progress fully understood. Policy-makers have therefore generally set out to try and influence aggregate demand rather than aggregate supply. Except in those economies that rely heavily on central planning, policy has instead tried to create an environment conducive to encouraging the fulfilment of entrepreneurial 'animal spirits'. It is also important to note that a supply orientation does not lend itself to a global approach as conveniently as does a demand orientation.

Pursuing this idea of the level at which policy is applied, there are three alternatives available: unilateralism, co-ordinated unilateralism and multilateralism. Unilateralism means that individual countries are left to deal with their own economic problems in isolation. During the 1970s and early 1980s this was the approach adopted. In general, governments showed themselves reluctant to expand domestic demand for fear of the effect on inflation and their balance of payments. Unilateral policy therefore tended to be contractionary. As might have been expected, the policy had a beneficial effect on inflation but an adverse effect on practically all the world's other economic problems. One is forced to ask whether the benefits of such a policy outweigh the costs and indeed whether there are not better ways of reducing inflation.

Co-ordinated unilateralism requires that countries agree to pursue a package of macroeconomic policies with the objective of raising world output and employment without creating larger balance of payments disequilibria. Although frequent economic summits bringing together the leaders of the world's most powerful Western economies have provided the forum for such co-ordinated expansion, co-ordination has failed to materialize, largely because of the fear that expansion means inflation and that not all countries will fulfil their obligations.

Various international policies could be pursued under the multilateral approach. These might set out to control the creation and distribution of international reserves, to improve the means of international financial intermediation, to modify the role of international agencies such as the IMF – through which many of the policies might be operated – and to change global average propensities to spend and save though redistributing world purchasing power away from countries with relatively high propensities to save and towards those with relatively high propensities to spend. This is the sort of approach favoured by the Brandt Commission.

The co-ordinated unilateralist and multilateralist approaches share the central feature that they explicitly recognize the interrelations between countries that exist through the world's trading and financial system, that actions by one country or group of countries affect others, an induced response in which then has a feedback effect on the initiators. This recognition of external effects is likely to make these approaches more efficient at dealing with global problems. However, financial policies should themselves not be isolated from other policies. They need to be seen as but one component of world economic policy, which also comprises trade policy. Financial and trade policies need to be co-ordinated. There is, for example, little point in providing deficit countries with more finance and therefore more time for correcting their deficits if the scope for adjustment through accommodating trade policies is not simultaneously provided. The degree of co-operation and co-ordination required clearly poses very significant practical problems, but the stakes are high, indeed the costs of failing to come up with a remedy for the world's ailing economy could be immense.

3 The World's Financial System in Perspective

Since the beginning of the 1970s there have been many fundamental changes in the world's financial environment. These changes include the collapse of the par value international monetary system, the move towards floating exchange rates, the growth in the importance of private international financial markets, and the rise in the price of oil, which has brought about a redistribution of the world's financial wealth and has caused large balance of payments disequilibria. In this chapter we briefly examine these changes. We also spend some time looking at the international monetary arrangements preceding them.

Because of their apparent obscurity there is perhaps a tendency to under-estimate the importance of world financial issues and to underplay the central significance of the international financial system. This is unfortunate, since, although the mechanisms through which the world financial system exerts its influence on the world economy may indeed be somewhat difficult to grasp or to quantify precisely, there can be little doubt that they exert a very real effect on both the level and distribution of world economic welfare.

Basically the international financial system is the system through which countries settle debts with each other. It establishes the environment in which countries possessing different currencies trade and lend, and encompasses a collection of institutions, rules and conventions which influence the way in which balance of payments disequilibria are corrected or financed. The world needs such a system primarily because it needs a set of arrangements through which transactions may be carried out between people in different countries who use different domestic currencies. In the same way as an efficiently operating domestic monetary system generates gains in welfare through the facilitation of specialization and exchange within a country, so an efficiently operating international monetary system generates benefits by facilitating specialization and trade between countries. Within such a system there must be a mechanism for determining the rate of exchange between different currencies, and for defining what reserve assets will be acceptable in settlement of debt.

1. KEY FEATURES OF WORLD MONETARY SYSTEMS

Any international financial system may be interpreted as comprising characteristics relating to, first, the way in which imbalances in international payments are corrected, or in other words the adjustment issue; second, the nature of reserve assets in the system, the way in which they are created, and the extent to which payments imbalances may be financed, or in other words the liquidity issue; third, the degree of central management that the system encompasses, including the question of whose responsibility it is to ensure that policies adopted by individual countries are globally consistent; and fourth, the degree of confidence that is held in the stability of the system.

From this list the concepts of adjustment and liquidity emerge as being quite fundamental to the discussion of world monetary systems, adjustment involving the correction of payments imbalances and liquidity involving their financing. From the viewpoint of the world monetary system as a whole the relation between adjustment and liquidity is an inverse one; the more adjustment that is undertaken, the less are the system's requirements for liquidity. Different world monetary systems may be based on different combinations of adjustment and liquidity. Under one system emphasis may be placed on the rapid correction of payments imbalances, while under another system more stress may be laid on financing imbalances.

However international financial systems are not just concerned with efficiency. There are also important equity issues. Not least of these is that of determining the appropriate distribution of adjustment obligations and of financing.

2. THE EVOLUTION OF THE WORLD MONETARY SYSTEM

The present world monetary system is a patchwork of design and *ad hoc* amendment and modification. Whilst in a number of ways the system certainly reflects some of the various all-embracing plans that have been put forward at different times, it also exhibits features which it owes to sudden events and considerations of expediency. It might be useful to trace the evolution of the world monetary system. Let us begin by examining the system incorporated within the classical macroeconomic model.

2.1 The gold standard

The gold standard existed before 1914, when countries fixed the value of their currency in terms of gold. Exchange rates between currencies were therefore fixed. Gold was shipped around the world to finance payments deficits, and central banks bought and sold gold in return for domestic currency. Furthermore, gold constituted the principal reserve asset.

One of the most appealing features of the gold standard mechanism in theory is that its workings are quite direct and automatic. The principles upon which it operates may be summarized briefly. Assume a world made up of two countries A(merica) and B(ritain). If A achieves a surplus on its balance of payments with exports of goods and services and autonomous capital inflows exceeding imports of goods and services and autonomous capital outflows, there will be a net inflow of gold into A and, because B is the only other country in the world, a related net outflow of gold from B. The stock of gold in A therefore rises and that in B falls. Assuming, as the classical model does, that changes in the stock of money will be reflected by changes in the general price level, prices will rise in A and will fall in B. Assuming further that the demand for imports and exports in both A and B is relatively elastic with respect to price, the demand for A's exports will fall and the demand for A's imports will rise. At the same time the demand for B's exports will rise and the demand for B's imports will fall; the price changes induced by changes in domestic money supplies automatically restore balance of payments equilibrium in both countries. The gold standard mechanism therefore ensures that in the long run all payments imbalances are corrected via the simple mechanism of the money supply rising in surplus countries and falling in deficit ones.

However, for the gold standard to function effectively, even in theory, a number of preconditions have to be fulfilled. First, domestic money supplies have to be tied to the stock of gold in some way, otherwise the domestic money supply will not necessarily reflect changes in the domestic stock of gold. Second, prices and wages have to be flexible in both an upward and downward direction. If prices and wages are downwardly inflexible, then a fall in the money supply might be reflected by a rise in unemployment instead of a fall in prices. Third, there has to be no demand to hold money as an asset, otherwise a change in the money supply might be compensated for by a change in the propensity to store money, with the result that there will be no effect or only a muted effect on the monetary demand for goods and services.

These conditions are familiar components of the classical model and are open to equally familiar criticism. Perhaps most strategically the assumption of permanent full employment, which in the form of Say's Law underlies the classical model, is invalid. In many instances the monetary contraction implied by a balance of payments deficit led to relatively high levels of unemployment. As a result, the cost of correcting a balance of payments deficit frequently expressed itself in terms of unemployment rather than falling prices. The cost of sticking to the gold standard's rules when expressed in terms of unemployment in deficit countries (and inflation in surplus countries) proved too high, and governments which, through the fiduciary issue of fiat money, had the option of allowing the domestic money supply to change independently of the domestic stock of gold often decided to suspend the 'rules of the gold standard game'. Where expansionary domestic monetary policy was used to offset the contractionary effects emanating from a balance of payments deficit, full employment was maintained, but the payments deficit persisted.

Although the balance of payments continues to exert an impact on the domestic money supply, in ways that will be examined in more depth later in the book, the gold standard as an automatic regulator of imbalances was superseded after the First World War. It had been suspended during hostilities, but there was an attempt immediately after the war to restore the gold standard, with some countries agreeing to hold more of their reserves in the form of currencies convertible into gold rather than in gold itself. However, the problem was that the attempt to return to fixed exchange rates was based on pre-war values that were no longer appropriate. Sterling in particular was overvalued and confidence was undermined as a result. Dissatisfaction with the rules of the game and the lack of confidence in the fixity of exchange rates, combined with the economic turmoil of 1929–31, resulted in the final abandonment of the gold standard.

This was followed by a period of unsatisfactory experimentation in world monetary affairs. The world split into currency blocs, some currencies floated, others pegged to gold, and trade and exchange restrictions and currency depreciations became increasingly used in largely unsuccessful beggar-my-neighbour attempts to gain competitive advantage. There were no longer any generally accepted rules but rather a free-for-all from which nobody seemed to be benefiting. There was a clear incentive to come up with something better.

2.2 The Bretton Woods par value system and the International Monetary Fund

The desire to improve on the chaos of the 1930s led to the Bretton Woods Conference[1] in 1944 and an attempt to devise a system which would provide a more permanent and acceptable framework for international transactions. Two plans dominated the conference: the Keynes Plan and the White Plan.[2] Keynes wanted a system whereby countries could correct their balance of payments disequilibria without simultaneously having to sacrifice domestic objectives such as full employment and economic growth. His plan called for an International Clearing Union to supervise international settlements, which would be made in a new international asset to be called 'bancor' that would initially be acquired in exchange for gold. Countries continually running surpluses would build up their holdings of bancor with the Clearing Union, while countries continually running deficits would eventually run out of bancor and might have to make use of the overdraft facilities that were to be available. By penalizing, through high charges, both those countries that consistently gained bancor (surplus countries) and those countries that consistently lost it (deficit countries), Keynes hoped to encourage both surplus and deficit countries to contribute to the process of correcting balance of payments disequilibria. As a vital component of the adjustment process Keynes envisaged that exchange rates would be altered quite frequently both in an upward direction where countries experienced persistent surpluses and in a downward direction where persistent deficits were the problem.

In contrast, White put more emphasis on internal adjustment and the management of domestic aggregate demand to correct imbalances, rather than adjustment through use of the exchange rate. A corollary of internal adjustment is that finance has to be provided whilst adjustment is being made. White advocated the establishment of a stabilization fund to provide such finance.

The system that emerged from Bretton Woods bore more resemblance to the White Plan than to the Keynes Plan. It was intended that the Bretton Woods system would generate benefits for international trade in the form of *stable* (though not necessarily *fixed*) exchange rates, whilst, at the same time, avoiding the deflationary rigidities of the gold standard mechanism. The system was designed to ensure a world of full employment and economic growth. To this end the system exhibited a number of broad features. First, adherents to the system agreed to maintain par values for their currencies expressed in terms of the dollar, which was in turn tied in value to gold. The value of a currency could, however, vary 1 per cent either side of par, thus creating a 2 per cent band around the par value. Second, the par value of a currency could be changed after consultation with other members of the system but only in the event of the member being in a situation of fundamental balance of payments disequilibrium – a situation which was not rigorously defined. Third, through the International Monetary Fund (IMF), which was set up in 1946, the Bretton Woods system provided short- to medium-term finance to those countries experiencing temporary balance of payments deficits while in the process of adjusting. Fourth, all members of the IMF agreed to dispense with exchange restrictions on transactions in the current account of the balance of payments, while allowing destabilizing capital flows to be countered by exchange controls. However, free convertibility was not actually achieved until 1958, and so the Bretton Woods system did not begin to operate fully until then.[3]

In order to carry out its lending functions the IMF clearly needed financial resources. These it was agreed should come from its member countries through subscriptions to the Fund. Each member's subscription is determined by its quota. The size of each member's quota within the Fund is in turn based on the member's level of national income, the value and variability of its trade and the level of its reserves. Until 1973 subscriptions were paid partly in gold and partly in a member's own currency, but since then the whole of the subscription may be paid in a member's own currency.

The drawing provisions of the Fund are somewhat technical, and over recent years have in certain details been subject to quite frequent modification. The fundamental features have, however, remained unchanged and may be described briefly. To begin with, it is an oversimplification to say that members borrow from the Fund. In fact they purchase the foreign currencies they require with their own currency, undertaking to buy back their own currency from the Fund at a later date with foreign currency which is acceptable to the Fund – acceptability in this context depending on how much of any particular currency the Fund has. The more it has, the less acceptable are repayments in this currency. Drawing rights now comprise a number of elements. These are summarized in Table 3.1. As the table shows, the various facilities may be differentiated from one another in terms of the degree of conditionality that applies to them, as well as the length of time within which the drawing has to be repaid. Drawings under the reserve tranche are completely free of conditions; drawings under the lower credit tranches are conditional, but the conditions are not very harsh; drawings under the higher credit tranches are subject to conditions that are quite demanding.

In the period between 1947 and 1969 the Bretton Woods system underwent a number of superficial as opposed to structural modifications. These had a basically common theme – namely to provide the international monetary system with more liquidity as and when needed and thereby to strengthen the system. The modifications included first the General Arrangement to Borrow, introduced in 1962, whereby the Group of Ten countries (Belgium, Canada, France, Germany, Italy, Japan, the Netherlands, Sweden, the United Kingdom and the United States) plus Switzerland undertook to provide the IMF with extra convertible currencies should the Fund find itself short of resources. Second, at the initiative of the Federal Reserve System in the United States, a set of bilateral swap agreements was established during the 1960s whereby central banks agreed to swap respective home currencies with the object of offsetting short-term and reversible private speculation against a particular currency. The swap agreements served to support the position of the dollar, which was the pivot of the Bretton Woods system, being the major currency with which central banks intervened in foreign exchange markets, the currency in which the value of other currencies was expressed, and the only currency convertible into gold. Other modifications to the Bretton Woods system were designed more specifically to defend the pound sterling. In particular, various agreements made through the Bank of International Settlements in Basle (and therefore known as Basle Facilities) attempted to ensure that the United Kingdom would be provided with sufficient foreign exchange to maintain the pound's par value. However, the 1968 Basle Facility also made a step in the direction of converting short-term and volatile sterling liabilities into longer-term and more

TABLE 3.1 *Financial facilities of the Fund, their conditionality and possible cumulative purchases (per cent of quota)*

	Present position		*With supplementary financing facility*	
	Tranche policy	*Extended facility*	*Tranche policy*	*Extended facility*
Before second amendment takes effect				
Gold tranche	25.0	25.0	25.0	25.0
Credit tranches				
4 × 36.25	145.0	—	145.0	—
1 × 36.25	—	36.25	—	36.25
Extended facility	—	140.00	—	140.00
Supplementary financing[1]				
3 × 34.0	—	—	102.0	—
With extended facility	—	—	—	140.00
Subtotal	170.0	201.25	272.0	341.25
Compensatory financing	75.0	75.0	75.0	75.0
Buffer stock financing	50.0	50.0	50.0	50.0
Cumulative total[2]	295.0	326.25	397.0	466.25
After second amendment takes effect				
Reserve tranche	25.0	25.0	25.0	25.0
Credit tranches				
4 × 25	100.0	—	100.0	—
1 × 25	—	25.0	—	25.0
Extended facility	—	140.0	—	140.0
Supplementary financing[1]				
1 × 12.5; 3 × 30	—	—	102.5	—
With extended facility	—	—	—	140.0
Subtotal	125.0	190.0	227.5	330.0
Compensatory financing	75.0	75.0	75.0	75.0
Buffer stock financing	50.0	50.0	50.0	50.0
Cumulative total[2]	250.0	315.0	352.5	455.0

1. In special circumstances a standby arrangement may be approved for purchase beyond these limits and the normal limitations under tranche policy; in such cases purchases will be made with supplementary financing. The amount of such additional finance will be quantified in relation to a member's need and the adequacy of its programme.
2. In addition, some members have used oil facility drawings. The average use by those members was equal to 75 per cent of quota.

DATA: IMF Treasurer's Department.

Tranche policies

Gold tranche

Condition-balance of payments need.

First credit tranche

Programme representing reasonable efforts to overcome balance of payments difficulties; performance criteria and instalments not used.

Higher credit tranches
Programme giving substantial justification of member's efforts to overcome balance of payments difficulties; resources normally provided in the form of standby arrangements which include performance criteria and drawings in instalments.
Extended facility
Medium-term programme for up to three years to overcome structural balance of payments maladjustments; detailed statement of policies and measures for first and subsequent 12-month periods; resources provided in the form of extended arrangements which include performance criteria and drawings in instalments.
Supplementary financing facility
Used in support of programmes under standby arrangements reaching into the upper credit tranche or beyond, or under extended arrangements, subject to relevant policies on conditionality, phasing, and performance criteria.
Compensatory financing facility
Existence of temporary export shortfall for reasons beyond the member's control; member co-operates with Fund in an effort to find appropriate solutions for any balance of payments difficulties.
Buffer stock financing facility
Existence of an international buffer stock accepted as suitable by Fund; member expected to cooperate with Fund as in the case of compensatory financing.

---

stable ones, with participants, in return for a guaranteed exchange value for their sterling balances, agreeing to maintain a proportion of their reserves in sterling.

A far more strategic modification to the Bretton Woods system was introduced at the beginning of 1970 – the Special Drawing Rights (SDR) facility. This was strategic not inasmuch as it aimed to augment the supply of international liquidity, since many other modifications had done precisely this, but inasmuch as it ultimately aimed to change the way in which international reserve assets were created. Previously the main channels through which this had been done were, first, the mining of gold and its acquisition by monetary authorities; second, the running of balance of payments deficits in the United States, which served to increase the quantity of dollars held by central banks outside the United States; and third, increases in the size of drawing facilities within the IMF. The SDR facility aimed to bring the creation of international reserves under more purposeful control.

The main features of SDRs are as follows. First, SDRs constitute a purposefully created reserve asset. Second, they are allocated to 'participants' in the scheme in relation to the participant's quota. Third, they are not backed by debt. Fourth, they are internationally acceptable in exchange for foreign currency. Fifth, their use is unconditional, although at first there was a provision for reconstitution which stated that over five years a participant's average holding of SDRs should not drop below 30 per cent of that participant's average cumulative allocation. Sixth, the transfer of SDRs between participants in return for foreign exchange takes the form of a book-keeping entry in the Special Drawing Account of the IMF, and transfers do not serve to reduce the total amount of SDRs in existence. Seventh, SDRs, which originally had a gold value guarantee, have since July 1974 had their value expressed in terms of a 'standard' basket of currencies. Eighth, SDRs acquired yield interest in the form of additional SDR allocations, and SDRs used have an interest rate now related to the market level. Ninth, SDRs may be used to repay previous purchases from the General Account of the IMF.

SDRs are primarily designed to be used in order to meet balance of payments needs, but, with particular application to the United States, they may also be employed, in certain circumstances, to buy back currency liabilities created by the past running of deficits. SDRs are not, however, supposed to be used for the sole purpose of changing the composition of reserves.

While the use of SDRs is unconditional inasmuch as the purposes of particular transfers are not subject to prior challenge, improper use of SDRs is discouraged by the fact that offending participants may be passed over in future SDR allocations, or may be required to reaccept the SDRs improperly used.

When an SDR transfer is activated, the IMF selects the participant from which currencies will be drawn by reference to certain criteria. The Fund will normally call upon countries with strong balance of payments positions or strong reserve positions, or countries which are endeavouring to reconstitute their SDR holdings. A 'primary criterion' of the Fund in the operation of the SDR scheme is to maintain over time equality between participants in the scheme in terms of the ratios of SDR holdings (or of excess SDR holdings) to total reserves.

2.3 Weaknesses of the Bretton Woods system and its eventual breakdown

Although normally associated with a period of successful world economic performance, with the benefit of hindsight it is clear that the Bretton Woods system was subject to a number of shortcomings. These may be classified under the headings of adjustment, and reserve creation and confidence.

2.3.1 Adjustment

Although in principle the Bretton Woods system was based on adjustable par values, in practice it operated as a fixed rate system: exchange rates were simply not altered very frequently. Payments imbalances were corrected by means of the internal management of demand in the case of deficit countries and, up to 1960, by means of trade liberalisation in the case of surplus countries, and not by movements in exchange rates. The concentration on demand management gave rise to associated problems. First, demand management policies did not always work as speedily as was hoped. Second, countries were frequently reluctant to sacrifice domestic objectives such as full employment and growth in order to achieve balance of payments equilibrium, particularly countries such as the US, where the trade sector was relatively very small. Third, the existence of what were effectively fixed exchange rates implied that countries did not have precise control over their domestic money supplies, since these could be affected by movements of money across the foreign exchanges. In any case under the Bretton Woods system it became increasingly difficult for countries to pursue independent monetary policies, since the level of domestic interest rates was largely dictated by what was being offered abroad. Finally the adjustment burden, which architects of the system had supposed would fall equally on both deficit and surplus countries, in fact fell more than proportionately on deficit countries.[4] The ability of such countries to postpone or avoid adjustment was effectively constrained by the finite level of their international reserves and the limits on their ability to borrow on acceptable terms.

By contrast disequilibria in the form of balance of payments surpluses did not produce symmetrical pressures to adjust, since surpluses implied the accumulation of reserves, something which is not subject to a finite limit. The only cost of persistent surpluses to the country concerned is the opportunity cost of holding reserves, namely the marginal productivity of the real resources which such reserves could be used to purchase. Similarly countries – and in particular the US – which were in a position to finance their deficits with their own currency because of its acceptability abroad, i.e. reserve currency countries, were at an advantage compared with other deficit countries, since they did not need to call on assistance from the IMF and were therefore not subject to the conditions and discipline imposed by that institution.

The inflexibility of the Bretton Woods system with regard to exchange rate adjustment, which at the outset was felt would inspire confidence and discourage speculation against exchange rate movements, in fact proved to do just the opposite. Different rates of economic growth and inflation meant that the adjustment of par values became inevitable. The infrequency of such adjustment implied that when exchange-rate changes did take place they were large and predictable. As a result, and in anticipation of the eventual change in par values, speculative flows of short-term capital were generated. Short-term capital flows were further facilitated by the full convertibility amongst the major currencies which existed at the beginning of the 1960s as well as by the development of the Euro-currency market through the 1960s, which enabled funds to move swiftly between countries. Combined with the growth in the stock of short-term mobile capital, these factors meant that speculative flows put increasing pressure on the fixity of exchange rates incorporated in the Bretton Woods system.

Speculators were presented with a one-way option as far as exchange rate changes were concerned. The direction of the change could easily be predicted and the only doubt related to the exact date on which the change would be made. Thus a speculator anticipating a devaluation of sterling could enter into a forward contract to sell sterling, hoping that by the time he needed the sterling to sell in order to fulfil his part of the contract he would be able to buy it in the spot market more cheaply. The only small cost associated with such speculative activity was that in the absence of devaluation the speculator would have to pay a slightly higher price for the sterling that he bought in the spot market than the price he received for it in the forward market. However the potential gain in the event of devaluation far outweighed this loss. Speculators would only have suffered heavy losses under the Bretton Woods system if they had forecast inaccurately the *direction* of the exchange rate movement and the rigidity of the system effectively ruled out this possibility.

2.3.2 Reserve creation and confidence

Another crucial weakness of the Bretton Woods system was that it failed to provide a systematic mechanism through which world reserves could grow in line with world trade. The growth in world reserves which occurred throughout the 1950s and 1960s resulted primarily from deficits in the US balance of payments and not from increases in the quantity of gold, the price of which was fixed, or IMF credits (see Chapter 5). For instance, over the period 1949–59, of the $8.5 billion increase in world reserves, $7 billion was provided by the US through the increase in its liabilities to foreign monetary authorities. Under the Bretton Woods system the US took on the role of supplying international reserves to the world economy, a role which had been unspecified in the Bretton Woods agreement. For a time all was well. Dollars were in great demand, since they were needed for transaction purposes – largely unaffected by the ravages of war the US was the major world producer of the goods that other countries demanded. In addition, there was an asset demand for dollars, since the interest paid on dollar holdings made them an attractive alternative to gold. The dollar problem in the 1950s was one of shortage.

But the system hinged on there being confidence in the dollar, and during the 1960s, particularly towards the end of the decade, confidence weakened. This decline in confidence reflected the basic dilemma which underlies any gold exchange standard. In order to be widely acceptable as an international reserve a national currency must be strong in the sense that devaluation cannot be contemplated. But at the same time, in order to make a contribution to the stock of reserves owned by other countries, the currency must be weak in the sense that the reserve centre country must run balance of payments deficits. With an expanding world economy the liabilities of the reserve centre will grow in relation to its own reserves. In the case of the US the ratio between its liquid external debt and its gold stock rose from 0.39 in 1950 to 1.18 in 1960 to 2.10 in 1965 and to 4.24 in 1970.

The increase in the debt/gold ratio and the decline in confidence was further exacerbated by the fall in the size of the US gold stock, which was caused by countries converting dollars into gold. This conversion may be conveniently explained by two factors. The first is internal portfolio adjustment. Where countries have a constantly increasing portfolio of international reserves and wish to maintain a constant ratio amongst the portfolio's constituent parts, one of which is gold, there will be a related increase in the demand for gold. Given that other supply channels were closed or slow to respond, and that the price of gold was fixed such that the market mechanism was not allowed to operate, the US tended to meet this demand from its own stock of gold, which as a result fell. The situation altered somewhat in

1968, when a two-tier gold system with both a fixed official price and a free market price replaced the London gold pool arrangements that had operated since 1961 and under which the official price had been supported by means of central banks augmenting supply. Although monetary authorities retained a *de jure* convertibility right, there was little doubt that the continued use of that right would lead to it being revoked. To all intents and purposes the world had moved on to a dollar standard.

The second explanation is that convertibility was activated mainly by Western European countries, and in particular by France, in an attempt to dissuade the US from pursuing internal policies which were viewed by these countries as being unsound and to their own disadvantage. The argument usually took the form that the US was exporting inflation. In addition, it was felt that under the Bretton Woods system the US achieved an unfair transfer of real resources to itself, since under this system non-reserve currency countries exchanged real goods and services for what were effectively the IOUs of the US. In fact there were many conflicts of interest under the Bretton Woods system not only between countries but also between different objectives or factions within countries. Thus, while European countries accused the US of running deficits which it financed by adding to its external liabilities, causing international reserves and the rate of world inflation to rise, the US maintained that it was in a situation of fundamental disequilibrium whereby it was forced to choose between the internal target of full employment and the external one of balance of payments equilibrium, and that either it should be allowed to devalue or surplus countries should revalue vis-à-vis the dollar. Whilst surplus countries did not like the capital inflows which their surpluses tended to generate and which tended to frustrate their domestic monetary policies, neither did they like the prospect of the competitive disadvantage that revaluation would imply for their exporters. An underlying weakness of the Bretton Woods system was that there was no consensus on the appropriate distribution of cost and benefits associated with the system. All participants had some reason to feel that the system imposed costs on them whilst conferring benefits on others.

As things turned out, it was the US which brought matters to a head following a run out of the dollar, by formally suspending the convertibility of dollars into gold on 15 August 1971 and at the same time by introducing an import surcharge in an attempt to improve the balance of payments. Domestic demand deflation to improve the balance of payments was ruled out. The suspension of convertibility forced other countries to make a choice between, on the one hand, accepting an increasing stock of inconvertible dollar balances and effectively moving on to a dollar standard, or, on the other, revaluing against the dollar. The initial choice was made at a conference held at the Smithsonian Institute in Washington in December 1971, the objective of which was to negotiate a multilateral monetary agreement.

2.4 The Smithsonian Agreement, its collapse and the move to floating

The main features of the settlement achieved were, first, an increase in the dollar price of gold, and thus, to the extent that other countries maintained the gold value of their currencies, an effective devaluation of the dollar relative to other currencies; second, a rearrangement of the relative central or par values of a number of currencies; and third, the introduction of wider bands around the new central values which permitted exchange rates to move 2¼ per cent either side of par. The Smithsonian Agreement demonstrated two important things. One was that in certain circumstances it was possible to gain a measure of multilateral agreement on international financial matters, and the second was that the dollar could be devalued.

For a relatively short period of time following the Smithsonian Agreement the world monetary system was on a dollar standard, with currencies convertible into dollars but dollars not convertible into gold. This state of affairs did not last, however, and by the end of 1973 the Smithsonian Agreement, and a subsequent attempt to strengthen it, had been abandoned.

It is interesting to ponder on the reasons for the failure of this attempt at multilateral reform. Basically they are that the agreement was not only unable to restore confidence in the stability of central values, but also insufficiently flexible to allow exchange rates to move towards their equilibrium values where these had failed to be established by discretion. The view that the rates chosen in 1971 were inappropriate is supported by the observation that balance of payments disequilibria remained uncorrected after the agreement. Failure to select equilibrium exchange rates and the uncertainty and instability to which this gave rise dictated a move towards floating as a matter of expediency. Furthermore, floating was a convenient way of neutralising the effect of divergent rates of inflation amongst countries on their balance of payments. The floating has been independent in the case of some countries, and joint in the case of others, the most notorious joint float being that of some of the countries of the European Economic Community. In certain instances the floating has been free from intervention, whilst in others it has been rather more managed.

2.5 Aspects of the period since 1973

2.5.1 The rise and fall of the 'grand design'

The 'grand design' approach to world financial reform was encapsulated in the Committee of Twenty,[5] which was established in July 1972 in order to draft a complete reform of the international monetary system covering issues such as the numeraire of the system, the method of reserve creation, the method and distribution of adjustment, and the amortization of reserve currencies. There was considerable disagreement within the Committee on almost all the aforementioned issues and, as a result, the policy suggestions that emerged were vague and operationally unhelpful. The C-20's Outline of Reform[6] supported an exchange rate system based on stable but adjustable parities, but with a provision for floating in particular circumstances; international settlement on the basis of the transfer of reserve assets; and liquidity based on the Special Drawing Right, with a gradual phasing out of reserve currencies and gold. More positively the C-20 advocated the establishment of an Interim Committee[7] to carry on a review of the international monetary system, and a Development Committee[8] to examine the special interests of developing countries. Furthermore the C-20 suggested a new method of valuing SDRs and a new 'extended' lending facility in the Fund. Whilst it is true that each of these ideas has subsequently been acted upon, by and large the deliberations of the C-20 were overtaken by events, in particular the large rise in the price of oil in 1973–4 and the related *de facto* move to floating.[9]

2.5.2 The rise in the price of oil and the move to the market place

While the quadrupling in the price of oil certainly put very great strain on the world's financial system by creating massive disequilibria in the form of large surpluses in the oil-exporting countries and large deficits in the oil-importing countries, it also demonstrated the robustness of the system and its considerable ability to meet the demands put upon it by a changing financial environment. The immediacy of the problems which the oil-price rise created effectively pushed any idea of a grand design type of reform to the back of the stage. Instead attention became focused on the specific problem of financing the oil deficits and of recycling the oil surpluses. In this context there was a very significant move to the market place. Oil funds were recycled largely by the private international banks via the Euro-currency market, with the oil-exporting countries lending their surpluses and the oil-importing countries borrowing from it in order to finance their deficits. The role of the IMF as an institution for financing deficits faded into relative insignificance. An additional implication of the rise in the price of oil was that it served to increase the nominal demand for reserves at a time when some evidence suggested that the world economy, certainly after it moved over to floating rates, possessed excess reserves.

The effect of the oil price rise on the dollar was two-edged. From one point of view it increased the transactions demand for dollars,[10] and alleviated some of the pressures on the dollar, but from another it tended to worsen the US balance of payments, particularly given the reluctance of the US to economize on oil consumption, and this adversely affected confidence in the dollar and in turn reduced the demand to hold dollars.

2.5.3 The move to legalized floating: the Jamaica Accord

By the mid-1970s it was clear that the grand design approach to international monetary reform had been abandoned in favour of more limited reforms concentrating on those areas where agreement had already been reached, even if the agreement was to disagree. The Fund's Articles of Agreement were amended to reflect the *de facto* changes that had occurred. At the fifth meeting of the Interim Committee held in Jamaica in 1976 it was agreed to accept floating as a legitimate instrument of economic policy – under the amended Articles IMF members are permitted to adopt whatever exchange rate policy (fixed or flexible) they consider appropriate. The IMF, however, retains an overseeing role, in principle exercising 'firm surveillance' over the exchange-rate policies of members, who themselves are supposed to be assisted in the execution of their exchange-rate policy by adherence to certain guidelines that the IMF has laid down.[11] The amendment also abandoned the official price of gold, leaving it to be determined solely by market forces.

2.5.4 *The move to a 'non-system'*

With the legalization of floating and the increasing importance of the private sector as a source of balance of payments financing, doubts were cast over the continuing role of the IMF. Certainly some powerful and influential governments appeared to be unconvinced of the necessity of having the IMF and to welcome the move to the market. In 1983 there were prolonged difficulties in raising the extra resources that were needed even to cover what was a real reduction in the Fund's activities, and for a time the Fund had to stop lending altogether. Thus, ten years after the Bretton Woods system had broken down, the Bretton Woods institutions – the World Bank as well as the IMF – came under threat. The world no longer possessed a 'system' as such. There was no generally agreed set of rules and practices which all countries followed. There was no universal exchange rate regime but a collection of managed and unmanaged floating, pegging to individual currencies or baskets of currencies, large and small devaluations and crawling pegs. There was no general agreement on the distribution of responsibilities for achieving international adjustment, and the creation of reserves was influenced by the vagaries of balance of payments disequilibria, the operation of the Euro-currency market and the price of gold, and the supply of international liquidity by the decisions of private banks.

However, the move from a centrally and officially managed system to an unmanaged non-system was already proving far from satisfactory by the early 1980s, both in terms of the exchange-rate regime, which it had been supposed would eliminate currency misalignment but in fact seemed to intensify instability and to generate a number of unforeseen problems, and the method of providing finance, which was supposed to be more flexible and efficient but in fact seemed at least to contribute to the serious debt problems that cropped up in a number of developing and Eastern European countries.

Dissatisfaction was sufficiently great in some academic and even official quarters as to lead to calls for a new Bretton Woods conference to consider the possibilities for future reform. It is to formulating an agenda of items that need to be resolved that the following chapter is devoted.

4 An Agenda for International Financial Reform

Dissatisfaction both with the way in which the world economy has performed since 1973 as well as with the operation of the international financial non-system since about the same time has led to considerable pressure for a major re-think concerning the organisation of the world economy. Advocates of such an initiative see it as covering many aspects of the relation between countries, but in particular finance and trade.

It is, of course, important to look at these issues together since by their very nature they are highly interdependent. Thus, the success of financial reforms to increase the flow of funds to developing countries is likely to be thwarted unless these countries are allowed to expand their exports in order to pay back loans. Similarly, to argue in favour of a system of free and liberal trade is somewhat hollow unless international finance is also made available to permit countries to cover temporary payments deficits without having to resort either to import controls or to large doses of demand deflation that will have a damaging effect on world trade.

Having noted the fundamental complementarity between finance and trade, this book concentrates fairly narrowly on international financial issues. However, the importance of accommodating trade policy should not be forgotton. The purpose of this chapter is to construct an agenda of items that may enter into any discussion of world financial reform, and to act as an overture to the rest of the book.

1. AGENDA ITEMS

1.1 International adjustment

Basically, adjustment relates to any aspect of a country's economic policy which strengthens the underlying balance of payments by encouraging a reallocation or a change in the level of spending, output and resources. Given this definition, all policies that reduce a country's demand for imports or raise its export earnings might, at first sight, seem eligible to classify as a form of adjustment. However, this is misleading. A further distinction needs to be made between *stabilization* and *adjustment*. The balance of payments may be stabilized through the suppression of import demand. Although the observed payments position may improve as a result of such policies, it does not necessarily follow that fundamental correction has taken place. Merely to deflate domestic aggregate demand until imports have been reduced to a total consistent with a given level of exports does not automatically constitute adjustment in the true sense of the word.

The means by which countries attempt to strengthen their balance of payments form a crucial element in any international financial system. Should governments rely on policies whose primary impact is to reduce aggregate demand; or instead focus on those that use the price system both to create incentives for people to change the pattern of their expenditure between different goods, imported or domestically produced, and over time, between consumption and saving, and to change the way in which resources are used? Or alternatively should they dispense with the price system as a method for allocating resources, and rely more heavily on direct planning to change the pattern of production and trade?

The answers to these questions have implications not only for the individual countries themselves but also for other countries, and therefore become of global concern. A system which emphasizes the internal management of demand as the major weapon for eliminating unsustainable payments deficits, and simultaneously attempts to maintain fixed exchange rates, is likely to have a demand deflationary bias, since it will be those economies that are in persistent deficit that will be forced to take corrective action. There is no equivalent pressure on surplus countries to expand out of disequilibrium, and the initial burden of correction is therefore unevenly distributed.

Although in principle flexible exchange rates overcome this problem of asymmetrical adjustment, inasmuch as the currencies of surplus countries appreciate in the same way as those of deficit countries depreciate, they bring with them additional problems. Should exchange rates be determined purely by market forces, or does this result in excessive and damaging instability which can only be eliminated by intervention in the foreign exchange market by the monetary authorities of individual countries? But if governments are to intervene, what factors should determine the nature of the intervention; should it be aggressive, setting out to change the direction in which rates are moving, or more passive, merely 'leaning against the wind' and modifying the movements that would otherwise occur? Does freeing exchange rates in practice have an inflationary effect, inasmuch as it removes the discipline imposed by losing reserves, and is it more likely to lead to currency depreciations than appreciations?

Taking the entire period since 1945, the world now has considerable experience with many types of adjustment policy. There have been periods of both essentially fixed and more flexible exchange rate regimes and it should therefore be possible to reach some conclusions on their relative merits and demerits. In addition, it should be possible to reach rounded judgements on the adjustment issue as a whole.

1.2 International liquidity

Any financial system, whether domestic or international, has to have reserve assets and to possess the means by which these are created. Where reserve creation is an imperfectly competitive activity, and returns exceed costs, there is also the question of how the resulting profits should be distributed. Furthermore, it is necessary to determine how many reserves should be created; at what level do they become deficient or excessive?

In looking to the future the past provides at least some sort of guide, and the international financial system has, at different times, tried various solutions to the problems listed above. Reserves have ranged from commodities, in particular gold, to domestic currencies, in particular the dollar, to a centrally created international asset – the Special Drawing Right. Reserves have been created as a result of gold production, increases in the price of gold, payments deficits in reserve currency countries, the activities of the Euro-currency market and decisions by IMF. Countries have settled debts with one another both by adding to their externally held liabilities and by transferring the ownership of reserve assets. The fact that only the liabilities of some countries have been accepted as a means of settlement has led to the accusation that the system is inequitable. Reserve levels have sometimes been viewed as being excessive and as a principal cause of global inflation, yet at other times their deficiency has been seen as a cause of world recession.

All financial systems have ways of moving finance from lenders to borrowers. The international financial system achieves this through private capital markets, in particular the Euro-currency market, and through the official sector by the IMF, the World Bank and bilateral aid. Much concern has been expressed about the destabilizing effects of the Euro-currency market, and about the debt problems that are often seen as being associated with the increased importance of the private sector in recycling finance, particularly to developing countries. Meanwhile, many of the arguments underlying the provision of aid to developing countries have been challenged. Clearly any review of international financial arrangements needs to discuss these issues.

1.3 The balance between adjustment and financing

Adjustment and liquidity issues are closely related. The less finance that is available, the more rapidly balance of payments deficits have to be corrected. It is therefore important that the appropriate blend of adjustment and financing is achieved. The perpetual financing of deficits in particular countries would be economically inefficient and in any case unacceptable to those countries providing the finance. On the other hand, the emphasis on the rapid correction of deficits that the unavailability of finance creates leads to globally higher levels of unemployment and lower levels of output than might otherwise be achieved. At certain times it may be appropriate to stress reforms which increase international liquidity and which therefore allow adjustment to take place slowly, whilst at others it may be appropriate to stress the need for more rapid adjustment. But by what means can such a global view be reached?

1.4 Global macroeconomic management

Evidence on the performance of the world economy since 1973 shows clearly that, although there may be differences in detail between countries, in broad terms the fortunes of countries are significantly interrelated. Inflation and recession have been global phenomena and have not been isolated in a limited number of countries. But if there are global economic problems, should there not be global solutions?

The logic of this view is appealing, first, since in the absence of an agreed global approach it is likely that the actions of individual countries will be pro-cyclical rather than counter cyclical, and, second, since variables which may be beyond the control of any one government individually may not be beyond the control of governments collectively. However, there is no well defined forum within which such a global view may be reached and under which appropriate action may be taken. The activities of the IMF and OECD, as well as the occasional summit meetings of world leaders, make some contribution in this direction, but on the basis of the evidence of world economic performance it seems clear that the rather *ad hoc* arrangements that at present exist are not satisfactory. The mechanisms through which macroeconomic management can be co-ordinated globally therefore represent an important agenda item.

1.5 The roles of the principal international financial institutions

The discussion concerning global macroeconomic management unavoidably opens up the whole question of what roles the principal financial institutions should play in the 1980s and beyond, bearing in mind that they were set up in the light of the economic problems of the 1930s. Undeniably the world situation has changed dramatically since then. The IMF, for example, which was established to oversee an international financial system based on essentially fixed exchange rates and to provide significant amounts of balance of payments finance, finds itself confronted with floating rates and able to provide a much smaller proportion of finance than can be provided by the private international banks. Indeed, paradoxically, at the same time as the need for a more global approach to macroeconomic management has grown, the extent to which the international financial system is centrally managed has diminished.

It is therefore an appropriate time to re-think and possibly redefine the terms of reference of institutions such as the IMF and World Bank, and also consider whether new institutional arrangements are required. One important component of such a re-think would be to consider the division of labour between the official sector and the private sector. What should be the role of the private banks and the private international capital markets?

1.6 Global versus regional approaches

Another part of the evolutionary story of the world's financial system has been the development of regional and other groupings. Thus, we have the north (the OECD, the industrial countries as represented by the Group of 10) and the south (the developing countries as represented by UNCTAD, or the Group of 77). Within the north there is the European Economic Community, while within the south there are various economic groupings. In the case of the EEC, policies which have tried to resist global trends have been adopted. Thus, as the world economy moved over to floating exchange rates, a number of European countries endeavoured to maintain a considerable degree of fixity amongst the values of their own currencies. The EEC has even introduced its own unit of account (the European Currency Unit) and taken measures that effectively monetize gold at a time when internationally policy was attempting to demonetize it.

The question arises from this of what is the appropriate spatial level for international financial policy? Should Europe or the south go their own ways or should an effort be made to arrive at a set of generally acceptable international financial arrangements?

1.7 Equity and efficiency: the north–south issue

In order to make any arrangements generally acceptable it may help to make them reasonably equitable. Certainly one of the causes of dissatisfaction with the Bretton Woods institutions in the eyes of developing countries is that they are dominated by and favour the north. Even amongst industrial countries there have been feelings at times that the system did not treat all of them evenly. While it is undeniable that the international financial system needs to be efficient, efficiency is not everything. The equity of the system is also an important issue for discussion. However, considerations of equity immediately raise an important constraint on the negotiating process. If existing arrangements have favoured one group of countries against another group, the second group will demand that reforms should redress the balance. Yet it will be precisely such reforms that the first group will resist. What prospects do reform proposals have in such circumstances?

2. THE MECHANICS OF REFORM: GRAND DESIGN OR PIECEMEAL?

From a negotiating point of view it may be easier to get agreement on reforms that merely modify rather than completely restructure the system. The available evidence would certainly seem to support this view. While the Bretton Woods conference is a clear exception, subsequent attempts to redesign the entire system have failed. Yet many relatively minor, and indeed some not so minor, modifications have been made. However, they have not attempted to alter the basic framework. Most of these modifications represented *ad hoc* responses to specific difficulties. But a problem with ad hoccery is that the more fundamental problems often remain unresolved, and may indeed be made worse. It is therefore important to keep an eye on the broad issues so that it can be ensured that piecemeal reforms move the system positively in the desired, rather than in the opposite, direction.

The danger is that continuing pressures to deal expediently with specific crises of one kind or another as and when they arise never permit this broader view to be formed. Thus the mechanics of international financial reform become preoccupied with coping with the oil crisis, or the recycling crisis, or the debt crisis, or whatever, and little time is invested in considering the underlying structure of the system. Of course part of the problem here is that while there is no immediate crisis, there is no perceived need for action, yet as soon as a crisis arises, attention focuses on dealing with the specific crisis. There is therefore rarely a time when it seems appropriate to undertake a fuller review of the issues. The most conducive environment is one in which, while there is no immediate crisis to overcome, there is also fairly general agreement that the system is not working efficiently. While the 1970s and 1980s have seen their fair share of short-term international financial crises that have required immediate action, there has also been a growing awareness of the fact that the underlying non-system has been allowed to slip into dissarray. The time may then be ripe for a reassessment.

The remaining chapters of this book endeavour to examine many of the agenda items identified in this one. Some items have chapters exclusively devoted to them while others are less fully examined. But it is hoped that what emerges is a review of many of the central policy issues in world finance.

Part II
International Financing

5 International Reserves: Supply, Demand and Adequacy

1. INTRODUCTION

International reserves are those assets that a country's monetary authorities can use either directly or by converting them into other assets to support the exchange rate when the balance of payments moves into deficit. The precise classification of reserves is, in fact, rather arbitary, although reserves are conventionally defined to incorporate gold, convertible foreign exchange, Reserve Positions in the International Monetary Fund (RPF) – credit that is automatically available – Special Drawing Rights (SDRs) and European Currency Units (ECUs).

International *liquidity* is a rather broader concept, being defined generally as access to the means of international settlement. From a functional point of view the liquidity available to a country is, in principle, measured by its ability to finance balance of payments deficits without having to resort to adjustment. Operationally therefore a country's liquidity position should include not only the customary forms of reserve assets but also items such as its ability to borrow, the foreign exchange holding of its commercial banks, the willingness of foreigners to hold its currency in the event of a payments deficit, and the extent to which increases in interest rates or changes in the term structure of interest rates encourage capital inflows without also having undesired domestic repercussions. It follows that at both the global level and the level of individual countries the value of international liquidity will exceed the value of international reserves. Assuming that one part of a country's international liquidity will be free of conditions and the other part not free, a sub-classification may be made between conditional and unconditional international liquidity. This is a particularly relevant distinction when discussing the lending policies of the banks and the IMF.

In this chapter we concentrate on international reserves, leaving international liquidity to be dealt with in the following one, where the activities of the Euro-currency market, the private international banks, and the IMF are discussed. The chapter begins by tracing the evolution of the principal reserve assets in the international financial system and by providing a statistical summary of the quantity, composition and ownership of international reserves. It then moves on to examine a series of questions relating to the future. What should be the numeraire of the system, should it be gold, dollars, or SDRs; or should the existing pattern of reserve assets be maintained? If changes are to be advocated, e.g. establishing the SDR as the principal reserve asset, how are these to be achieved? Having determined what the principal reserve asset(s) should be, and having examined the means by which the transition can take place, a further question is whether the quantity of reserves should be controlled and if so how? In discussing this question the issue that dominated the debate over international liquidity during the 1960s will also be examined, namely the adequacy or inadequacy of international reserves. This discussion highlights the close interrelation between many issues conventionally listed under the heading of international reserves, or liquidity, or financing, and the efficiency of international adjustment, comprising in part the nature of the exchange rate regime.

2. INTERNATIONAL RESERVE ASSETS

As noted above, there are a range of assets in the international financial system that are normally included in most definitions and calculations of reserves. Some of these, basically certain foreign currencies or foreign exchange, may be directly used to buy goods and services or other currencies; others, including that part of a country's borrowing from the IMF that may be drawn automatically and unconditionally, SDRs and ECUs may not be directly used in such a way but first need to be swapped into foreign exchange.

All the aforementioned components of reserves share the feature that they may be used relatively quickly should the need arise: they are all relatively liquid. Gold is rather more ambiguous in this respect. In principle countries might pay off their debts in gold or could sell it in order to raise the necessary foreign exchange. In practice, however, gold is not used in this way and is not therefore a very liquid asset. Monetary gold, as opposed to gold used for commercial and industrial purposes, is no longer shipped around the world, and large sales of gold by monetary authorities would clearly depress its price, something that substantial holders of gold would normally be anxious to avoid.[1] Still, the principle remains and gold is counted as a reserve asset rather than merely as a speculative commodity stock.

However, this is not the end of the story. Although, as we noted in Chapter 3, the official price of gold was abandoned in 1976, there is as yet incomplete unanimity amongst authorities as to how to value their holdings of gold.[2] It can clearly make a considerable difference if gold is valued for official purposes at SDR 35 per ounce when the market price is somewhere in the region of SDR 400–500 per ounce.

2.1 The quantity and composition of reserves

Although by 1950 the Bretton Woods system had been set up and the gold standard had been discarded, gold still had a very important role in the international financial system and was by far the largest single reserve asset. Indeed gold was much more important than all the other reserve assets combined. This was still the situation as late as 1967. However, between 1969 and 1976 gold as a percentage of total reserves fell dramatically from 49.5 per cent to 15.9 per cent. Over the same time the significance of foreign exchange grew rapidly from 42.0 per cent to 72.2 per cent. Not surprisingly, it is the changing relative importance of gold and foreign exchange that is the central feature of this period. SDRs, first created in 1970, failed to account for a significantly large proportion of total reserves, nor did Reserve Positions in the Fund, though there were some variations in the importance of these components as SDR allocations were made and as IMF quotas were periodically increased.

Another important, though related, feature of this period was the large increase in total reserves in the early 1970s. This took place in spite of the fact that the amount of gold and RPF fell. Its cause was in small part the allocation of SDRs but much more significantly an increase in foreign exchange.

As Table 5.1 reveals, after 1976 the picture becomes more complicated and depends significantly on how gold is valued. Using

TABLE 5.1 *Official holdings of reserve assets, end of selected years 1973–82 and end of March 1983*[1] *(billions of SDRs)*

	1973	*1977*	*1978*	*1979*	*1980*	*1981*	*1982*	*March 1983*
All countries								
Total reserves excluding gold								
Fund-related assets								
Reserve positions in the Fund	6.2	18.1	14.8	11.8	16.8	21.3	25.5	29.4
Special drawing rights	8.8	8.1	8.1	12.5	11.8	16.4	17.7	17.5
Subtotal, Fund-related assets	15.0	26.2	22.9	24.3	28.6	37.7	43.2	46.9
Foreign exchange	102.7	203.6	223.9[2]	249.7	296.8	304.8	294.6	293.3
Total reserves excluding gold	117.7	229.8	246.9[2]	274.0	325.4	342.5	337.8	340.2
Gold[3]								
Quantity (*millions of ounces*)	1,022	1,029	1,037	944[4]	952	952	947	947
Value at London market price	95.0	139.8	179.9	367.1	440.2	325.0	392.2	364.1
Industrial countries								
Total reserves excluding gold								
Fund-related assets								
Reserve positions in the Fund	4.9	12.2	9.6	7.7	10.7	13.5	17.1	20.7
Special drawing rights	7.1	6.7	6.4	9.3	8.9	11.9	14.1	14.1
Subtotal, Fund-related assets	12.0	18.9	16.0	17.1	19.6	25.4	31.2	34.8
Foreign exchange	65.7	100.0	127.2	136.1	164.3	159.7	153.2	155.1
Total reserves excluding gold	77.7	118.9	143.1	153.2	183.9	185.2	184.4	190.0
Gold[3]								
Quantity (*millions of ounces*)	874	881	884	789[4]	788	788	787	787
Value at London market price	81.3	119.6	153.4	306.7	364.2	269.1	326.0	302.6

TABLE 5.1—*continued*

	1973	*1977*	*1978*	*1979*	*1980*	*1981*	*1982*	*March 1983*
Oil-exporting countries								
Total reserves excluding gold								
Fund-related assets								
Reserve positions in the Fund	0.3	5.4	4.4	3.0	4.1	5.8	6.7	7.4
Special drawing rights	0.3	0.4	0.5	1.0	1.2	1.8	2.1	2.0
Subtotal, Fund-related assets	0.6	5.8	4.9	4.0	5.3	7.6	8.8	9.4
Foreign exchange	10.2	55.2	40.1[2]	51.0	66.9	72.4	66.8	60.5
Total reserves excluding gold	10.8	61.0	45.0[2]	55.0	72.2	80.0	75.6	69.9
Gold[3]								
Quantity (*millions of ounces*)	34	34	36	37	40	42	42	42
Value at London market price	3.1	4.8	6.3	14.2	18.5	14.2	17.4	16.2
Non-oil developing countries								
Total reserves excluding gold								
Fund-related assets								
Reserve positions in the Fund	0.9	0.5	0.9	1.0	2.1	2.0	1.7	1.3
Special drawing rights	1.4	1.1	1.2	2.1	1.7	2.7	1.6	1.4
Subtotal, Fund-related assets	2.4	1.6	2.1	3.2	3.8	4.7	3.3	2.7
Foreign exchange	26.8	48.4	56.6	62.6	65.5	72.7	74.6	77.7
Total reserves excluding gold	29.2	49.9	58.7	65.8	69.2	77.3	77.8	80.3

TABLE 5.1—*continued*

	1973	*1977*	*1978*	*1979*	*1980*	*1981*	*1982*	*March 1983*
Gold[3]								
Quantity (*millions of ounces*)	114	114	117	118	124	122	118	118
Value at London market price	10.6	15.5	20.2	46.2	57.5	41.8	49.7	45.4

1. 'Fund-related assets' comprise reserve positions in the Fund and SDR holdings of all Fund members and Switzerland. Claims by Switzerland on the Fund are included in the line showing reserve positions in the Fund. The entries under 'Foreign exchange' and 'Gold' comprise official holdings of those Fund members for which data are available and certain other countries or areas, including Switzerland. Figures for 1973 include official French claims on the European Monetary Co-operation Fund.
2. Beginning with April 1978, Saudi Arabian holdings of foreign exchange exclude the cover against a note issue, which amounted to SDR 4.3 billion at the end of March 1978.
3. One troy ounce equals 31.103 grams. The market price is the afternoon price fixed in London on the last business day of each period.
4. The decrease recorded in the quantity of countries' official gold holdings from the end of 1978 to the end of 1979 reflects mainly the deposit by the members of the European Monetary System of 20 per cent of their gold holdings with the European Monetary Co-operation Fund. The European currency units issued in return for these deposits are shown as part of the countries' official foreign exchange holdings.

SOURCE: International Monetary Fund, *International Financial Statistics*.

its old defunct official price, the dominance of foreign exchange continues beyond 1976. On this basis by 1982 gold accounted for only just over 9 per cent of total reserves, Fund-related assets (RPF and SDRs) for 10.5 per cent, and foreign exchange for 80.3 per cent. However, when the market price is used, gold as a proportion of total reserves rises to 43.8 per cent in 1982. Indeed in the period 1979–81 gold valued at its market price accounted for 55.4 per cent of total reserves, foreign exchange for 40.3 per cent and Fund-related assets for a paltry 4.2 per cent.

Of course the choice between using the market price or the old official price also has a dramatic effect on the total value of reserves. First, because the market price is so much higher, using it serves to increase the value of global reserves. Second, because the market price fluctuates quite markedly, total reserves become more unstable than they would otherwise be. Again from Table 5.1 it may be seen that the market price of gold rose from SDR 117.1 per ounce in 1976 to SDR 440.3 per ounce in 1980, then fell back to SDR 271.6 per ounce in 1982.

Variations in the total value of international reserves have been a particularly significant feature of the eighties. Before 1980, and with only an isolated exception, total reserves had continually grown, largely as a result of the growth of foreign exchange and latterly gold when valued at its market price. After 1980, however, first the absolute value of gold and then the absolute value of foreign exchange declined, with the result that between 1980 and 1982 total reserves fell by almost 23 per cent. This decline sparked off considerable debate about the adequacy of reserves and the need for additional allocations of SDRs, questions to which we return later in this chapter.

Before an attempt is made to explain the developments catalogued above, two other developments need to be mentioned. The first relates to the introduction of the ECU as a new form of asset in 1979. Members of the EEC receive ECUs in return for paying a proportion of their gold and reserve currencies into the European Monetary Co-operation Fund. Although this mainly affects the composition of reserves, it also represents a net addition to reserves inasmuch as the EMCF values gold at a market-related price.

The second development relates to the changing composition of official foreign exchange reserves. In 1976 over 85.4 per cent of these were held in dollars or Eurodollars and 14.6 per cent in other currencies. By 1981 only 63 per cent were held in a dollar form.

Meanwhile holdings of other currencies such as the Deutsche mark, the yen and the Swiss franc accounted for 21 per cent, and holdings of ECUs for 16 per cent. Central banks seemed to be gradually diversifying the range of reserve currencies they held, and moving away from dollars.

The explanation of the changes so far reported lies in a combination of factors, including changing institutional arrangements, changing patterns of trade and investment, the changing conduct of economic management and related changes in the distribution of balance of payments surpluses and deficits, changing preferences amongst the holders of official reserves, and the changing exchange rate regime.

Changing institutional arrangements include the introduction of SDRs in 1970, the abandonment of the official price of gold in 1976, the introduction of ECUs in 1979 and occasional increases in IMF quotas. Of course such changes in themselves only provide an intermediate explanation, since there is the more fundamental question of why the changes were made. In the case of SDRs it was the desire to devise a more satisfactory method of reserve creation; in the case of gold the desire to eliminate the large and almost certainly unsustainable difference between the market and official prices and to demonetize it; and in the case of ECUs the desire to move along the road towards European monetary unification. Increases in Fund quotas were fairly automatic, being designed to maintain the Fund's resources and reviewed every few years. But in 1983 the US Congress was very reluctant to vote through the necessary legislation, and the increase was delayed by a prolonged debate about the role of the Fund, and some domestic US political issues.

Changes in the location of deficits and surpluses have a significant bearing on the quantity and composition of foreign exchange. Where a country whose currency other countries are prepared to hold is in deficit, the significance of that currency in total foreign exchange holdings will tend to rise. Thus, the quantity of dollars, marks or yen in the system will at least *to some extent* reflect the state of the US, German and Japanese balance of payments. However, this again is only a partial and intermediate explanation. Holdings of currencies do not perfectly match balance of payments changes; indeed the accumulation of reserves by non-reserve centre countries does not even require deficits in the reserve centres.[3] Moreover, there is the problem of explaining the state of the balance of payments. For example, one explanation of the big increase in the dollar component of foreign exchange reserves in the early 1970s is that the US government was pursuing fairly easy monetary policy, which resulted in large US deficits. Similarly, it might be suggested that the declining relative importance of the dollar in the late 1970s and early 1980s reflected the strengthening US payments position. Again the volume of externally held Deutche marks increased in the late 1970s and early 1980s when Germany was experiencing a deficit in its balance of payments, but was at the same time reluctant to finance this by running down reserves. Previously Germany and Japan had opposed allowing their currencies to be used as reserve currencies.

Turning now to the preferences of reserve holders, in one sense these do not change, since there is no doubt a continuing preference for a portfolio of assets yielding a relatively high return and a relatively low risk. It is therefore not this preference that changes but rather the combination of assets that is seen as best fulfilling it.

In principle, monetary authorities might be expected to speculate on the future price of gold, and to switch between reserve currencies, depending on the relative interest rates on offer and their expectations of what is going to happen to exchange rates and thus the prices of currencies expressed in terms of other currencies. In practice, as the data on gold holdings in Table 5.1 confirm, official holders do not speculate with gold. Nor does it seem that official holders actively switch the composition of their foreign exchange in order to maximize return. Such activity would lead one to expect that holders would have a relatively undiversified mixture of currencies at any particular time but that they would make quite frequent changes in the identity of the currencies held. But if the move catalogued above implies that individual countries are holding diversified portfolios, this suggests, in contrast, that holders have been primarily concerned with minimizing the risk of loss associated with holding an undiversified portfolio of currencies in an environment of flexible exchange rates. They have not wanted to be in a situation where all their foreign exchange is in one currency the value of which might suddenly fall. Diversification at the level of individual countries is a risk-averting strategy.

In fact there are a range of factors influencing the composition of a country's official currency holdings. Return and risk may not be the most important ones. Other influences are the nature of a country's exchange rate arrangements, its pattern of trade, a reluctance to destabilize the international financial system, agreements between countries not to hold each others currencies as reserves, such as exists under the European Monetary System, and plain inertia. A country whose currency is pegged to the dollar, which trades heavily with the US, and which has traditionally held most of its foreign exchange in the form of dollars is more likely to hold a high proportion of its foreign exchange in dollars than is another country which has a floating exchange rate, and therefore little need to intervene in the foreign exchange market, and fewer trading ties and historical connections with the US. Industrial countries exhibit the strongest revealed preference for dollars as opposed to other currencies, non-oil LDCs a rather weaker preference, and oil-exporting LDCs the weakest preference of all.

2.2 The ownership of reserves

Information on the ownership of reserves is also contained in Table 5.1. In 1982 industrial countries held 64 per cent of RPF, 74 per cent of SDRs, 51 per cent of foreign exchange, and 83 per cent of gold, excluding that held by the EMCF. One of the principal changes since 1950 has been the declining ownership of reserves by the US. In 1950 the US owned over 50 per cent of total reserves, largely because its gold holdings accounted for 68.5 per cent of the total amount of gold held by members of the IMF. During the late 1950s and 1960s European countries, in particular France and to a lesser extent Germany, swapped dollars for gold. As a result, reserve holdings in the US declined and those in France and Germany increased. By 1970 the US held just under 30 per cent of total official stocks of gold, Germany held 10.7 per cent and France 9.5 per cent, but the US still had the largest holdings of reserves. By 1980 this situation had changed – if gold is valued at SDR 35 per ounce. On this basis Germany then held 11.5 per cent of total reserves, France 6.8 per cent, the US 6.0 per cent, Italy 5.7 per cent, Japan 5.7 per cent, Saudi Arabia 5.2 per cent, the UK 4.7 per cent, Switzerland 4.3 per cent and the Netherlands 3.0 per cent.

The changing ownership of reserves can again be explained by a combination of factors. The exchange of dollars for gold by France and Germany has already been noted, with gold counting as reserves in all countries but dollars only counting as reserves when held outside the US. An additional factor has been the distribution of surpluses and deficits throughout the world. Countries that have run persistent payments surpluses, such as Japan, Germany and recently

Saudi Arabia, have been able to build up their reserves, though of course it is the reasons behind the surpluses that provide the ultimate explanation. Other countries have borrowed from the Euro-currency market to increase their reserves. Another factor to bear in mind is the increase in the price of gold since 1976. Since the ownership of gold is highly concentrated, with just ten industrial countries holding nearly 80 per cent of total official stocks, the increase in its price has widened the inequality in the ownership of reserves – when these are defined to include gold at its market price. In turn this has been a bone of contention between developing countries, which hold a relatively large proportion of their reserves in foreign exchange and own relatively little gold, and developed countries. It is an issue to which we return in Chapter 11, where we also look at the idea of changing the way in which SDRs are allocated so that a larger proportion of these go to developing countries.

3. THE NUMERIARE DEBATE: GOLD VERSUS FOREIGN EXCHANGE VERSUS SDRs

The current combination of reserve assets in the international financial system was not devised or planned. It instead reflects the result of a process of evolution. From an initial position of dominance after the Second World War gold became progressively less important throughout the fifties and sixties. With the demand for reserves increasing more rapidly than the output of gold and with the official price of gold fixed, excess demand was met by increased external holdings of dollar liabilities. However, dissatisfaction with this method of reserve creation ultimately led to the introduction of SDRs.

One issue that crops up in any debate about international financial reform is what should be the principal reserve asset or the numeraire in the system? Should attempts be made to resurrect gold; should a dollar standard be accepted; or should measures be taken to encourage the establishment of the SDR as the principal reserve asset? However, a further question is should there be one principal reserve asset at all? Is it not better to have multiple reserve assets, and within this arrangement multiple reserve currencies? In this section we examine the arguments and counter-arguments associated with the various options.

3.1 Gold

Gold does have certain attractions. It has a value in use as well as in exchange and this, as well as its being the traditional international reserve asset, creates confidence. Furthermore, as noted in Chapter 3, the gold standard adjustment mechanism has the appeal of automaticity; there are established rules which, if followed, imply that disequilibria will be corrected. The need for reserves is therefore kept to a minimum.

Against this, gold has important shortcomings as a reserve asset. First, it has to be dug out of the ground and then stored, and this is costly. Moreover, it is possible to avoid these costs and derive a 'social saving' by using assets which are cheaper to produce.

Second, the benefits from using gold are not equally or even remotely equally distributed throughout the world. There are profits to be made from producing reserve assets. These arise where their value, in terms of their command over goods and services, is greater than their costs of production. Even though relatively costly to produce, the value of gold exceeds its production costs. Because of the geographical concentration of gold deposits, the production of gold is imperfectly competitive and gold producers therefore derive monopoly profits or 'seigniorage'. When it is recalled that the Soviet Union and South Africa are major producers, it may clearly be seen that there will be political resistance to using gold as the principal reserve asset.

Third, assuming for a moment that the official price of gold is fixed, the level of world economic activity will tend to adjust to the quantity of gold in the system. If the quantity of gold expands more rapidly than the quantity of other goods and services, inflation is the likely result, whereas if the quantity of gold expands less rapidly than the demand for it, recession and unemployment are likely to follow.

One apparent way out of the dilemma is to let the price of gold fluctuate. Indeed there was a lengthy debate during the 1960s over whether the supposed inadequacy of international reserves should be met by raising the official price of gold. The debate, though an intriguing one, is largely of historical interest. Critics of the plan argued that it would reward the gold hoarders and encourage further hoarding of gold by creating the expectation that the price would be raised further in the future, something that the increased hoarding would itself make more likely. Nowadays, of course, there is no official price of gold to raise, and the market price moves in a manner typical of most commodities, i.e. there are big swings in the price of gold. Therefore an international financial system based on gold valued at its market price would experience large variations in the value of its reserve asset and this could do little other than augment uncertainty and instability. The counter-argument that the variations in price would simply reflect the fact that the value of reserves is adjusting to the underlying demand for them holds little water when it is remembered that variations in demand are also likely to reflect speculation.

3.2 Foreign exchange: individual and multiple currencies

Using national currencies as international reserve assets overcomes some of the deficiencies associated with gold. Most significantly there is the social saving to be made. The size of this is positively related to the amount of reserves created and the marginal productivity of the resources freed from producing gold and negatively related to the administrative costs of servicing the paper money. With a fixed official price of gold the significance of the social saving associated with the use of currencies will rise as the value of international reserves increases, since it is reasonable to assume that there are increasing costs associated with mining gold and decreasing costs associated with producing paper currencies. If currencies can fulfil the functions of an international reserve asset just as well as gold, global economic efficiency suggests that they should be used instead of gold. In this sense the use of foreign exchange has made gold a 'barbarous relic'.

However, while a growing world economy needs additional reserves, even though other factors such as the efficiency of payments adjustment and the incidence and size of payments disequilibria will also affect this need, it is possible to create reserves at too rapid a rate. One deficiency of relying on a currency as the principal reserve asset is that its supply will be related to the state of the reserve currency country's balance of payments and may not have much to do with the needs of the international financial system for additional reserves. It cannot be assumed, therefore, that the growth in foreign exchange always reflects an increase in the demand for it.

Apart from the lack of central and purposeful control over the quantity of foreign exchange, there is again the question of the distribution of seigniorage. As with gold, there are profits associated with the production of a reserve currency. Indeed since the costs of producing paper currencies are relatively small, the profits are likely to be relatively high. In a system based on foreign exchange the seigniorage goes primarily to the countries which produce the currencies that perform the reserve asset role. By definition these will be countries that are relatively rich and economically strong, since such strength is a precondition for reserve currency status. In a sense, then, a system based on foreign exchange is unavoidably inequitable.

On the other hand, the benefits of reserve status can be overstated. First of all, interest is paid on the balances of currency held; even though this will itself be paid in currency, it represents an additional claim on the real resources of the reserve currency country. Second, being the world's banker imposes constraints on the conduct of domestic economic policy, since crises of confidence in the currency have to be avoided where possible.

It is partly because of these constraints that countries such as Germany and Japan had been reluctant to see their currencies used as reserves. However, as explained earlier, one feature of the late 1970s and early 1980s was the move towards multiple reserve currencies and away from the more exclusive use of the dollar. While allowing reserve holders to diversify their portfolios of assets and to reduce the risks that had been increased by the move to floating exchange rates, a multiple reserve currency system does present the additional worry that instability may be caused by holders switching the composition of their reserves between different currencies in the expectation of changes in interest rates and exchange rates. To the extent that the system facilitates destabilizing speculation – a phenomenon discussed in more detail in Chapter 10 – it suffers from a significant potential weakness. Inefficiencies in the allocation of resources will result where speculation, under the framework of a multiple reserve currency system, shifts exchange rates away from the levels that would be determined by underlying real economic competitiveness. The additional uncertainty generated by unstable exchange rates can have adverse consequences for the growth of world trade and prevent the additional welfare gains that would be derived from it.

A further problem with a multiple reserve currency system is that the compositional multiplicity of currencies can in practice turn out to be rather limited. Under such a system reserve growth largely depends on running payments deficits in reserve currency centres; it therefore tends to take place in the form of relatively weak currencies. It seems to be one of the fundamental inconsistencies of the multiple currency reserve system that there will be a shortage of strong currencies into which it might be anticipated that central banks would wish to move, and a superfluity of weak currencies from which it might be anticipated that there would be an outward movement. Combined with the uncertain effects on the growth of reserves and the lack of systemic management associated with multiple reserve currencies, these deficiences provide good reason to examine alternative reserve assets.

3.3 Special Drawing Rights

SDRs, which in fact account for such a small proportion of total international reserves, in theory have many advantages over the other more important reserve assets. However, for the most part these advantages can only be derived if the SDR can be established as the principal reserve asset rather than as just one asset amongst many. Its attractions include, first, that the creation of SDRs can be controlled centrally and purposefully by the IMF. The quantity of SDRs can in principle therefore be modified according to the needs of the system. The same cannot be said either of gold or foreign exchange.

Second, because of this measure of central control, the international community can choose the appropriate distribution of the seigniorage associated with SDR creation. Broadly speaking, there are two methods by which this may be done. Seigniorage may be used by the IMF, as the issuer of SDRs, to achieve some generally agreed international objective such as the alleviation of poverty. Thus, there are the proposals for an SDR aid link mentioned in previous chapters and discussed more fully in Chapter 11. Alternatively, it may be allocated to the holders of SDRs either by means of paying them a sufficiently high rate of interest or by distributing SDRs on the basis of the long-run demand for reserves in individual countries, thus ensuring that in the long-run initial recipients hold rather than spend them and benefit from the additional security provided by extra reserves.

In practice SDRs have been allocated on the basis of IMF quotas, the supposition being that these reflect the long-run demand for reserves in different countries. The vast majority of SDRs have therefore been allocated to developed countries. However, since some recipients, in particular the developing countries, have in fact been persistent net users of SDRs and have thereby acquired an unrequited net inflow of real resources, they have derived some additional proportion of the seigniorage associated with SDRs. There has, then, been an informal link even in the absence of a formal one. However, the increase in the early 1980s in the rate of interest charged on the net use and paid on the net acquisition of SDRs up to a market-related level from the previously very low level has served to change the distribution of seigniorage. Now net users receive rather less of it and acquirers rather more than they did before.

Third, SDRs are a sophisticated reserve asset and are accepted by agreement rather than because they have value in use or represent the liabilities of any particular country. Furthermore, their value, determined as it is by the average value of a weighted basket of hard currencies, is more stable than that of either gold or individual currencies – though it is true that countries may be able to devise a preferable made-to-measure combination of currencies in which to hold their reserves.

Finally, with the SDR as the principal reserve asset there would not be the international financial instability caused by monetary authorities switching the composition of currency holdings. A major weakness of a multiple reserve currency system could therefore be avoided.

The problem with the SDR does not so much relate to its deficiencies as a reserve asset – indeed as noted earlier the IMF is already committed to establishing the SDR as the principal reserve asset and has accepted the logic of its superiority – as to the means by which its pre-eminence may be achieved. Part of the difficulty here is tied up with the functions that money is normally expected to perform, as a medium of exchange, a unit of account, and store of wealth. At present the usefulness and therefore the attraction of SDRs is limited by comparison with foreign exchange. Significant changes will almost certainly be needed if the SDR is to achieve the status of the principal reserve asset. These changes are discussed in Section 5.2 of this chapter, which deals with the policy options available. However, before moving on to these issues, there are a number of other issues in the debate about international reserves that need to be discussed.

4. THE ADEQUACY OF INTERNATIONAL RESERVES

For the sake of argument let us assume that the SDR is established as the principal reserve asset. The next question immediately arising is 'how many SDRs should be created?' Even if SDRs continue to fulfil only a secondary (or even a tertiary) role, the question remains of when should SDR allocations be made. How can one judge whether the world economy needs extra reserves? Furthermore, how can one judge whether individual countries possess adequate reserves?

There are both quantitative and qualitative approaches to these questions. Furthermore, the conclusions reached are likely to depend on whether exchange rates are fixed or flexible.

4.1 Reserve adequacy and the exchange rate regime

The general presumption is that fewer reserves are needed with flexible rates than with fixed rates. Indeed, theoretically, with a perfectly flexible exchange rate system no reserves are needed at all, since disequilibria are immediately corrected by movements in exchange rates. Reserves are only required when monetary authorities are attempting to maintain an exchange rate above its market equilibrium level, since in such circumstances they have to purchase any excess supply of their own currency that is coming on to the foreign exchange market. Under a managed float, reserves will be needed by the authorities in order to intervene in the foreign exchange market. It is possible that such floating may cause an increase in destabilizing private speculation which, with the authorities endeavouring to minimize short-run fluctuations in the value of the currency, will serve to increase the need for reserves.

Furthermore, it may be argued that with flexible exchange rates the consequences of reserve inadequacy or excess reserves may be offset by changes in domestic credit creation. Countries can determine their target money supply growth and then so control domestic credit creation as to ensure that this is achieved. Domestic monetary targets can be insulated from the effects of reserve changes, which then become less important. However, in practice there are likely to be significant constraints on the extent to which the exchange rate may be used as a policy instrument for achieving a money supply target and in these circumstances the level of reserves is still important. What techniques have been used for evaluating the adequacy of reserves?

4.2 Quantitative approaches

4.2.1 Ratios

This approach takes the level of, and changes in, the ratio between reserves and some other variable as an indication of the adequacy of reserves. Most commonly the ratio between reserves and imports has been used. Over time and within a country reserve adequacy is then measured by changes in the ratio. Across countries the relative values of ratios are taken as reflecting the relative adequacies of reserves.

However, the theoretical justification for evaluating reserve adequacy in this way is not compelling. Reserves constitute an inventory held against balance of payments deficits rather than an active transactions balance which is used to finance trade. Unless deficits grow in proportion to trade, it is incorrect to argue that a fall in the ratio between reserves and imports necessarily implies growing reserve inadequacy. The fall might equally well reflect the fact that the need for reserves to cover balance of payments disturbances rises less than proportionately to the level of trade, the existence of excess reserves in the base year, or economies of scale in reserve holding.

Although some attempts have been made to salvage the reserve-import measure of reserve adequacy from these criticisms by allowing for trend movements and stock adjustments in reserves, the general conclusion has to be reached that the R/M ratio is a very unsubtle means of evaluation.

The same holds for various other ratios which relate reserves to the domestic money supply, liquid liabilities held by foreigners, or a country's net external balance. None of them provides a rigorous explanation of what constitutes the optimum value for the particular ratio chosen or indeed what factors most significantly influence such an optimum value. It therefore becomes highly suspect to reach either cross-sectional or time series conclusions on the basis of ratios alone. Although the global reserve-import ratio has fallen over the post-war period, no conclusions about the adequacy of reserves may be reached until the optimum ratio is defined.

4.2.2 Cost-benefit: the theory of the optimum quantity of reserves

An alternative approach based on the costs and benefits of reserves attempts to overcome this deficiency. Again in principle it may be applied at both the global and individual country levels. Let us look at the global analysis first.

Microeconomic theory tells us that in order to achieve maximum economic welfare goods should be produced up to a point at which the marginal cost of producing them equals the marginal benefit from consuming them. This same notion of optimality may be applied to the output of international reserves.

The theoretical analysis is illustrated in Figure 5.1. MCPR represents the marginal cost of producing reserves; it is assumed to be both low and constant. MBR represents the marginal benefit derived from holding reserves. This schedule has been drawn as sloping downwards from the left to the right, suggesting that the marginal benefit falls as the stock of reserves rises. The reasoning behind this is simply that reserves are held as a form of security against the future. They enable a country to finance temporary balance of payments deficits without having immediately to resort to adjustment. But as more and more reserves are held, the likelihood that additional reserves will be needed declines. Thus, although the accumulation of reserves may confer extra security, the size of the additional security conferred falls. There are, in other words, diminishing returns to reserve holding. The optimum quantity of international reserves (Q^{opt}) exists at point A where the marginal cost of producing them equals their marginal benefit. To the left of point A the marginal benefit derived from extra reserves exceeds their cost of production, and welfare will be increased if extra reserves are produced. To the right of point A the marginal cost of producing reserves exceeds their marginal benefit, and the world has too many reserves.

Once a decision has been made about the optimum quantity of reserves, the next problem is to ensure that this quantity is willingly held. How many reserves monetary authorities will demand to hold will depend on the marginal opportunity cost of holding reserves, which may be interpreted as being equal to the rate of return on other assets. In Figure 5.1 this is represented by the MCHR schedule. As drawn, it is assumed to be constant. According to Figure 5.1 monetary authorities will demand reserves up to the point at which the marginal benefit they derive from extra reserves equals the marginal cost of holding them. This occurs at point B in Figure 5.1, where a quantity of reserves Q' will be demanded. But it may be seen fairly easily that point B lies to the left of point A. As things stand, monetary authorities will demand a quantity of reserves less than the optimum. In order to ensure that the optimum quantity of reserves is demanded a rate of interest will have to be paid on reserves so that the sum of the financial return to holding reserves (as represented by the rate of interest on them) and the security yield from holding them equals the marginal cost of holding them. By paying a rate of interest on reserves equal to r the MBR schedule is shifted upwards and to the right until it cuts MCRH at point C, where the demand for reserves equals Q^{opt}. The size of the gain in world welfare which results from this exercise is represented by the shaded triangle in Figure 5.1. For each unit of reserves lying between Q' and Q^{opt} the marginal benefit of reserves exceeds the marginal cost of their production – though, as can be seen, the net addition to welfare falls as Q^{opt} is approached.

A number of questions arise from this analysis. One is 'what is the appropriate rate of interest on reserves?' Fortunately the answer to this is quite straightforward. Assuming that reserves are paper currencies or SDRs, the cost of actually producing them will be low. For the optimum to be attained it follows that the marginal benefit from reserves will also have to be low. It further follows that in these circumstances the rate of interest on reserves will approximately have to equal the return on other assets if the optimum quantity of international reserves is to be willingly held. A second question is whether it is possible to apply the concept of the globally optimum

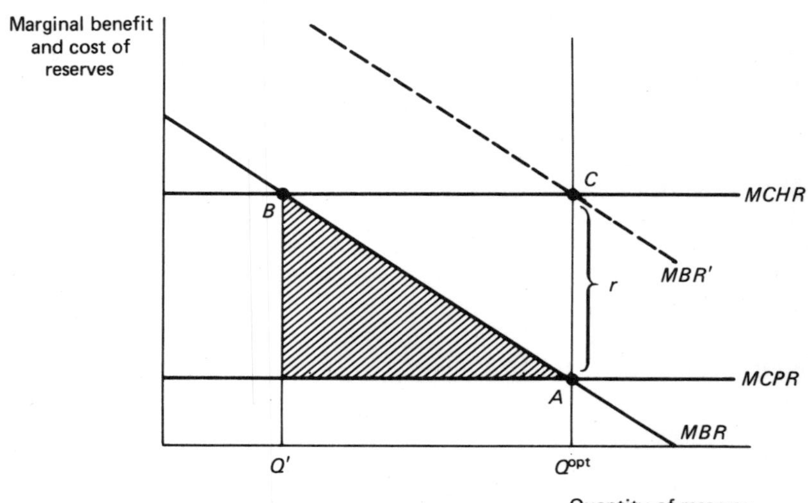

FIGURE 5.1 *Marginal cost and benefit of reserves*

quantity of international reserves in practice. Is it operationally possible to define the actual optimum quantity of reserves?

The practical estimation of the optimum stock of international reserves is hampered more by the difficulties of estimating the benefits of holding reserves than with those of estimating the costs of producing them. Indeed the cost of producing reserves in terms of printing extra dollars or making additional entries in the Special Drawing Account of the IMF may be fairly easily calculated. However, the marginal benefit of reserves depends on the costs of the adjustment thereby avoided and this may depend on the method of adjustment used. Indeed in some cases adjustment may be required and its avoidance in these circumstances is a cost not a benefit. The marginal benefit also depends on the preferences of monetary authorities as between various types of adjustment and financing, and these are something to which it is even more awkward to give quantitative precision. In practice, therefore, whether the existing stock of reserves is globally optimal is frequently judged on the basis of certain macroeconomic criteria which are taken to be broadly consistent with the existence of either excess or deficient reserves – see the next section.

The cost–benefit approach has more frequently been used to estimate the adequacy of reserves in particular countries. Again the approach attempts to identify the costs and benefits of holding reserves and to calculate the level of reserves at which marginal cost equals marginal benefit. Most empirical studies adopting a cost–benefit approach have used the reciprocal of the marginal propensity to import to reflect the cost of adjustment (and thus the marginal benefit of reserves) and the difference between the social return on capital, somehow measured, and the return on reserves to represent the marginal cost of holding them.

However, such an approach is open to a number of criticisms. First, reserve adequacy is usually judged purely on the basis of random variations in the current account of the balance of payments; the problems caused by secular changes and by capital movements are largely ignored. Second, the use of the reciprocal of the marginal propensity to import as a means of estimating the cost of adjustment implicitly assumes that such cost may be expressed in income terms and that adjustment takes the form of expenditure-reducing policies. There may in practice be important distributional issues. Furthermore, if expenditure-switching policies imply lower (or indeed higher) adjustment costs, then the use of the import propensity will serve to misrepresent the optimum level of reserves. Third, given the difficulties of estimating the social return on resources, the marginal cost of holding reserves is often rather arbitrarily chosen.

A general conclusion on the cost–benefit approach to reserve adequacy, then, is that while it is theoretically sound, difficulties arise in finding suitable empirical proxies for the theoretical determinants identified and in making the approach operational.

4.3 Qualitative approaches – the symptoms of non-adequacy

The basic idea behind the qualitative or symptomatic approach to the adequacy of reserves is as follows: a shortage or excess of reserves will exert an impact on certain key economic variables either directly, through, for instance, affecting the domestic money supply, or more indirectly by encouraging the pursuit of particular policies. By observing the policies that are pursued and the performance of certain key economic variables, one may reach conclusions about reserve adequacy.

In terms of policies, some combination of contractionary demand management, incomes policy, exchange rate depreciation, foreign aid curtailment, foreign exchange controls, import tariffs, quotas, non-tariff barriers, and export subsidies are seen as consistent with inadequate reserves. In terms of economic variables, some combination of high unemployment, high interest rates and a depreciating exchange rate are expected. On the other hand, a combination of expansionary demand policies, exchange rate appreciation, import liberalisation, export taxes, controls on capital inflows, inflation and low interest rates would be symptomatic of excess reserves.

Although the qualitative approach is initially appealing, and may be helpful, it has a number of important shortcomings. First, the symptoms of adequacy are not rigorously derived from a precise theoretical model which explains the relation between reserve levels and other economic variables; indeed it is in the nature of the qualitative approach that it lacks precision.

Second, the symptoms observed may be caused by factors other than the inadequacy or excessiveness of reserves. Thus, for example, it is unrealistic to believe that the disbursement of foreign aid will be influenced solely by the current level of reserves; indeed in this particular case not only economic but also political factors will exert an influence.

Third, the qualitative approach implies that the level of reserves constitutes an important, and indeed almost central, policy objective, and that governments will adjust domestic and external policies in order to change a country's level of reserves. Although in particular cases this may be true, it is unlikely to be universally true.

Fourth, even the observation that certain economic and policy variables seem to change along with changes in the level of reserves does not necessarily mean that these changes were brought about by the variation in reserves. Thus, to say that inflation is associated with a rise in reserves is quite consistent with the view that inflation increases the demand for nominal reserves to which supply then responds, and not just that the increase itself causes inflation.

Fifth, if countries are not as concerned about gaining reserves as they are about losing them, there is the possibility of an asymmetrical policy response. Thus, although in terms of a deterministic cost–benefit model a country may hold excess reserves, it does not automatically follow that expansionary policies will be adopted in an attempt to reduce the level of reserves. It is, however, much more likely that inadequate reserves will result in contractionary demand policies simply because of the constraint imposed by a finite level of reserves.

Sixth, different symptoms may simultaneously point in opposite directions. High levels of unemployment, taken as being indicative of deficient reserves, may co-exist with high rates of inflation, which would normally be taken as being indicative of excess reserves. The symptoms of adequacy and inadequacy may then be *positively* related. As another example of this, exchange rate depreciation, which is taken as suggesting reserve inadequacy, may generate inflation, which is taken as suggesting just the opposite. Finally, as noted earlier with flexible exchange rates, the connection between reserve changes and inflation becomes much looser as the degree of domestic control of the money supply increases.

4.4 Distributional aspects of reserve adequacy

4.4.1 Between countries

As already noted, the quantitative and qualitative approaches may in theory be applied at the level both of individual countries and the world as a whole. The severe data problems associated with applying the cost–benefit approach at the global level have, however, meant that in general this approach has been reserved for judging reserve adequacy in individual countries, while the ratio approach or the qualitative approach has been adopted at the global level. Unfortunately, such measures at best give but a first indication of the adequacy of reserves. Indeed even an accurate *indication* may be attained only if other variables do not vary. A change in the exchange rate regime over time will, for example, almost certainly affect the adequacy of a given level of reserves; a situation may arise where, even though the reserve-import ratio has fallen, a simultaneous move towards floating rates means that the level of reserves is much less significant. Again the whole pattern of reserve adequacy may change, even though the global ratio between reserves and imports remains the same, if the distribution of reserves and/or trade, changes.

Another important conclusion is that individual cases of deficient and excess reserves can co-exist with any given global situation. It is quite possible, then, that the problem of international reserve adequacy is more a distributional one than an aggregate one. Between 1973–4 and 1981–2 the ratio of non-gold reserves to imports for non-oil developing countries fell from 21 per cent to 15 per cent and for oil-exporting countries from 96 per cent to 57 per cent. For industrial countries the ratio remained unchanged at about 15 per cent. Including gold, the ratio rose from 37 per cent to 39 per cent for industrial countries but fell from 31 per cent to 24 per cent for non-oil developing countries and from 114 per cent to 68 per cent for oil-exporting countries.

4.4.2 Between components

Different reserve assets may not be regarded by their holders as being perfect substitutes for each other. It is possible, then, that while reserves in total are adequate, deficiencies exist in terms of the amounts of the individual components of that total. Given the problems associated with the use of gold and foreign exchange as reserves, a case may be made that there is a maldistribution between the components of international reserves. Such distributional problems can clearly exist even though in aggregate the level of international reserves is adequate. Indeed this was the rationale for additional allocations of SDRs at the end of the 1970s.

4.5 Empirical evidence on reserve adequacy

Empirical evidence supports the view that while some countries hold inadequate reserves, others maintain reserves above the level that would be deemed adequate on the basis of some deterministic model. In terms of global adequacy there was a general consensus towards the end of the 1960s that a world shortage of international reserves existed – a view ostensibly supported by the growing incidence of exchange rate depreciations, the pursuit of deflationary economic policies in many countries and the decline in the global ratio between reserves and imports. Pressure to increase reserves culminated in the introduction of the SDR scheme.

In the early 1970s there was the substantial increase in global reserves referred to earlier, and for two years the reserve-import ratio actually increased before again falling after 1972. However, with the move to flexible exchange rates in 1973 and the acceleration in the world rate of inflation, the evidence could at first glance be seen as being consistent with the hypothesis that the *global* volume of international reserves had become excessive at least until the early 1980s. However, care has to be exercised in reaching this conclusion, since the falling R/M ratio and the high level of unemployment might suggest otherwise. Furthermore, in theory the move to flexible exchange rates should weaken the link between reserve growth and inflation.

Whatever one's view on the global adequacy of reserves, problems of distribution undoubtedly remain. Some countries, in particular the industrial countries and oil-exporting countries, seem to possess adequate or even excess reserves, while other countries, particularly the poorer non-oil developing countries, seem to possess inadequate reserves. In such circumstances the policy implication is that reserve inadequacy will be more appropriately dealt with by some form of redistribution than by an increase in the global quantity of reserves. We return to this issue in Chapter 11.

4.6 Demand versus supply determined reserve creation: is reserve adequacy really a problem?

As implied above, there is an argument that concern over the adequacy of reserves is uncalled for. One strand of the argument is that the quantity of reserves adjusts to the demand for them; reserves are demand-determined.

Certainly balance of payments surpluses can reflect the demand for additional reserves in the countries running them; reserve currency countries may then meet this demand by financing the related deficits through the creation of extra externally held liabilities. The supply of reserves then increases. Furthermore, even reserve creation organised through the IMF responds, in an indirect way, to the demand for reserves.

Another strand of the argument is that with flexible exchange rates any increase in the size of international disequilibria is offset by changes in exchange rates, and therefore no additional reserves are required; with flexible rates the system can adjust to any level of reserves. As a result, the quantity of reserves becomes much less significant, although there is then the question of how much adjustment is optimal.

While the above arguments cannot be dismissed, they can be overstated. For instance, during the era of fixed exchange rates in the 1950s the existence of a dollar glut was hardly consistent with the demand determination thesis. Nor has the adoption of more flexible exchange rates exerted a discernibly downward impact on the demand for reserves.

It would appear that supply factors still have a significant impact. Moreover, questions relating to the composition and distribution of reserves remain important ones that need to be addressed in any future reform of the international financial system.

What is perhaps more true is that the quantity of international *liquidity* is demand-determined. With a high degree of international capital mobility, countries short of reserves may be able to borrow in the capital markets of the world and thereby sustain expenditure above levels that would otherwise be possible. Control over the total quantity of reserves, even if it could be achieved, may therefore turn out to be an ineffective means of influencing macroeconomic policy. The distinction between individual countries is important here. Some countries with little access to commercial credit undoubtedly have to modify their economic policies because they are short of reserves. In any case, as explained above, there is at present no accepted system for controlling the global quantity of reserves, so the whole question is somewhat hypothetical unless a system of control can be devised.

Before moving on to look at this and other policy issues, we must examine two remaining questions more fully. First, since we have frequently referred to the demand for reserves, can we be more specific about the factors that are likely to influence it? Second, what is the connection between reserves and inflation? If reserves are demand-determined, does this mean that increases in the supply of reserves will be non-inflationary because all that will happen is that a larger proportion of a given demand for liquidity will simply be met by reserves?

4.7 The demand for reserves

The demand for international reserves can be related positively to the benefits of holding them and negatively to the costs. The benefits can be expressed in terms of the adjustment that, at least in the short run, is avoided. The larger the costs of adjustment are, the greater will be the benefits from holding reserves. A first determinant of the demand for reserves is, then, the cost of adjustment, or, in more conventional demand theory language, the price of substitutes.

Demand will also be positively related to the size and incidence of the need to adjust, and this depends on the size and frequency of balance of payments deficits. An important determinant of this will be the structure of the economy. For example, a highly diversified economy may not encounter disequilibria as often as one whose exports are highly concentrated; it may therefore hold relatively fewer reserves.

If, while yielding benefits, reserves could be held without cost, countries would demand an infinite amount. There is, however a price to pay for holding reserves. Again conventional demand theory leads us to expect that the demand for reserves will be negatively related to their price, which is the opportunity cost of holding them expressed in terms of the spending on real resources that is sacrificed.

Demand theory also tells us that demand depends on tastes and preferences. Monetary authorities will have preferences between financing a deficit and correcting it. Countries wishing to avoid sudden adjustment will tend to have a relatively high demand for reserves.

Finally the demand for reserves may depend on wealth and income. If reserves are a superior good, their income elasticity of demand will be positive. Indeed the security that reserves provide might be seen as a luxury good, and it might therefore be anticipated that the income elasticity of demand for them would be high. On the other hand, to the extent that there are economies of scale in holding reserves, the proportionate amount by which holdings rise as income rises will fall.

In effect we have now derived a theoretical demand for reserves function which is quite consistent with elementary demand theory. The demand for reserves is hypothesized as being associated with the price of reserves, the price of substitutes, the level of income, and the preferences of monetary authorities.

4.8 The relation between the quantity of international reserves and world inflation

Just as some economists explain domestic inflation in terms of changes in the domestic supply of money, there are those who believe that world inflation may be explained by changes in the quantity of international reserves. However, the rather more obscure transmission mechanism existing at the international level makes the relation between the quantity of reserves and the global rate of inflation less straightforward than that at the domestic level.

Basically the chain of causation between changes in the quantity of international reserves and the world rate of inflation consists of two links. The first is the link between international reserves and money supplies in individual countries, and thus in aggregate the world money supply. The second is the well documented link between domestic money supply growth and domestic rates of inflation.

Under the gold standard, changes in reserves had a fairly direct impact on the domestic supply of money. Under a gold-exchange-SDR standard, the relation is much looser and more tenuous but may nonetheless exist to the extent that an increase in reserves exerts a positive influence on the domestic money supply if recipients of foreign exchange convert it into domestic currency, or if an increase in reserve holdings encourages monetary authorities to pursue policies that are more expansionary, or if SDR allocations which are spent rather than held activate idle foreign exchange and thereby support a higher level of global monetary expenditure. Things, however, are not quite that simple.

First, as noted above, the quantity of reserves may not be purely exogenously determined but may instead be demand determined. Therefore increases in reserves need not necessarily be inflationary.

Second, an excess supply of reserves which, according to a monetary interpretation, is translated into inflation may result from a reduction in the demand for reserves just as much as from an increase in their supply. Thus, for example, while the oil price rises of 1973–4 and 1979 reduced the real supply of reserves because of the cost inflation they caused, they also reduced the real demand for reserves because of the demand deflation they caused.

Third, simple explanations which point to simultaneous increases in reserves and world inflation may confuse causation with correlation. They also need to explain why world unemployment has also risen and why inflation has sometimes increased ahead of reserves.[4]

Fourth, the rate of inflation associated with any given stock of reserves may vary with the distribution of reserves and the differing propensities of their owners to spend them.

Fifth, from a policy point of view the idea that world inflation may be controlled by controlling the quantity of reserves flounders because, as noted above, reserves are only one component of international liquidity. While it is difficult enough to control world reserves, it is even more difficult to control the quantity of international liquidity.

Sixth, but very importantly, with floating exchange rates countries can in principle determine their own inflation rates by setting the rate of growth of domestic credit and then permitting the exchange rate to adjust so as to eliminate any external influence on the domestic money supply. Flexible rates break the link between reserves and domestic money supplies and therefore the rate of inflation. Indeed, in the sense that under a flexible exchange rate regime countries have more autonomy over the formulation of their domestic policy, the adequacy of reserves as an element in the debate over global inflation becomes much less important.

Finally there is the well documented disagreement over the connection between domestic money supply and inflation that need not be examined here.

5. POLICY ISSUES

If the importance of reserve adequacy as an issue can be overstressed, perhaps the major policy question so far raised becomes 'What should the principal reserve asset be?' In this section we examine two related policy issues. Assuming that gold will remain a fairly passive reserve asset, these are, first, how can the world deal with the deficiencies associated with multiple currencies, and, second, how in practice can the IMF's stated objective of making the SDR the principal reserve asset be achieved in practice? A third key policy issue – the distribution of reserves – is discussed in Chapter 11.

5.1 Multiple reserve currencies, reserve harmonization and guidelines for currency management

Some of the consequences of a combination of multiple reserve currencies and flexible exchange rates are clearly undesirable. Switching the composition of reserves can accentuate, and in practice does appear to have accentuated, fluctuations in exchange rates around their equilibrium levels. Moreover, exchange-rate instability accentuates the desire to switch the composition of reserves. While deviations from equilibrium exchange rates will lead to inefficiencies in the allocation of resources, a multiple currency system offers no offsetting benefits in terms of controlling reserve creation or generating appropriate adjustment.

One possible approach to dealing with the problem of multiple reserve currencies that has been canvassed is to harmonize the composition of reserves, with countries agreeing to hold them in certain fixed proportions. The central problem with such a scheme is that countries are being asked to sacrifice the freedom of choice that is to them the main attraction of multiple reserves. If countries can be persuaded to hold their reserves in a specific combination of currencies, why not hold SDRs instead, since these are valued on the basis of a weighted average of currencies?

A second approach is to establish guidelines for reserve use to ensure that exchange-rate instability is minimized. This scheme would mean establishing target zones for bilateral exchange rates. Currency switching would then by agreement be conducted to ensure that rates did not move outside the target zones or were shifted back if they did move outside. Thus countries decumulating reserves would be encouraged to sell an overvalued currency, while countries accumulating reserves would buy undervalued ones.

The problem with this scheme is that, while it is not advocating a return to fixed exchange rates, it is calling for a relatively high degree of centrally agreed management of flexible rates which may be difficult to achieve if it is seen by countries as eliminating the benefits of flexible rates. Furthermore, some method of determining equilibrium rates would be needed, and the target zones would need to be modified as these changed. If this was not done, the old problem of fixed rates would be recreated and intervention by monetary authorities in the foreign exchange markets would prevent rather than encourage the realization of equilibrium rates. The stability of exchange rates is not the prime objective, since to stabilize exchange rates at the wrong level leads to global inefficiency. What is required is stability around equilibrium rates. The track record of the international community in selecting what are the equilibrium rates and ensuring that these are implemented is not good. Indeed it was failure in this area that was in part to blame for the collapse of both the Bretton Woods system and the subsequent Smithsonian agreement.

5.2 Establishing the SDR as the principal reserve asset

If shoring up the multiple reserve currency system is regarded as a second best solution and making the SDR the principal reserve asset as the first best, the question arises as to how this objective can be achieved. Achieving it depends on two elements. First, the SDR needs to be made more attractive as an asset. Second, a mechanism for moving from the existing state of affairs to an SDR-based system needs to be found.

5.2.1 Making the SDR more attractive

While it may be necessary to make the SDR more attractive, there are reasons for not making it too attractive. Reserve assets need to be sufficiently attractive that they are willingly held but not so attractive that holders are reluctant to use them should a balance of payments need arise.

But what makes a reserve asset attractive? There are a number of elements relating to value, the interest rate paid to holders and charged to users, and the usefulness of the asset, especially in terms of its degree of liquidity or the speed with which it may be used to settle obligations.[5] In its short existence there have been a number of reforms made to the SDR relating to each of these facets of attractiveness. The valuation method has been changed to make the value of SDRs more stable, the rate of interest has been increased, and the usefulness of the asset has been widened as more institutions have been designated as holders; but there is scope for further reform.

Value. The current method of valuation described in the appendix and the table therein makes the value of SDRs more stable than individual currencies comprising the SDR basket. This stability will appeal to risk-avoiders, though risk-taking central banks may prefer to speculate through the currency composition of their reserves on making a larger appreciation in the value of their reserves. Similarly, because the weighting of currencies in arriving at the valuation of SDRs does not always mirror the trading and financial importance of particular currencies to particular countries, they may prefer to construct their own currency cocktails. However, what is more appropriate for one country may be less appropriate for another, and a compromise is unavoidably called for. With low rates of inflation in those countries whose currencies determine the value of SDRs and their importance in world trade and finance, the compromise used in the current method of valuation is probaly quite reasonable. Should it be desired to encourage the value of SDRs to rise through time, however, one way would be to increase the relative weight of appreciating currencies and reduce the weight of depreciating ones, creating an asymmetrical basket.

Interest. However, a better way to increase the yield on SDRs may be to alter the interest rate paid on them. As noted in earlier sections, there are theoretical reasons associated with the optimum supply of reserves for paying a market-related interest rate on SDRs. Central banks will not regard them as competitive if the yield they offer is much lower than that on offer elsewhere. However, the question of the interest rate on SDRs raises a number of points. If the objective is to find the equilibrium rate at which the demand for SDRs to hold equals their supply, will this be approximated by a rate related to capital market rates? If SDRs are less useful than other assets and holders are sometimes constrained by institutional regulations on the use of SDRs from adjusting their holdings of SDRs to the desired levels, and if at the same time the domestic market rates used for estimating the interest rate on SDRs are below those in the Euromarket, there may be a case for offering a higher rate – without making it so high as to discourage use. Furthermore, although holding SDRs is less risky than holding any single currency, it may easily be more risky than holding a custom-made combination of currencies. In such circumstances the argument that, because of its low degree of risk, the SDR can afford to offer a lower than market rate of interest becomes less compelling. On the other hand, since the quantity of SDRs and the uses to which they may be put are subject to international control, since the currency components of SDRs may not always be easily available in the world's money markets, and since there are lower transactions costs associated with the SDR than with an equivalent home-made cocktail of currencies, there may also be a case for a rate below the market-related one. Rather than trying to select the equilibrium rate, there may be an argument for establishing a market in SDRs under the auspices of the IMF in which the equilibrium rate would be determined by the forces of demand and supply.

Usefulness and liquidity. Having a market, and possibly also a futures market, in which SDRs were traded would also increase their liquidity. By eliminating some of the rules and regulations relating to the use of SDRs that currently exist, and by widening still further the institutions that can deal in SDRs, possibly to include commercial banks, their usefulness and attractiveness could be significantly increased. At present holders must have a balance of payments need before they can use SDRs and countries are usually designated to acquire SDRs in exchange for currencies. No great willingness to build up stocks of SDRs has been shown by central banks. There may, then, be a case for enhancing the liquidity of SDRs by encouraging their free use rather than by imposing designation. Removal of the balance of payments need criterion would remove the anomaly that SDRs are a more liquid asset for some holders than others.

To become a fully fledged reserve asset, and more particularly a fully fledged international money, SDRs would need to perform the functions of money and act as a medium of exchange and unit of account as well as a store of wealth. It may be unrealistic to expect that goods could be bought and sold by means of SDRs – although with commercial banks holding SDR deposits they could become more generally acceptable as a means of settling obligations – but certainly there is considerable scope for denominating a range of transactions outside the IMF in terms of SDRs. Already this private role for SDRs has begun to evolve and 'commercial SDRs', which use the basic basket method of valuation but which often use different interest rates, have come into existence. Indeed the relation between official SDRs and commercial SDRs needs to be investigated. Will, for example, commercial SDRs crowd out official SDRs? More generally the whole question of the private sector's use of SDRs and transferability between private and official sectors needs to be thought out. But undoubtedly there is potential here for making

SDRs more useful. Combine all this with the usefulness of the SDR as a currency peg, expressing the values of currencies in terms of SDRs, and as an asset in which intervention in foreign exchange markets may be conducted, and there is clearly considerable room for manoeuvre with respect to SDRs.

However, the principal appeal of the SDR is not just to create yet another reserve asset which then co-exists on more equal terms with foreign exchange but rather to replace foreign exchange with SDRs.

5.2.2 Transition to an SDR-based system: reserve currency and gold consolidation

There are two elements in such a transition. First, new supplies of reserves would have to be met by SDR creation rather than by reserve currency countries expanding the quantity of their externally held liabilities or by the revaluation of gold stocks. The settlement of obligations would need to proceed through the transfer of assets between countries, i.e. asset settlement, rather than an increase in the liabilities of certain countries. Second, apart from working balances, existing stocks of reserve currencies would have to be swapped or substituted for SDRs. Some form of substitution account would be required. Various proposals for such an account have been put forward from time to time.

By examining these proposals it is possible to extricate the main issues that have to be resolved. The first concerns the identity of the assets to be deposited with the account. While most schemes have concentrated on the substitution of currencies, the scheme could in principle also operate for gold.

The second problem concerns the nature of the asset to be issued by the account in exchange for deposits. In some early versions it was assumed that this would be the SDR proper. In later versions emphasis switched to a separate SDR-denominated asset. To be an acceptable substitute for foreign exchange the asset would need to be attractive both in terms of the range of institutions that would be permitted to deal in it and its marketability. While it may be more expedient to introduce a new asset strictly for the purpose rather than to try and make appropriate modifications to the SDR, the ramifications of this decision for the distribution of the costs and benefits associated with the account are central.

The third problem relates to the degree of compulsion that would be used to encourage participation in the scheme. The choice ranges from a completely mandatory scheme under which countries would be required to surrender a fixed proportion of their holdings of reserve currencies in exchange for SDRs, to a completely voluntary scheme under which participation would be left to the discretion of individual countries. The argument against compulsion is that it reduces freedom of choice with regard to the composition of a country's reserves. The argument against voluntary schemes is that there is no guarantee that they will achieve the objective of bringing about a reduction in reserve currency balances. While it may be easier to reach agreement on a voluntary basis, this may simply mean that effectively no account is introduced. If this is the case, the price of having a voluntary account may well be the need for restrictions on central banks' freedom of choice in selecting the composition of their reserves. If it is accepted that the international community in general will benefit from the activities of the account, there may be a case for not leaving its success to the discretion of individual countries.

While for the international community as a whole the social benefits of the scheme may exceed the social costs, for individual countries private benefits may be less than private costs. If the non-participation of important individual countries means that the account will be ineffective, then there may be a case for compulsion. Another argument in favour of compulsion is that under a voluntary scheme there would tend to be purely speculative movements into the account from reserve currencies. The irreversibility of transactions, which seems to be an agreed principle in all versions of the account, would, however, reduce the likelihood of this becoming a major difficulty and, even if it did, it would be fairly easy to deal with, simply by requiring countries to give a period of notice before substitution. Voluntary participation need not then imply that participation would be left completely open. Participants could voluntarily accept a programme of substitution extending over a number of years. In any case, provided SDRs are made sufficiently attractive to potential holders, the degree of compulsion would become largely irrelevant, since countries would be anxious to substitute SDRs for reserve currencies.

A fourth problem relates to the time period over which the account is to be implemented. At one extreme the scheme could be introduced on a once-for-all basis. The implication would be a sudden and large conversion of foreign exchange for SDRs. While there would be no change in the total quantity of reserves, there would be a dramatic change in their composition. The alternative would be to substitute SDRs for foreign exchange holdings gradually and progressively. Under this variant there would be no large creation of SDRs at any particular time and the problem of damaging confidence in the SDR as an asset that might be associated with a large allocation would thereby be avoided. The longevity of the account would clearly depend on the annual rate of substitution. It would also depend on whether there was a simultaneous movement, within the international monetary system, towards an asset settlement method of international payment. One implication of failing to achieve a movement of this kind would be that the substitution account might be called upon to convert new foreign currency balances as well as old ones. It would, therefore, need to exist on a continuing basis.

How long the substitution account would exist also depends on the fifth issue, namely, what happens to the currencies that are deposited with the account. The question here is whether they should be amortized or not. Amortization could occur at a fixed annual rate or it could be related to either SDR acquisition or the balance of payments position in reserve currency countries. The relation to SDR acquisition or the balance of payments could in turn either be symmetrical, having the capacity to slow down as well as speed up amortization, or asymmetrical, with there being a fixed minimum rate of amortization. However, more recent discussions of the substitution account within the IMF seem to have moved away from the concept of amortization altogether, and it is envisaged that the account would simply invest its stock of currencies.

Attention has instead focused on the financial arrangements that would underpin the account; this is the sixth principal problem area. A key issue relates to the financial objectives of the account, whether it is to make a profit, break even or make a loss – in which case there is the question of how the loss would be covered. Whereas the prime purpose of a substitution account is to change the composition of reserves, its activities would have incidental ramifications for the total quantity of reserves.

Assuming, for example, that currencies deposited with the account were to be invested in the issuing country and that interest were to be paid to the account in the same currency, and assuming further that interest were to be paid on SDRs issued by the account in the form of SDRs, the total quantity of reserves would rise at a rate equivalent to the interest rate on SDRs expressed as a fraction of total reserves. If, on the other hand, interest on the account's holdings of currencies were to be paid in SDRs, then this would have the effect of reducing the total quantity of reserves as compared with a system where interest was paid in the issuer's own currency. Whether total reserves would actually fall would depend on the rate of interest paid to the account by reserve centres as compared with that paid by the account to recipients of SDRs. A profit for the account would imply a reduction in total reserves; a loss would imply an increase in total reserves; and a break-even situation would imply no change in total reserves. Apart from the effect on total reserves, the profitability of an SDR-based account would, in principle, seem to be largely irrelevant, since payments in excess of receipts could be covered by an additional creation of SDRs. The likelihood of a loss being incurred by the account would depend significantly upon whether reserve currency amortization were to be incorporated within the scheme. With a once-for-all scheme which included amortization, the income of the account would diminish through time as the account's stock of reserve currencies fell. Since the level of interest payments by the account would remain constant, it would experience increasing deficits over time. On the other hand, with a progressive scheme interest payments would gradually rise while interest receipts would remain constant over the lifetime of the account. The end result, however, would be the same and the size of the account's deficit would tend to rise. Without amortization the likelihood of a loss would be considerably reduced, since under a once-for-all scheme the account's capital stock would remain intact, while under a progressive scheme it would rise in conjunction with liabilities.

The foregoing discussion of the issues to which the concept of reserve currency consolidation gives rise reveals that, while the basic notion is fairly straightforward, the exact details can vary widely. The effects may therefore depend importantly on the precise mechanism by which consolidation is induced. A version of the substitution account which introduces a new SDR-denominated asset, an infinite lifetime, and no amortization of reserve currencies, might have a harmful effect on certain strategic objectives of international monetary reform, such as the establishment of the SDR as the principal international reserve asset, and the achievement of a more symmetrical distribution of the adjustment burden by an asset settlement as opposed to the liability creation method of international payment.

Furthermore, the operation of the account would not be independent of the exchange-rate regime that existed. With managed floating, reserve centres could be put in a position where they were obliged to swap SDRs for holdings of their currency acquired by other countries through foreign exchange intervention of which the reserve centre disapproved. This could happen where a country was endeavouring to depreciate its own currency against that of a reserve centre. In such circumstances agreement on establishing a substitution account would probably rest on also establishing a code of conduct for exchange-rate management and some system for IMF surveillance of intervention.

The objective of making the SDR the principal reserve asset in the international monetary system not only implies a reduced role for reserve currencies but also a reduced role for and perhaps the eventual demonetization of gold. This could again be aided by the activities of a substitution account. The basic mechanism by which a gold substitution account would operate would be similar to that for reserve currencies. Broadly speaking, gold would be exchanged for SDRs. The implications of such substitution for the total quantity of reserves depends on the SDR price paid for the gold deposited and the price at which gold is valued for the purpose of calculating reserves. Clearly, if gold is valued for reserve purposes at its now defunct, relatively low, official price, and the substitution account pays the market price, then the effect of the substitution will be to raise the level of international reserves. Where, however, reserve gold is valued at the market price, then an increase in reserves would only occur if the account were to pay a price above the market one. If the account paid the market price for the gold deposited, the effect on total reserves would be zero, whereas if the account paid a price below the market one, the effect would be to reduce total reserves. In this latter case an additional allocation of SDRs could be made to make good the shortfall in reserves. Many similar problems occur with the substitution of gold as with the substitution of reserve currencies. A central one is what to do with the gold once it has been acquired. With no monetary role, there would be no point in holding it. A programme of selling gold for non-monetary purposes would, however, need to take into account the effects on the price of gold, since this in turn would influence the book profits of the substitution account. Rapid sale leading to a large fall in the price of gold would lead to losses. In any case the termination of a monetary role for gold might lead speculators to offload their stocks in the self-fulfilling expectation of a fall in price.

5.3 Regional reserve assets

The previous two sections have focused on reforms at the international level. Other reforms could occur at a more disaggregated regional level. Chapter 11 discusses proposals for introducing a southern currency. Meanwhile the ECU already exists. There are circumstances under which this could evolve and become an attractive and more widely accepted international reserve asset. Much depends on how far Europe moves along the road towards monetary union. A somewhat fuller examination of European monetary arrangements is, however, deferred until Chapter 10.

APPENDIX: SDR VALUATION

The following is quoted from the IMF Annual Report, 1981:

> In its communiqué issued after the meeting in Hamburg, Germany, on April 25, 1980, the Interim Committee endorsed the objectives of simplifying and further enhancing the attractiveness of the SDR as an international reserve asset and generally expressed the view that it would be desirable for the interest and valuation baskets for the SDR to be identical. Since 1974, the SDR valuation basket had comprised 16 currencies and the interest rate basket 5 currencies. After extensive discussions, the Executive Board decided in September 1980 to adopt the 5-currency basket for determining both the value of and interest rate on the SDR. The new basket came into effect on January 1, 1981.
>
> The agreed initial weights of the currencies in the basket – 42 per cent for the U.S. dollar, 19 per cent for the deutsche mark, and 13 per cent each for the French franc, Japanese yen, and pound sterling – broadly reflect the relative importance of these currencies in international trade and payments, based on the value of the exports of goods and services of the member countries issuing these currencies and the balance of these currencies held as reserves by member of the Fund over the five year period 1975–79. These agreed initial weights were converted into units of each of the 5 currencies in the new basket by using London noon exchange rates averaged over the three months ended December 31, 1980. As on previous occasions when the method of valuation of the SDR was changed, the continuity of value was preserved by ensuring that the

value of the SDR on the last working day when the old basket was in use (i.e., December 31, 1980) was the same using both the old and new baskets. An illustrative calculation of the value of the SDR is given in the accompanying table.

SDR Valuation, 30 April 1981

Currency (1)	*Currency Amount Under Rule O–1* (2)	*Exchange Rate*[1] (3)	*U.S. Dollar Equivalent*[2] (4)
U.S. dollar	0.54	1.0000	0.540000
Deutsche mark	0.46	2.2145	0.207722
French franc	0.74	5.2540	0.140845
Japanese yen	34	215.13	0.158044
Pound sterling	0.071	2.1404	0.151968
			1.198579
	SDR value of US$1 =		0.834321
	U.S. dollar value of SDR =		1.19858

1. Middle rate between buying and selling rates at noon in the London exchange market as determined by the Bank of England, expressed in currency units per U.S. dollar except for the pound sterling, which is expressed in U.S. dollars per pound sterling.
2. The U.S. dollar equivalents of the currency amounts in column (2) at the exchange rates in column (3)—that is, column (2) divided by column (3) except for the pound sterling, for which the amounts in the two columns are multiplied.

SOURCE: *IMF Annual Report, 1981.*

From January 1, 1981, the U.S. dollar rate for the Japanese yen used in the daily calculation of the value of the SDR is obtained from the London exchange market rather than the Tokyo market. As all the exchange rates used for calculating the value of the SDR are now obtained from the London market, it is easier for dealers in obligations denominated in SDRs to replicate the SDR in the private market.

The object of the change in the valuation basket is to simplify the SDR, making it more useful as a unit of account, and thereby to facilitate the wider use of SDR-denominated assets and liabilities in financial markets and in international transactions, resulting in a wider role for the SDR in the international monetary system. The 5-currency basket retains the properties of stability and representativeness that characterized the 16-currency basket, while providing a greater likelihood of constancy in the currency composition of the basket.

The list of currencies used in determining the value of the SDR, and the amount of each of these currencies, will be revised every five years beginning January 1, 1986, unless the Fund's Executive Board decides otherwise, so as to include the currencies of the five member countries of the Fund with the largest exports of goods and services during the five-year period ending 12 months before the effective date of the revision (for example, 1980–84 for the revision effective January 1, 1986). However, a currency will not replace another currency on the list unless the value of the exports of the country issuing the former currency over the relevant five-year period exceeds that of the country issuing the latter currency by at least 1 per cent. The amounts of the currencies in the revised valuation basket for the SDR will reflect both the values of the exports of goods and services and the balances of these currencies held by other members. These two factors will be assigned a similar relative importance to that given them in arriving at the agreed percentage weights of the current SDR basket.

6 Short-term Capital Markets, the Private Banks, and the IMF

1. INTRODUCTION

Whereas the 1960s were dominated by concern over the global adequacy of international reserves, other aspects of international liquidity came to the fore in the 1970s and 1980s. Much attention has, for instance, been paid to the Euro-currency market, attempting to explain its growth and examining its implications for controlling world reserves, the world's money supply, and international financial stability. Not unrelated to this, the activities of the private international banks have come under close scrutiny as, during the 1970s, they played the major role in recycling the OPEC surpluses that resulted from increases in the price of oil, but then started to backtrack as a number of the countries to which they had lent encountered debt problems.

However, discussion of the role of the private banks cannot for long be divorced from a wider discussion of the other channels through which finance is moved around the world. These include the activities of large multinational companies which make direct investments in a number of countries, as well as (and along with other private dealers) making short-term speculative investments based on international differences in interest rates and their expectations as to how particular exchange rates are likely to move. Other channels also include the public or official sector, comprising national governments and central banks as well as the principal international financial organisations such as the IMF, the World Bank and the regional development banks.

This chapter reviews many of these issues. However, it excludes a discussion of that portion of international capital flows that results from direct investment by companies or the provision of trade credit.

Section 2 provides a brief resumé of the Euro-currency market, Section 3 examines the activities of the private banks, while Section 4 discusses lending by the public sector and in particular by the IMF. A review of foreign aid is deferred until the next chapter.

In many areas of economics it is helpful to bear in mind the distinction between efficiency and equity, and the analysis of capital flows is no exception. Some finance may flow almost exclusively for humanitarian reasons, with the objective of raising the well-being of the globally relatively poor at the expense of the globally relatively rich: although it is unlikely that much so-called aid can be explained in this way. More generally, however, international capital movements result from the fact that the pattern of saving and investment throughout the world is such that in some countries the demand for funds for investment exceeds the supply while in others there is excess saving. Subject to certain administrative controls and other constraints associated with perceived risk or political difficulties, saving will tend to move to where the rate of return on investment, or the marginal productivity of resources, is highest, and this may well be in a country other than the one in which the saving is undertaken. There is therefore nothing necessarily inefficient about international lending and borrowing nor about the markets through which it occurs; indeed the world as a whole stands to benefit from these activities.

2. THE EURO-CURRENCY MARKET

The principal market through which short-term capital moves is the Euro-currency market. Yet the evolution of this market has been a fairly recent phenomenon, dating from the end of the 1950s when full convertibility between currencies was introduced.[1] The market deals in deposits made with a bank in a currency other than that of the country in which the bank is located. It began life by essentially being a market in offshore dollars (dollars held outside the United States),[2] but although the dollar has remained the currency in which most (about 70 per cent) Euro-currency deals are conducted, other strong currencies such as the Deutsche mark, Swiss franc and yen have also become important.

The initial lenders on to the market are usually large public institutions, some central banks, though not those of the main industrial countries, and companies or banks with surplus funds. The funds are deposited with commercial banks which often lend the money to other banks. Indeed these 'inter-bank' transactions are a very significant aspect of the Euro-currency market. Ultimately, however, the funds find their way to a borrower outside the banking system. Again this is likely to be a large state or private enterprise finding itself currently short of finance. Up until the early 1970s the principal lenders and borrowers were to be found in the industrial countries. However, following the first major oil price rise in 1973, many OPEC countries had surplus oil revenues (in dollars) that they were unable to absorb, and placed these on the Euro-currency market. At the same time, and also largely as a result of changed oil prices, non-oil developing countries had large balance of payments deficits to finance, and for a time developing countries became the largest single group of borrowers from the market. Subsequently the dominance of the European countries as both lenders and borrowers has been re-established.

Other key features of the market are that it operates on short maturities, usually six months or less, with only small profit margins. The profits made result mainly from the amount of business that is done rather than the unit profit.[3] Furthermore, there is little transformation of maturity between lender and borrower, though the demand by borrowers for longer-term loans has been met by the banks offering to roll over loans on the understanding that the rate of interest will be adjusted in the light of changes in world interest rates and therefore the rate that the bank is itself having to pay on deposits.

2.1 The evolution of the market

The development of the Euro-currency market, certainly up until the mid-1970s, has been fairly extensively covered in the literature. Through the 1950s and 1960s the deficit in the US balance of payments had created a large pool of dollars held outside the US, sometimes in countries such as the Soviet Union that were reluctant to put them back in the US. At the same time legislation in the US which aimed at controlling capital outflows strictly constrained the ability of US banks to lend abroad, while controls on the interest rate they could offer depositors limited their ability to bid for deposits within the US. In addition, as US-based multinational companies grew, it became convenient for them to do business with banks in the countries in which they were operating – not least to escape US controls.

As mentioned above, the Euro-currency market received a large boost from the oil price rise in 1973. This increased the supply of funds on the market – with the 'low absorbing' OPEC members looking for an outlet for their revenues that would give them a high degree of liquidity without the risks as they saw them of placing the money in the US, and also raised the demand for funds – with many deficit non-oil developing countries being attracted by the ease of access of Euro-currency credits and the lack of formal policy conditions on the loans which borrowing from the IMF would have required. Meanwhile, significant economies of scale, as well as the fact that Euro-currency business does not necessitate banks having to hold a large proportion of their deposits as reserves to cover withdrawals, enabled them to offer competitive rates which were attractive to both lenders and borrowers.

As Table 6.1 reveals, the Euro-currency market grew very rapidly between 1976 and 1980 whether measured in gross terms or after netting out inter-bank transactions. Annual growth rates of around 25 per cent in international bank credit were the norm for the 1970s. However, the table also reveals that this rate of growth was not maintained into the 1980s, when it dropped to under 5 per cent per annum. Indeed the market actually began to stagnate in 1983, showing very little, if any, growth.

What insight does this more recent period provide in explaining the development of the market? Amongst the contending explanations the first introduces the concept of the Euro-currency multiplier. This suggests that, as with a national banking system, banks operating in the Euro-currency market can create credit. The conventional money multiplier which is applied to domestic financial intermediation suggests that total deposits D depend on the cash base in the system C, the preferences of the general public for cash as opposed to bank deposits α, and the reserve ratio with which the banks comply β, or in other words the proportion of deposits that are held by the banks in the form of cash. The multiplier is then expressed as:

$$\frac{\Delta D}{\Delta C} = \frac{1}{\alpha + \beta}$$

Provided that the values of α and β are stable, the value of the multiplier will also be stable.

Initially such analysis may seem to provide a potential explanation

TABLE 6.1 *Euro-currency market size (measured by foreign-currency liabilities at end of period, billions of dollars)*

	1976	*1977*	*1978*	*1979*	*1980*	*1981*	*1982*	*June 1983*
By market centre:								
European centres	406	511	656	867	1,045	1,202	1,273	1,239
United Kingdom	201	232	290	385	485	590	636	635
France	50	64	80	101	124	134	140	127
Luxembourg	34	46	55	76	84	82	83	79
Belgium	20	22	37	48	62	73	72	74
Netherlands	21	27	38	47	55	57	55	52
Italy	17	23	30	37	46	49	43	37
Switzerland	17	20	30	34	35	35	34	34
Austria	—	10	13	18	23	23	25	25
Germany	14	16	21	25	25	26	24	23
Spain	7	9	12	17	21	24	19	17
Sweden	3	4	5	8	11	13	13	14
Denmark	—	2	2	3	3	4	4	4
Ireland	—	2	2	2	4	4	4	4
Unallocated	22	34	41	66	67	88	121	114
United States[1]	—	—	—	—	—	46	147	171
Japan	35	36	48	61	100	123	124	126
Canada	21	25	33	40	54	66	65	67
Offshore banking centres	133	168	212	265	325	424	448	453
Bahamas	79	90	105	112	126	150	132	137
Singapore	17	21	27	38	54	86	103	105
Bahrain	6	16	23	29	38	51	59	57
Hong Kong	6	8	16	21	32	43	53	54
Cayman Islands[2]	12	16	18	27	33	42	47	46
Panama	11	15	20	33	35	42	43	43
Netherlands Antilles	2	2	3	5	7	10	11	11
By currency of denomination:								
U.S. dollar	476	562	703	887	1,138	1,446	1,633	1,641
German mark	70	104	141	193	190	184	189	175
Swiss franc	24	35	43	62	83	110	100	98
Japanese yen	2	4	9	15	17	24	27	29
British pound	6	10	15	23	36	30	26	25
French franc	5	7	11	17	22	17	18	20
Dutch guilder	5	8	11	13	12	14	17	20
Other currencies[3]	7	10	16	23	26	36	47	48
By type of entity:								
Non banks	109	135	174	245	327	428	474	489
Official monetary institutions	80	100	115	145	150	132	90	84
Other banks[3]	406	505	660	843	1,047	1,301	1,493	1,483

TABLE 6.1—*continued*

	1976	*1977*	*1978*	*1979*	*1980*	*1981*	*1982*	*June 1983*
Gross market size	595	740	949	1,233	1,524	1,861	2,057	2,056
Interbank liabilities within market area	281	361	471	655	819	1,002	1,125	1,111
Net market size	314	379	478	578	705	859	932	945

1. International banking facilities only.
2. US bank branches only.
3. Includes unallocated.

SOURCE: *World Financial Markets*, Morgan Guaranty, January 1984.

of the rapid growth of the Euro-currency market during the 1970s, since Eurobanks hold only small working balances. However, further thought reveals that the analogy between a national banking system and the Euro-currency market which is implied by multiplier analysis is largely inappropriate and misleading. First, Euro-currency deposits are more like time deposits than the demand deposits to which multiplier analysis is applied. Second, a large proportion of the recorded gross size of the market relates to inter-bank transactions which do not create credit but are merely sophisticated financial intermediation. Third, the Euro-currency market is not like a national banking system, since recipients of Euro-currencies may not redeposit them with the Eurobanks. In national banking systems almost all the recipients of payments that are financed by bank loans will deposit the money they receive back in a bank that is part of the system. In the case of the Euro-currency market, while some recipients may indeed place the funds back in the market, most will convert their receipts into the relevant national currency. Whether the funds return to the Euro-currency market then depends on what the central bank which has bought the foreign currencies in exchange for domestic currency does with them. However the central banks of the Group of Ten countries have agreed not to increase their deposits in the Euro-currency market, so this option is ruled out for them. The end result is that there is likely to be a high leakage of funds from the Euro-currency market, and this has the effect of drastically reducing the size of any multiplier that may be at work. Furthermore, to the extent that the leakage varies, the value of the multiplier will be unstable. Given that the multiplier is likely to be small, and probably little above one, the principal explanation of changes in the size of the market must be found elsewhere.

The multiplier formula suggests that other explanations may lie in changes in what is the equivalent of the cash base, i.e. the quantity of externally held currencies, or changes in the preferences of the holders of these currencies as between the various ways in which they may be used.

The attractions of the Euro-currency market have already been described, including its convenience, its lack of regulation, its high degree of liquidity and the competitive interest rate on offer. Although, as they became more widely acknowledged, these factors may have accounted for the early growth of the market, they seem less likely to explain the continuing and rapid growth in the 1970s, nor the relative and then absolute decline in the 1980s. They are factors better equipped to help explain the level of business rather than changes in the level of business.

So what about an explanation based on the state of the US balance of payments and the quantity of externally held dollars? Does the rapid growth and subsequent levelling off in the Euromarket reflect changes in the US payments deficit? Again at first glance there might seem to be something in this argument, since a persistent US deficit implies an increase in dollar liabilities. Furthermore, the period of rapid Euromarket growth broadly coincided with a period when the US balance of payments was weak, while the slower growth coincided with a period when it was stronger. However, the apparent simplicity of the argument is again rather misleading.

First, a persistent US deficit only provides the *potential* for the *Eurodollar* segment of the market to grow. When the evidence presented in Table 6.2 is examined more closely, it is found that the

TABLE 6.2 *US balance of payments and the growth of the euromarket*

Year	*US balance of payments (official settlements basis) ($bn)*	*% Growth of euromarket (net)*
1974	−8.73	37.5
1975	−5.15	15.5
1976	−10.56	26.9
1977	−34.86	26.9
1978	−30.10	30.3
1979	10.87	24.4
1980	−7.24	21.8
1981	−1.66	16.0
1982 (1st half)	0.95	2.7

SOURCE: *BIS Annual and Quarterly Reports*.

connection between the US deficit and the growth of the Euromarket is far from precise. The market continued to grow even when there was a US surplus. There would therefore appear to be other factors at work which determine the extent to which externally held dollars find their way onto the Euromarket rather than being converted into the domestic currencies of holders via the spot market.

Second, the Deutsche mark and yen segments of the market have grown even though Germany and Japan have generally maintained substantial balance of payments surpluses. Thus, although the state of the US balance of payments is clearly a relevant factor in discussing the growth of the Euromarket, it is more of a permissive than a causative influence. Events in the Euromarket therefore seem to be exclusively susceptible to none of the explanations so far discussed.

Instead the growth of the market would seem to reflect changes on both its demand and supply side, with these being influenced by the rate of world economic growth, the size and distribution of payments disequilibria, changes in the location of externally held dollars, and differences and changes in the preferences of holders, which are affected by a combination of economic and political factors such as relative interest rates and perceived risk. The rapid growth of the 1970s can be explained in large part by the big global imbalances, the location of the surpluses, the preferences of OPEC, which strongly favoured the Euromarket,[4] and the willingness of the banks to lend to certain non-oil developing countries. Similarly the slower growth of the 1980s reflects the global recession, the changing pattern of disequilibria which saw the size of OPEC surpluses eroded, the increased riskiness of Euro-currency lending as perceived by the banks as the debt problem became more widely acknowledged, and the growing instability of the international financial system. To the extent that the debt problem has been accentuated by rising real interest rates, the stance of US monetary policy may also be listed as a significant factor in explaining the fortunes of the Euro-currency market.

2.2 The mechanics of the market and the effect on international reserves

With the significance of inter-bank transactions, the mechanics of the Eurocurrency market can seem exceedingly complicated and something of a mystery story. However, the basics of what goes on are reasonably straightforward. First a currency, or a claim to it, gets outside the country of denomination either as a result of trade or investment. Second, the currency is deposited with a bank outside the country of denomination which then on-lends the deposit. Third, since the eventual borrowers may not want the particular foreign currency in which the loan is denominated, they will convert it into domestic currency via the relevant central bank, and as a result international reserves and the domestic money supply will increase.

Indeed borrowing from the Euro-currency market offers deficit countries a way of financing their deficits while protecting or even building up their reserves. As a result Euro-currency activity can exert a significant impact on total international reserves. Suppose that a country faced with a deficit decides to finance it by Euro-currency borrowing. While its reserves will be protected, the reserves of those countries which eventually receive the borrowed Euro-currencies will rise. A net addition to world reserves therefore takes place because of the reclassification of Euro-currencies as reserves.

2.3 Problems and policies

Considerable concern has been expressed over the Euro-currency market. It has been seen by some commentators as possessing a number of undesirable characteristics. First, by raising world liquidity and the international velocity of circulation of money it is seen as having serious inflationary consequences. To a certain extent this criticism has to be accepted. The purpose of the market is essentially to intermediate between lenders and borrowers in order to activate balances and to finance expenditure and this clearly has consequences for world aggregate monetary demand. However, in a period of recession this expansionary impact may be seen as beneficial; during the 1970s the market was applauded for neutralizing the deflationary impact of the rising price of oil. Furthermore, most worries over the inflationary consequences of the market have been generated by fears that the credit multiplier associated with its operation is very high. But, as has already been established, these fears are almost certainly unfounded.

Second, it is argued that by increasing the international mobility of capital the Euromarket reduces the national independence of monetary policy. Differential interest rates generate capital flows which then induce policy changes which eliminate the interest rate differentials. Countries can therefore find their domestic monetary policies being frustrated by capital movements. While this argument is stronger under a fixed exchange rate regime, even under flexible rates a related worry remains, namely that the market increases the degree of international financial instability. This is because it is extremely susceptible to changes in expectations. Default by one important borrower may not only be transmitted across a number of banks via the inter-bank market but may also lead to banks trying to withdraw from other countries with a number of knock-on results.

Part of the problem of the Euromarket is often seen as the absence of central regulation (the equivalent of a central bank to a national banking system) and a lender of last resort. However, since lending, borrowing, the currency of denomination, and the banks are likely to relate to a number of different countries, it is difficult to see how the responsibility for the good order and conduct of the market could exactly be defined. Yet even the underlying problem may be overstated. While no formal regulations exist, growing experience on the side of the operators in the market, combined with a measure of prudential supervision by individual central banks, and a general unwillingness by central banks as a group to allow the market to flounder, significantly reduces the likelihood of its collapse.

A final problem relates to whether the placement of funds through the Euromarket has been efficient or equitable. These are issues to which we turn in the following section. Before moving on to them, however, it needs to be remembered that the Euromarket has generated considerable benefits. It is a flexible and adaptable financial market that has mobilised a large volume of privately held currencies for use in international trade. It has provided an important source of balance of payments financing for a number of countries and has helped maintain global levels of economic activity. By increasing the usefulness of currencies, and in particular the dollar, it has probably reduced pressure on the dollar and stabilized the international financial system. And, of course, its very existence suggests that participants benefit from it.

3. THE PRIVATE INTERNATIONAL BANKS

One of the most noticeable aspects of international finance since 1973 has been the changing role of the private international banks operating largely through the Euro-currency market. During the 1970s quantitatively they played the principal role in recycling finance from OPEC to the non-oil developing world. However into the

TABLE 6.3 *External lending and deposit-taking of banks in the BIS reporting area,* 1978–82[1] (*billions of U.S. dollars*)

	1978	*1979*	*1980*	*1981*	*1982*
Destination of lending[2]	90	125	160	165	95
Industrial countries	38	69	96	99	57
Oil-exporting developing countries	15	7	6	2	8
Non-oil developing countries	24	40	49	51	25
Centrally planned economies[3]	7	6	5	5	−4
International organizations and unallocated	6	3	4	8	9
Sources of funds[2]	90	125	160	165	95
Industrial countries	68	66	103	141	102
Oil-exporting developing countries	3	37	41	5	−19
Non-oil developing countries	14	13	8	9	5
Centrally planned economies[3]	2	5	1	—	2
International organizations and unallocated	3	4	7	10	5
Change in net claims[4] on	—	—	—	—	—
Industrial countries	−30	3	−7	−42	−45
Oil-exporting developing countries	12	−30	−35	−3	27
Non-oil developing countries	10	26	41	42	20
Centrally planned economies[3]	5	1	4	5	−6
International organizations and unallocated	3	—	−3	−2	4

1. The data on lending and deposit-taking are derived from stock data on banks' claims and liabilities (net of redepositing among banks in the BIS reporting area) that include valuation changes owing to exchange rate movements. Data on adjusted flows are provided by the BIS, but the distribution of those adjusted flows among the major groups of countries according to Fund classifications is a Fund staff estimate.

   The BIS reporting area comprises all banks in the Group of Ten countries, Austria, Denmark, Ireland, and Switzerland and the branches of US banks in the Bahamas, Cayman Islands, Hong Kong, Panama, and Singapore.
2. The distribution of global figures by major groups of borrowers (depositors) was derived from BIS data. For industrial countries, gross claims (liabilities) were reduced by redepositing among banks in the reporting area but increased by claims on (liabilities to) offshore centres. The latter thus were assumed, in the absence of information on the country distribution of onlending from (deposit taking by) offshore centres, to represent lending to (deposit taking from) industrial countries. For the other groups of borrowers and depositors, net claims (liabilities) were equated to gross claims (liabilities).
3. Excludes Fund member countries.
4. Lending minus sources of funds.

SOURCE: *IMF Annual Report, 1983.*

eighties the banks became more reluctant to lend and often had to be coerced to do so by central banks. The general pattern of bank borrowing and lending is shown by Table 6.3. How can one explain this changing picture, and does experience suggest that there are deficiencies associated with relying so heavily on the private sector?

3.1 Explaining the pattern of bank lending

There are basically two related approaches to explaining the pattern of international financial flows. The first distinguishes between the significance of demand and supply factors. The central question here is whether flows are determined by the demands of borrowers with supply being relatively elastic and responding quite passively to demand; or whether flows are in fact supply-constrained, with borrowers unable to raise additional finance and the banks rationing credit.

In the former case the concept of a foreign exchange constraint is relatively meaningless. Constrained by factors other than the availability of foreign exchange, countries decide on an optimum combination of economic growth and external debt and then simply borrow what they require.

In the latter case the availability of foreign exchange is the binding constraint, with countries having to modify their domestic aspirations and policies to be consistent with the quantity of funds they can attract. Here it is the banks that are the active participants, with the borrowers adjusting to whatever volume of finance is provided.

The second approach focuses instead on whether the flow of funds is rationed through price or in some other way. Is the rate of interest at which countries borrow from the banks the market clearing rate, or are there market imperfections such that there is excess demand or excess supply at the prevailing interest rate?

Looking initially at the first distinction between demand and supply side factors, we see, as might be anticipated, a mixture of evidence. Some of the poorest countries of the world have had to make significant sacrifices in living standards as a result of balance of payments pressures and it is difficult to believe that they would not have opted for more financing and less adjustment had the choice been there. In fact the choice has not been there, since the banks have with few exceptions deemed such countries uncreditworthy. The supply of commercial finance for these potential borrowers has been inelastic with respect to the rate of interest, or more accurately the spread over LIBOR and therefore the unit profit on lending. Such supply inelasticity is not difficult to explain. The banks are clearly concerned not only about the price of a loan but also about the prospects of getting repaid. For some borrowers, as the price of a loan increases, so the probability of repayment declines, and the risk of default increases such that the expected return falls. Indeed for this reason a situation where banks are more likely to lend at a lower price than at a higher one may arise. It is feasible that the supply schedule of commercial loans is backward bending above a certain interest rate.[5] The banks' assessment of the probability of repayment or default hinges on their evaluation of the borrower's creditworthiness, to which we return in a moment.

For the better off developing countries and Eastern European countries that were in the 1970s deemed creditworthy by the banks, the supply constraint was much less effective. Indeed during the 1970s the banks actively set out to increase the demand for loans. In these cases the situation looks much more like one of excess supply than excess demand, and there have been examples, such as India in the early 1980s, where countries were not prepared to borrow nearly as much as the banks were prepared to lend. Furthermore, what sketchy econometric analysis has been undertaken lends some additional support to the idea of a demand constraint on capital flows.[6] However, this work has been based on data drawn from the 1970s. With the arrival of debt difficulties the constraining influence of credit rationing has almost certainly increased; for while the borrowers' demand for funds has remained strong – not least because of the need to finance debt – the banks' assessment of these countries' creditworthiness has been adversely affected, and in combination with growing concern over their exposures and capital asset ratios their enthusiasm for lending has declined. No doubt even a proportion of the lending that was undertaken by the banks in the early 1980s was motivated by the desire to reduce the threat of default from which they would stand to lose; again therefore the importance of demand and supply factors has varied over time.

Turning to the significance of the price element in explaining the pattern of financial flows, it is important first of all to clarify exactly what the price of a loan is. It comprises two elements: the rate of interest (LIBOR) and the spread. The interest rate is essentially determined by world market forces, whereas the spread reflects the banks' assessment of country-specific risk. Normally loans perceived by the banks as carrying a lower risk will have a lower spread. It is also important to note the distinction between the real and the nominal price of a loan. In the 1970s even though nominal interest rates were relatively high, the rapid rate of inflation meant that real rates were low. In the 1980s, on the other hand, and because of the marked decline in the rate of inflation, real rates rose even though nominal rates fell. This rise in real interest rates is consistent with both a swift upward movement in the demand for funds and a fall in their supply. At the same time spreads, having narrowed during the second half of the 1970s, began to widen in the 1980s, reflecting the banks' growing perception of the risk associated with lending to developing countries. Although in this instance the risk was seen as one of default, the banks had already introduced floating interest rates, whereby the price of a loan adjusts to movements in world interest rates, partly in an attempt to protect their real rate of return against the risk associated with a variable rate of inflation. In addition, the ramifications of default on any one bank had been reduced by the introduction of syndicated lending. Under this arrangement a large number of banks participate in any one loan, thereby spreading the risks.

This brief review of the underlying theory of international capital movements comes up with few surprises. It has been seen that both demand and supply factors are important in explaining capital flows, although their relative importance may vary over time and between countries; there may therefore be no simple general theory that is universally applicable. In addition, while the level of real interest rates and the size of spreads are far from irrelevant and may be used by banks on occasions as a weapon of competition, they fail to reflect fully the range of factors that influence the willingness of banks to lend and, indeed, the willingness of countries to borrow. In the latter case the demand for loans will be affected by the size of current payments deficits, expected future ability to pay – which will be affected both by domestic factors, such as the scope for adjustment, and international factors, such as the level of world aggregate demand (though interest rates themselves will be influenced by this) – governments' inter-temporal preferences between current and future expenditure, and, paradoxically, existing debt commitments. However, it is to the banks' assessment of country creditworthiness that we now turn, since this has an important bearing on the distribution and pattern of bank lending.

3.2 Creditworthiness

As already mentioned, there is little doubt that differential creditworthiness is to some extent picked up by differences in the size of the spreads on loans. There is plenty of empirical evidence which supports the view that spreads are positively related to default risk.[7] Yet it remains unlikely that the whole of the banks' assessment of creditworthiness is subsumed within the spread; bankers are certainly of the opinion that there is an additional availability constraint. Either way it is instructive to consider what factors they will take into account when assessing a country's creditworthiness.

Of course what the banks are essentially concerned about is whether they will be repaid. In reaching a view about this many pieces of information will be relevant. Amongst the factors they may look at are a country's natural endowments, its degree of export and import diversification, its export and import growth, its level of international reserves, the volume and structure of its existing debt and the previous conduct of its debt repayment, the availability of other sources of finance (from, for example, the IMF), the scope for balance of payments correction, and the willingness of the government to take unpopular measures and of the population to accept them.

In estimating the risk of default the banks will use this information to examine both the ability and the willingness of the borrower to repay. Ability to repay will depend in the first instance on the productivity of the loans. For domestic loans the requirement is that the marginal efficiency of investment exceeds the rate of interest. Where international lending is concerned, the borrowing country also has to be able to earn the necessary foreign exchange. Banks will therefore be worried where countries use loans to expand consumption or where, even though the savings ratio is high, export performance is poor. Generally speaking, however, they will be looking for a high rate of economic growth and often a growth of output across the whole economy which exceeds the rate of interest on loans (there is a further analysis of debt capacity in Chapter 8).

However, there may be circumstances in which it is a country's short-run *liquidity* position that raises the risk of default and inhibits its ability to repay rather than its longer-term *solvency* as reflected by the growth of output. As a guide to this, banks are likely to examine a country's ratio of reserves to imports or debt service payments, its rate of export growth, and its ratio of exports to debt service. They may also look at the scope for export expansion or import compression. Interestingly, and in comparison with the analysis above, creditworthiness may, in the latter instance, rise as a country's rate of economic growth falls. Indeed in many cases where countries have lost creditworthiness a deflationary package of policies, usually though not always under the auspices of the IMF, is a precondition for further financial support.

Even where borrowers are able to repay loans, it is possible to conceive of circumstances in which they may see it as being to their advantage to default. This would be a rational decision if the benefits from so doing (in terms of the capital and interest that remains unpaid) outweigh the costs (in terms of future unavailability of credit that would no doubt result from such action). Since the benefits of default will be derived in the short term with the full costs only being felt in the long term, and since politicians tend to have short planning horizons, the risk of such default cannot be completely dismissed; and there is little doubt that some of the most heavily indebted countries, where the benefits of default are correspondingly large, have considered it. The thing is that it is in just such countries that the costs are also likely to be large. Furthermore, although the benefits may be calculated with some precision, the exact size of the costs is uncertain. Since most politicians are probably risk-averse, they will be under pressure to avoid default if possible. Thus, it is not surprising that where the default option has been considered, it has also usually been rejected.[8]

3.3 The shortcomings of bank lending

Although it must be conceded that bank lending has made a vital contribution to balance of payments financing since 1973, experience has also revealed a number of shortcomings associated with it. These relate both to efficiency and equity.

Before moving on to examine them, we must ask whether the banks themselves will decide to remain in the business of balance of payments financing or whether they will return to concentrating on project-oriented financing. Two related factors are at work here. The first relates to country risk. Almost certainly during the 1970s the banks under-estimated this. They did not appreciate how vulnerable borrowers were to variations in the world demand for their exports, to changes in their terms of trade, or to changes in world interest rates and exchange rates. Nor did they fully foresee how these factors were going to move.

The second relates to their own risk and is affected by their degree of exposure in developing countries and their own capital–asset ratios. Commercial bank shareholders have become increasingly concerned that the banks have overlent to developing countries in general and to specific developing countries in particular.

Almost certainly the falling capital–asset ratios of the banks that occurred during the 1970s and early 1980s were seen by their shareholders and the various regulatory agencies as a weakening in their balance sheets. The banks therefore began to regard it as imprudent to allow the ratio to fall further if they were to retain confidence.

While the net exposure (assets minus deposits) of the banks in developing countries has been small, at about 8 per cent, net claims have been high in relation to developing country exports. Furthermore, the growth in net exposure was rapid at the turn of the decade, rising by more than 600 per cent between 1977 and 1982. Moreover, aggregation can be misleading. Most international lending has been concentrated in relatively few banks and has been made to relatively few countries, and for some American banks their loans to Brazil and Mexico alone have exceeded their total equity, which has clearly made them reluctant to extend their loans. For as long as other banks were prepared to enter the business of lending to developing countries, bank lending in aggregate was able to increase, but when such opportunities for expansion had been exploited, further growth relied on the elasticity of supply, and, as noted above, this may be low or even negative.

Considerations such as these lead back to the question of the efficiency of bank lending. World economic inefficiency will result if bank lending is unstable, if it is unrelated to the underlying productivity of resources throughout the world, and if there are external costs associated with it.

It is certainly unstable. The banks moved rapidly into balance of payments financing following the rise in the price of oil in 1973–4 and then endeavoured to extricate themselves in the 1980s. In general terms they were quick to lend to developing countries following the (temporary) upsurge in commodity prices, and anxious to reduce their lending as borrowers encountered declining terms of trade and debt difficulties. Such instability is enhanced by the tendency towards herd behaviour that characterises the banking community. Withdrawal by one bank can quickly encourage other banks to follow suit rather than to offset the withdrawal by lending more themselves or at least to maintain the level of their lending. Another dimension of this is that all banks will have an incentive to get out at the first whiff of repayment problems, yet not all of them will be able to do so, since such behaviour would certainly induce default.

As the above discussion implies, lending may be only loosely related to the underlying strength of an economy or the marginal productivity of resources. Banks may have imperfect information and may misinterpret what information they do have; they may be unduly influenced by transient and often largely cosmetic factors or, in syndicated loans, by the views and prestige of the 'lead' bank. This can of course work both ways. On some occasions banks may overlend yet on others they may underlend. Either way short-term capital is unlikely to be efficiently allocated throughout the world by the banks.

Furthermore, as noted in an earlier section, factors which alter the creditworthiness of one country can have an influence on the willingness of banks to lend to other countries, and this may be quite unrelated to the economic performance and prospects of these countries. For example, a fall in the price of oil will create debt problems for oil producers such as Mexico and Venezuela, and will damage their credit rating with the banks. But as a result of debt problems in these countries, the banks may become more risk-averse and less prepared to lend to other countries whose economic prospects actually improve as oil prices fall, because the price of a major import has fallen and because a falling oil price tends to increase world aggregate demand and therefore the demand for their exports. The lack of simultaneity in the debt-servicing capacity of borrowers suggests that such a response is irrational; though to the extent that the withdrawal of funds itself creates a liquidity-based debt problem in the affected countries, it may seem rational after the event.

Another externality associated with bank lending relates to its global consequences. If banks pull out from providing balance of payments finance and nobody else steps in to take their place, the result will be that borrowers will have to correct their deficits more rapidly. They can do this by deflating domestic aggregate demand and, thus, the demand for imports or by introducing import controls. Either way the countries that provide these imports will experience a reduction in their exports and a deterioration in their balance of

TABLE 6.4 *Euro-currency bank credits – by country of borrower (credits with a maturity of one year or more, publicly announced, in millions of dollars)*

	1976	*1977*	*1978*	*1979*	*1980*	*1981*	*1982*	*1983*
Industrial countries	11,255	17,206	28,950	27,248	39,100	86,022	42,471	38,367
Australia	12	360	212	941	2,475	1,680	4,721	2,979
Belgium	—	—	40	1,000	2,833	360	1,172	883
Canada	885	3,292	5,705	1,845	1,743	4,112	3,838	958
Denmark	607	868	2,242	1,205	1,720	1,661	789	1,586
Finland	300	314	550	92	1,040	463	631	283
France	587	2,325	1,915	2,955	1,745	3,912	5,703	1,708
Greece	323	204	509	1,010	1,333	1,063	770	1,085
Ireland	434	440	616	687	237	1,361	401	765
Italy	355	1,024	2,485	3,708	6,268	6,030	3,657	2,950
New Zealand	—	538	480	540	675	476	3,411	70
Norway	473	182	1,517	935	685	713	1,769	970
Portugal	50	122	677	887	745	1,590	1,388	849
South Africa	650	—	150	52	388	287	1,479	752
Spain	2,037	1,973	2,426	4,184	5,457	3,242	1,849	3,013
Sweden	440	1,446	1,872	1,263	1,370	1,867	649	3,188
United Kingdom	1,671	1,992	3,899	795	1,470	747	1,635	1,304
United States	677	826	1,206	2,348	6,719	54,784	6,516	12,862
Yugoslavia	125	488	962	2,086	1,359	684	719	615
Other[1]	1,629	812	1,487	715	838	1,014	1,374	1,547
Developing countries	15,017	20,976	37,302	47,964	35,054	45,264	41,519	32,999
Latin American countries	8,664	9,917	21,332	28,077	24,103	30,152	26,719	15,309
Argentina	958	849	1,461	2,965	2,506	2,534	1,565	1,750
Brazil	3,232	2,814	5,634	6,278	4,158	5,751	5,716	4,475
Chile	208	591	1,045	867	1,322	2,204	1,194	1,319

TABLE 6.4—*continued*

	1976	*1977*	*1978*	*1979*	*1980*	*1981*	*1982*	*1983*
Colombia	110	43	882	754	608	1,030	741	459
Ecuador	87	385	952	593	1,209	934	815	431
Mexico	1,993	2,727	7,250	8,243	5,971	7,530	7,953	5,138
Panama	152	147	553	155	385	255	378	413
Peru	395	189	—	596	480	1,407	1,069	500
Venezuela	1,185	1,666	2,054	6,830	6,715	7,559	6,799	237
Other[2]	344	506	1,501	796	749	948	489	587
Asian countries	2,830	4,277	7,921	10,551	7,142	10,288	8,403	8,849
Hong Kong	85	408	390	680	407	664	33	—
India	—	50	75	50	771	377	284	809
Indonesia	470	817	1,118	1,061	1,435	725	1,250	1,497
Korea	738	1,265	2,651	3,258	1,917	2,824	2,923	3,245
Malaysia	207	212	858	1,168		1,725	1,909	950
Pakistan	—	27	76	214	300	350	455	365
Philippines	970	698	2,073	2,067	1,056	1,257	635	815
Thailand	100	140	192	543	676	692	268	349
Other	260	660	488	1,510	580	1,674	646	819
Middle Eastern and African countries	3,523	6,782	8,049	9,336	3,809	4,824	6,397	8,841
Algeria	643	723	2,576	1,906	40	—	26	1,964
Egypt	108	250	60	19	203	63	353	300
Ivory Coast	155	265	73	435	135	499	434	30
Morocco	641	797	605	500	420	774	326	294
Nigeria	—	1,000	825	1,373	1,330	1,802	2,042	1,853
Turkey	170	34	100	3,036	—	100	277	1,078

TABLE 6.4—*continued*

	1976	*1977*	*1978*	*1979*	*1980*	*1981*	*1982*	*1983*
United Arab Emirates	55	1,086	726	401	101	363	93	901
Other	1,751	2,627	3,084	1,666	1,580	1,223	2,846	2,421
Centrally planned countries	2,503	3,394	3,767	7,325	2,809	1,791	765	1,212
China	—	—	—	3,395	181	370	43	10
East Germany	215	832	642	796	303	470	8	392
Hungary	300	300	700	260	550	550	340	683
Poland	525	19	374	849	800	—	—	—
Soviet Union	282	234	650	—	—	25	374	68
Other[3]	1,181	2,009	1,401	2,025	975	376	—	59
International Organizations[4]	74	190	160	275	429	302	150	1,321
Total	28,849	41,766	70,179	82,812	77,392	133,379	84,905	73,899

1. Includes multinational organizations.
2. Includes unallocated.
3. Includes COMECON institutions.
4. Includes regional development organizations.

SOURCE: *World Financial Markets,* Morgan Guaranty, January 1984.

payments which they, in turn, may have to correct. A vicious circle of deflation, recession, protectionism, and falling world trade can become entrenched, though most countries stand to lose by it.

But at the same time is it really the banks' responsibility to ensure that things do not go wrong in this way? They will undoubtedly see their principal responsibility as being to their shareholders, and they are likely to take the view that these interests are best served in an uncertain world environment by trying to maximize short-run private profit; it may be unreasonable to expect them to assume the global role of maximizing world economic welfare.

The concept of welfare moves us on to the question of the distribution of bank lending. As Table 6.4 shows in aggregate terms, this has been heavily skewed, being concentrated in industrial countries and a relatively narrow range of middle- and high-income developing countries. While it has been claimed that the failure to normalize for country size leads to the degree of concentration being exaggerated – with small countries borrowing less simply because they are small, and in relation to their economic size actually borrowing as much as bigger countries – much depends on the sample of countries selected and the time period studied. The fact remains that the banks have usually deemed low-income countries uncreditworthy. Indeed for a time towards the end of the 1970s the poorest countries were actually net depositors on to the Euro-currency market rather than net borrowers from it, and it is still true that a large number of poor countries borrow very little from the banks even in proportion to their size.

Again, however, it is unreasonable to criticize the banks for the inequitable distribution of their lending. After all, they are not charitable institutions. Indeed on the contrary they would be more open to criticism were they to lend to countries that seemed to have little chance of repaying the loans. At the same time the elements of market failure remain, not only with respect to equity but also in terms of inefficiency. If bank lending fails to meet the requirements of the perfectly competitive market solution, should so much of the recycling of world capital be left in the hands of the banks; or should international agencies be more responsible for it?

4. THE INTERNATIONAL MONETARY FUND

Along with its contribution to balance of payments adjustment to be discussed in Chapter 9, the Fund provides short-term financial

TABLE 6.5 *Selected IMF financial activities by type and country, 1976–83 (millions of SDRs)*

	Financial year ended April 30								
	1976	*1977*	*1978*	*1979*	*1980*	*1981*	*1982*	*1983*	*1976–83*
					By Type				
I. General Resources Account									
Gross purchases[1]	5,267.4	4,749.7	2,367.3	1,239.2	2,210.8	4,385.9	6,960.2	10,258.2	37,438.7
Net purchases[2]	(4,966.6)	(3,899.6)	(−1,861.8)	(−3,267.2)	(−1,041.8)	(1,924.2)	(4,950.3)	(8,703.1)	(18,173.0)
II. Administered accounts									
Trust fund loans	—	31.7	268.2	670.0	961.7	1,059.9	—	—	2,991.5
Oil facility subsidy account payments (grants)	13.8	27.5	25.0	19.1	27.8	50.1	9.3	2.5	175.1
Supplementary financing facility subsidy account payments (grants)	—	—	—	—	—	—	22.9	44.3	67.2
III. SDR allocations	—	—	—	4,032.6	4,033.2	4,052.5	—	—	12,118.3
Total	5,281.2	4,808.9	2,660.5	5,960.9	7,233.5	9,548.4	6,992.4	10,305.0	52,790.8
					By Country (I, II, III)				
Industrial countries	2,391.3	2,198.1	1,438.8	2,593.7	2,617.6	2,543.9	—	54.0	13,837.5
United States	—	—	—	874.1	874.1	857.3	—	—	2,605.5
United Kingdom	1,000.0	1,700.0	1,250.0	304.2	304.2	298.3	—	—	4,856.8
Italy	780.2	—	90.0	129.0	128.9	126.5	—	—	1,254.6
Others	611.1	498.1	98.8	1,286.4	1,310.4	1,261.8	—	54.0	5,120.6

TABLE 6.5—*continued*

	Financial year ended April 30								
	1976	*1977*	*1978*	*1979*	*1980*	*1981*	*1982*	*1983*	*1976–83*
Developing Countries	2,889.9	2,610.8	1,221.7	3,367.2	4,615.9	7,004.3	6,992.4	10,251.0	38,953.3
Oil-exporting	—	—	—	369.3	369.3	380.3	—	65.1	1,184.0
Non-oil developing	2,889.9	2,610.8	1,221.7	2,997.9	4,246.6	6,624.0	6,992.4	10,185.0	37,769.3
Africa	580.5	635.3	336.6	861.7	1,262.6	1,472.9	1,999.9	2,072.1	9,221.6
Asia	882.0	603.8	435.4	1,011.5	1,197.4	3,448.3	3,163.5	3,106.1	13,848.0
Europe	611.5	340.1	271.6	249.0	765.8	981.2	1,326.0	1,188.1	5,733.3
Middle East	133.6	199.5	143.1	289.7	152.4	75.7	.8	25.2	1,020.0
Western Hemisphere	682.3	832.1	35.0	586.0	868.4	646.0	502.2	3,794.4	7,946.4
All countries	5,281.2	4,808.9	2,660.5	5,960.9	7,233.5	9,548.4	6,992.4	10,305.0	52,790.8
Gold distribution[3]	—	209.7	212.6	220.4	230.8	—	—	—	873.5
Profits from gold sales distributed to developing countries[4]	—	—	222.6	70.6	302.4	400.2	—	—	995.8

1. Excluding purchases in the reserve tranche.
2. Excluding purchases and repurchases in the reserve tranche; net repurchases (–).
3. Valued at SDR 35 per fine ounce.
4. Distribution in US dollars. SDR amounts based on SDR/US dollar rate in effect at time of distribution.

SOURCE: *IMF Annual Report, 1983.*

assistance to countries experiencing temporary payments difficulties through its General Account, and long-term finance through its Special Drawing Account.

4.1 The General Account

The various facilities within the General Account were listed and briefly described in Chapter 3, Table 3.1. This reveals that whereas the Fund makes some resources available with few conditions, and not very stringent conditions at that, the majority of finance is only available after the borrowing country has negotiated a reasonably detailed programme of policies with the Fund. The implementation of the programme is then monitored through a series of quantified performance criteria, and, since Fund loans are phased over time, later instalments are only paid if the borrower keeps within these performance criteria. Furthermore, some Fund finance is available only if payments difficulties have been caused in particular ways: for instance, a temporary shortfall in export receipts in the case of the Compensatory Financing Facility.

Since Fund lending is financed by members paying subscriptions and making loans to it, the Fund effectively recycles international finance. After the mid-1970s most of this recycling was from the industrial countries and those members of OPEC with large payments surpluses (in particular Saudi Arabia) to the non-oil developing countries. This general pattern of lending has, however, been interrupted by the occasional large loan to an industrial country, such as the 1976 credit to the United Kingdom. Furthermore, the identity of those developing countries receiving Fund support has changed over the years.

4.2 The quantity and pattern of Fund lending

Table 6.5 provides information on both the volume and destination of Fund lending. A number of features concealed here warrant mention. First, the quantity of international lending undertaken by the Fund is relatively small. Second, it varies from year to year, expanding quite rapidly sometimes and then contracting or growing more slowly. Third, the balance between low and high conditionality finance varies over time, as shown by Table 6.6. Fourth, the

TABLE 6.6 *Low-conditionality and high-conditionality purchases, 1976–83 (billions of SDRs)*

	Financial year ended April 30							
	1976	*1977*	*1978*	*1979*	*1980*	*1981*	*1982*	*1983*
I. Low-conditionality purchases	5.09	2.97	0.41	0.64	1.05	1.56	1.65	4.12
First credit tranche	0.29	0.78	0.09	0.13	0.16	0.78	0.02	0.03
Oil facility	3.97	0.44	—	—	—	—	—	—
Compensatory financing facility	0.83	1.75	0.32	0.46	0.86	0.78	1.63	3.74
Buffer stock facility	—	—	—	0.05	0.03	—	—	0.35
II. High-conditionality purchases	0.18	1.78	1.96	0.59	1.15	2.82	5.31	6.14
Credit tranche	0.17	1.59	1.85	0.35	0.93	1.90	2.73	3.68
Extended Fund facility	0.01	0.19	0.11	0.24	0.22	0.92	2.58	2.46
III. Total I + II	5.27	4.75	2.37	1.24	2.21	4.39	6.96	10.26

1. Less than SDR 5 million.

SOURCE: *IMF Annual Report, 1983.*

destination of lending has also varied over time; some countries have been almost perpetual users of Fund resources, whereas others only turn to the Fund infrequently.

The quantity of Fund finance may be conveniently assessed against both the size of global payments deficits and the size of private sector recycling. During the second half of the 1970s Fund credit financed little over 5 per cent of the combined current account deficit of the principal clients, the non-oil developing countries. Meanwhile, commercial credit financed more than 40 per cent of it. During 1980 and 1981 the banks supplied fifteen times as much finance as did the Fund to this group of countries. Although 1982 and 1983 found the banks unwilling to expand their lending – indeed repayments exceeded new loans – there was no matching increase in the availability of Fund finance.

However, while it is true that in relation to both the global size of payments deficits and the recycling activities of the banks the Fund has been an insignificant source of finance, such a conclusion is misleading. The relative significance of the Fund has varied from year to year and from country to country. In 1976, for example, as well as in the early 1980s, it was a quantitatively not insignificant lender in aggregate. Furthermore, for some countries which do not have access to commercial credit the Fund is an important, if not the only, source of short-term finance. Even for countries which do attract commercial credit, Fund lending, which may appear small by comparison, may raise the creditworthiness of the borrower, thereby having a catalytic effect on commercial flows.

As with commercial lending, variations in the year-to-year lending of the Fund may be explained by a combination of demand and supply side factors. On the demand side changes in the size and causes of payments deficits will affect the quantity of finance which countries are eligible to draw. Similarly, changes in the nature of the conditions that the Fund attaches to finance may make potential borrowers more or less willing to borrow from it. It may not simply be chance, for example, that the period of slack Fund lending following 1976 coincided with a period when the Fund was tending to emphasize the need for devaluation, a policy that is unpopular with many governments.

On the supply side the capacity of the Fund to lend is affected by the quantity of its resources, which are in turn affected by the size of Fund quotas, by the rules defining eligibility to draw under various facilities, and by the views of the executive directors on which loans should or should not be made. Moreover, decisions which affect the proportion of finance available on a low- as opposed to a high-conditionality basis are also likely to influence the use made of Fund credit. As the supply or conditionality price of Fund finance rises, so it is likely that the demand for it will fall. It is not surprising to find, for instance, that 1976 was a bumper year for Fund lending. Not only were many primary producers experiencing export shortfalls, but the CFF had been significantly liberalised in 1975, with the result that countries were eligible to draw more from the Fund.

Both demand and supply side factors also influence the destination of Fund lending. Some countries will simply be ineligible to draw on the Fund. Others, though eligible, may decide not to borrow because they are able to find alternative sources of finance which they prefer. Still others may be turned away by the Fund after failing to come up with a mutually acceptable programme of policies. The varying use of Fund credit by the countries of Latin America may, for instance, be explained in these terms. Up until the 1970s these countries had been very significant clients of the Fund. During the 1970s a combination of quite reasonable economic performance, dislike of Fund conditionality, and the availability of commercial credits led them to ignore the Fund. In the 1980s, however, deteriorating economic performance, declining terms of trade, rising real interest rates, and the banks' insistence that further loans would only be made if IMF programmes were put in place, left them with little alternative other than to borrow from the Fund.

In contrast the least developed countries of Africa and Asia, with few exceptions, such as India, never had much option other than to borrow from the Fund, and for a time at the beginning of the 1980s were the principal recipients of Fund loans. As noted earlier, in the case of India the banks would have been prepared to lend more than the Indian government was prepared to borrow. Anxious to avoid the debt problems that it saw emerging in Latin America, the government instead put in for, and received, a large loan from the Fund.

4.3 The Fund and the banks: the catalytic effect

As noted above, even though the absolute amounts of finance provided by the IMF may be relatively small, the adjustment programmes it validates may result in much larger inflows in the form of aid or Euro-currency credits. There is some regression evidence available which supports a positive correlation between Fund drawings and Euro-currency credits. However, it is also clear that drawings from the Fund and the acceptance of the related conditionality need in itself be neither a necessary nor sufficient condition for access to commercial loans. Some countries at some times have borrowed heavily from the Euro-currency market while making no use of the Fund; others have borrowed quite heavily from the Fund while borrowing relatively little commercially. The negotiation of an IMF-supported programme sometimes leads to an inflow of commercial finance and sometimes does not. Borrowing from the Fund is clearly not seen by the banks as a completely adequate guarantee of creditworthiness, even though they put great store by IMF activities when considering their own lending strategy to some countries.

The relation between the banks and the Fund came to the fore after 1982 as a number of the larger developing countries which had previously relied on private capital encountered debt problems. The negotiations to which these 'crises' led revealed the complex interrelation between the Fund and the banks, with the banks deferring the rescheduling of their loans until Fund programmes had been worked out, and the Fund trying to ensure that private finance would be forthcoming should it go ahead and commit its own resources.

While the Fund can claim that its relations with all member countries are essentially similar, the skewness of commercial lending implies that the nature of the relation between the Fund and the banks will vary between countries. In some low-income countries which have a balance of payments need for finance, and which have been able to negotiate an IMF programme but which are deemed a high risk by private banks, the Fund will be on its own and the catalytic effect will in practice be non-existent. In better-off developing countries or industrial countries that are deemed independently creditworthy it will be the banks that may be on their own, at least for protracted periods. In still other countries both the Fund and the banks may be simultaneously lending. It is quite possible therefore that the Fund may be supporting the private sector in one context, yet acting as a substitute for it in another.

4.4 The Special Drawing Account

SDRs were discussed more fully in Chapter 5, since, along with that part of General Account resources that can be drawn down unconditionally – the reserve tranche – they count as international reserves. However, it may be noted here that, first, SDRs are only a small proportion of total international financial flows, and, second, their distribution is based on IMF quotas, which means that a large proportion of them are allocated to industrial countries that are in balance of payments surplus.

5. REMAINING ISSUES

This chapter has concentrated on the short-term movement of capital. Within this it has focused on commercial flows; although there has also been some discussion of the IMF, which lends at various rates of interest, ranging from the concessionary to the almost commercial. A major gap in the analysis so far relates to the longer-term movement of capital and it is to this that the next chapter turns. However, it has to be recognised that Euro-currency lending, and indeed Fund lending, may effectively be rather longer term than at first sight it seems. The banks may, for instance, lend for, say, only three or six months but on the clear understanding that the loans will be rolled over or renewed when they expire. Similarly, the Fund may negotiate a series of standby arrangements, with the result that a deficit country may be continually borrowing from the Fund over a protracted period of years.

7 Foreign Aid and the Private Bond Market

The previous chapter concentrated on short-term financial provision through the commercial banking sector and the official sector. We now turn to examine longer-term flows of finance. Most of the chapter will focus on foreign aid, but we begin with a brief discussion of long-term lending through the private bond market.

1. THE BOND MARKET

Whereas the Euro-currency market has a relatively short history, the conventional way of raising long-term capital has been by issuing bonds. While the bond market has in the past been important for industrial countries, developing countries have raised only relatively small amounts of finance from it. Indeed for the vast majority of developing countries the bond market is really of no practical significance. Tables 7.1 and 7.2 provide information on some of the principal features of the international bond market, including the main types of bond issued and the principal borrowers.

There are a number of factors accounting for the pattern and size of bond lending. First, the access of potential borrowers to the capital markets of many countries is impeded by an often complex range of rules and regulations. Many developing countries in particular find it extremely difficult to break into these markets. Indeed it is only Mexico and Brazil, and to a lesser extent Argentina, Venezuela and in 1982 and 1983 Malaysia, that have had any real success in raising bond finance. Second, lenders find it unattractive to tie up money in long-term contracts with fixed nominal interest rates when variations in the rate of inflation mean that the real rate of interest is uncertain. It is hardly surprising that in an era of accelerating inflation and falling real interest rates lenders are reluctant to buy bonds. At the same time borrowers are unwilling to issue bonds if high nominal interest rates are accompanied by falling inflation and therefore by rising real interest rates. It is precisely because the short-term Euro-currency market enables the problems of fluctuating inflation to be circumvented that it has been so popular.

Unless ways of dealing with this problem are introduced, by index linking interest rates, it is difficult to see how the bond market will expand. Potential reforms directed towards increasing the appeal of the bond market are discussed in Chapter 8, but for the present we turn to another channel through which international financial flows occur, namely foreign aid.

2. FOREIGN AID

While some international capital flows can be explained by commercial considerations, other flows occur at interest rates often well below the market level. Governments or private bodies in one country sometimes lend on concessionary terms, or even provide out and out grants, to the governments of other countries, either directly (bilaterally) or through the intermediation of an international agency such as the World Bank or one of the regional development banks (multilaterally). Because the donor is located outside the recipients's country, and because the finance is concessionary, such flows are referred to as 'foreign aid'.

Although, in the past, foreign aid has flowed between developed economies, as was the case after the Second World War when the United States helped to finance economic reconstruction in Europe, it is more normally nowadays thought of in terms of developed industrial economies providing financial assistance to developing countries, with the assumed intention of helping their economic development.

2.1 Types of aid

2.1.1 Bilateral and multilateral

More than 80 per cent of aid is bilateral. The basic reason for this is that donors prefer it, because they can decide to whom it goes and usually also the purpose for which it is used. Furthermore, bilateral aid is more easily tied.

TABLE 7.1 *The international bond market (New issues with a maturity of three years or more, publicly offered or privately placed in the period, $ million)*

	1976	*1977*	*1978*	*1979*	*1980*	*1981*	*1982*	*1983*
Eurobonds	14,479	17,771	14,125	18,726	23,970	31,616	51,645	48,488
By category of borrower								
US companies	586	1,130	1,122	2,872	4,107	6,178	12,567	6,046
Foreign companies	5,323	7,347	4,540	7,183	9,032	12,882	13,372	16,621
State enterprises	4,138	4,667	3,291	4,524	5,839	7,496	14,650	11,241
Governments	2,239	2,936	3,643	2,433	3,045	2,629	7,683	8,495
International organizations[1]	2,193	1,691	1,529	1,714	1,947	2,431	3,373	6,075
By currency of denomination								
US dollar	9,276	11,627	7,290	12,565	16,427	26,830	43,959	38,406
German mark	2,713	4,131	5,251	3,626	3,607	1,277	2,588	3,776
Canadian dollar	1,407	655	—	425	279	634	1,201	1,039
Dutch guilder	502	452	394	531	1,043	529	645	735
French franc	39	—	103	342	986	533	4	—
Japanese yen	—	111	121	116	304	368	374	212
British pound	—	218	234	291	974	501	748	1,915
European composite units	99	28	165	253	65	309	1,980	2,095
Special drawing rights	—	—	32	107	39	446	—	—
Other	443	549	535	470	246	189	146	305
Foreign bonds outside the US	7,586	8,777	14,359	17,749	14,521	13,817	20,451	22,786
By category of borrower								
US companies	28	40	245	217	307	592	1,971	1,420
Foreign companies	1,654	1,421	2,110	3,463	3,157	3,384	4,376	7,872
State enterprises	2,439	2,427	3,163	3,284	2,830	3,701	5,488	4,305
Governments	1,307	2,043	5,771	7,663	4,086	2,762	3,577	3,129
International organizations[1]	2,158	2,846	3,070	3,122	4,141	3,378	5,039	6,060

TABLE 7.1—*continued*

	1976	*1977*	*1978*	*1979*	*1980*	*1981*	*1982*	*1983*
By currency of denomination								
Swiss franc	5,359	4,970	5,698	9,777	7,617	8,285	11,432	14,103
Japanese yen	226	1,271	3,826	1,833	1,088	2,457	3,418	3,793
German mark	1,288	2,181	3,779	5,379	4,839	1,310	2,952	2,614
Dutch guilder	597	211	385	75	259	481	956	1,085
British pound	—	—	—	—	168	746	1,214	520
Luxembourg franc	—	29	201	237	266	84	160	144
Other	116	115	470	448	284	454	319	527
Foreign bonds in the US	10,604	7,428	5,795	4,515	3,429	7,552	5,946	4,400
By category of borrower								
Canadian entities[2]	6,138	3,022	3,142	2,193	2,136	4,630	3,180	2,145
European entities[2]	900	1,208	1,527	915	610	710	650	585
International organizations[1]	2,275	1,917	459	1,100	550	1,375	1,700	1,220
Other	1,291	1,281	667	307	133	837	416	450
Total	32,669	33,976	34,279	40,990	41,920	52,985	78,042	75,669

1. Includes regional development organizations.
2. Includes private companies, state enterprises, and governmental borrowers.

SOURCE: *World Financial Markets*, Morgan Guaranty, January 1984.

TABLE 7.2 *Principal borrowers in the international bond market (new issues with a maturity of three years or more, publicly offered or privately placed in the period, $ million)*

	1976	*1977*	*1978*	*1979*	*1980*	*1981*	*1982*	*1983*
Industrial countries	24,183	23,741	24,744	31,716	32,588	40,861	62,992	59,766
Australia	1,081	1,074	1,218	593	539	991	2,250	2,360
Austria	682	1,384	1,927	1,218	1,859	1,557	1,668	1,261
Belgium	134	297	37	537	227	527	211	1,148
Canada	9,336	5,276	4,764	4,197	3,797	10,648	11,979	7,487
Denmark	995	796	1,018	752	1,125	695	1,269	1,719
Finland	332	358	952	699	392	672	815	861
France	2,720	1,944	1,286	2,106	2,820	3,156	8,456	6,447
Germany	374	567	174	609	455	279	1,101	3,070
Ireland	20	86	83	179	331	517	625	955
Italy	85	300	240	338	904	1,108	2,214	1,549
Japan	2,165	1,978	3,467	5,775	5,309	6,928	8,397	13,917
Netherlands	455	681	251	832	1,575	630	894	946
New Zealand	497	567	744	553	293	1,107	1,375	455
Norway	1,406	1,888	2,751	1,955	892	530	832	664
Portugal	—	50	—	—	50	30	206	76
South Africa	76	33	400	235	363	92	374	543
Spain	244	376	319	433	426	444	747	1,443
Sweden	1,111	1,574	876	1,530	3,244	2,050	2,479	3,751
United Kingdom	1,067	1,915	1,365	1,181	1,733	1,408	1,201	1,386
United States	493	1,354	2,973	6,767	5,587	6,770	14,538	7,389
Yugoslavia	71	120	141	96	37	—	—	—
Other[1]	839	1,123	658	1,131	620	722	1,361	2,339

TABLE 7.2—*continued*

	1976	*1977*	*1978*	*1979*	*1980*	*1981*	*1982*	*1983*
Developing countries	1,789	3,533	4,447	3,263	2,629	4,886	5,073	2,473
Latin American countries	744	2,545	2,620	2,091	1,988	3,658	2,480	71
Argentina	—	43	253	517	260	195	—	—
Brazil	268	732	843	930	349	60	91	—
Chile	—	—	—	82	103	30	—	—
Colombia	—	—	—	—	75	20	35	—
Ecuador	—	8	—	—	100	—	—	—
Mexico	448	1,282	568	363	544	3,012	1,919	—
Panama	14	27	211	111	25	25	—	21
Peru	—	—	—	—	—	25	—	—
Venezuela	—	438	588	55	398	291	385	—
Other[2]	14	15	157	33	134	—	50	50
Asian countries	659	549	667	702	429	1,068	2,145	2,190
Hong Kong	—	129	—	—	30	70	40	50
India	—	—	30	45	65	271	225	60
Indonesia	—	—	102	85	45	97	482	328
Korea	59	69	65	44	68	323	172	556
Malaysia	10	43	141	151	—	—	807	831
Philippines	385	129	170	175	70	99	50	—
Singapore	205	154	70	25	—	30	125	70
Thailand	—		69	177	86	93	63	255
Other	—	25	20		65	85	181	40

TABLE 7.2—*continued*

	1976	*1977*	*1978*	*1979*	*1980*	*1981*	*1982*	*1983*
Middle Eastern and African countries	386	439	1,160	470	212	160	448	212
Algeria	109	167	721	208	—	—	—	—
Egypt	—	—	—	—	30	—	75	—
Israel	119	111	220	170	144	117	200	135
Ivory Coast	10	—	—	—	14	—	—	—
Morocco	44	28	61	22	24	—	—	—
United Arab Emirates	—	42	—	20	—	—	20	—
Other	104	91	158	50	—	43	153	77
Centrally planned countries	71	248	30	75	65	75	65	75
China	—	—	—	—	—	—	65	50
Hungary	—	174	—	—	65	20	—	—
Poland	71	74	30	56	—	—	—	—
Other[3]	—	—	—	19	—	55	—	25
International organizations[4]	6,626	6,454	5,058	5,936	6,638	7,163	9,912	13,355
Total	32,669	33,976	34,279	40,990	41,920	52,985	78,042	75,669

1. Includes multinational organizations.
2. Includes unallocated.
3. Includes COMECON institutions.
4. Includes regional development organizations.

SOURCE: *World Financial Markets*, Morgan Guaranty, January 1984.

2.1.2 Tied and untied

The practice of 'tying' is very widespread, applying to more than three-quarters of foreign aid. Tying is basically of two types: project tying and procurement tying. Tying aid to the foreign exchange costs of particular projects is popular with donors because it is felt to increase the recipient's accountability. Furthermore, donors can ostensibly see what they are getting for their money and in some sense there is a visible assurance that the resources are being 'properly' used. Finally, project tying may facilitate procurement tying, thereby helping donors to increase their exports.

Recipients, on the other hand, find project tying less attractive, since it forces them to come up with a series of large-scale projects requiring a significant foreign exchange content. Left to their own devices they may prefer to undertake a larger number of smaller-scale projects, because these are seen as more efficient in terms of their use of scarce local resources and appropriate technology, as less time-consuming administratively, as needing a smaller import content, and as having lower recurrent costs. Recipients therefore favour programme aid, where they have more discretion as to how the finance is used. However, the inflexibility that project tying enforces on recipients can be overstressed, since they may be able to use aid in support of a project which was going to be undertaken in any case, thus freeing foreign exchange to be used for some other purpose outside the influence of the donor. To an extent aid is 'fungible'.

Procurement tying has the effect of tying the spending of aid to purchases from the donor. It therefore imposes a constraint if, left with a free choice, the recipient would have spent the money elsewhere. Procurement tying springs primarily from a desire by individual donors to protect their own balance of payments by increasing exports. However, to a certain extent the balance of payments gains from procurement tying as perceived by individual donors may be illusory. First, given the geographical pattern of expenditure by aid recipients as a group, aid is in any case and in aggregate de facto mostly tied to expenditure in donors as a group. Second, tying may induce retaliation by other donors, thus eliminating the relative gain from it. Third, by limiting spending in third countries, procurement tying may reduce exports to these countries below what they would otherwise have been. Finally, there is again the question of fungibility; imports that would have been bought in any case may now be formally related to the aid provided

To the extent that they can avoid the implications of procurement tying by means of such import switching, recipients may not be too bothered about it. However, the scope for switching is almost certainly rather limited for most developing countries, which frequently depend heavily on one particular donor and which hold relatively small amounts of 'free' foreign exchange. From their point of view the costs of procurement tying result largely from the fact that they may initially have to pay a higher price for goods bought from the donor than from elsewhere, and subsequently a higher price for spare parts and service contracts. Furthermore, they may not only have to buy goods that are relatively expensive but also not best suited to their needs, embodying, for instance, inappropriate technology. These negative effects may then be spread throughout the economy by the inter-linkages between projects. In effect, therefore, procurement tied aid may be reinterpreted as a form of subsidy to exporters in the donor country.

2.1.3 Financial, food and technical

Total aid takes a variety of different forms. About 20 per cent of Official Development Assistance (ODA) comes in the form of technical assistance (training personnel, financing fellowships, scientific, social and economic research), and nearly 30 per cent in the form of grants covering both food aid and debt forgiveness. The rest is made up of bilateral lending or contributions to multilateral institutions.

Another element of aid, which lies outside ODA, is that provided by various charity organisations. Although these may be permanently active in a number of poor countries, they tend to make their largest impact when dealing with disaster relief.

2.2 The measurement of aid

One of the problems when discussing foreign aid is that there is no single international financial flow called 'aid'. Instead there are various types of international financial flow, some public, emanating from governments, official agencies or multilateral institutions, and some private, emanating from private firms, or foundations and charities. Some of these flows are purely commercial and would not normally be counted as aid, even though they may well assist the recipient. Others are grants. In between comes a wide spectrum, neither purely grants nor purely commercial.

These flows may be converted to a common denominator by calculating the grant element. A loan includes a grant element if the discounted present value of the repayment of the loan and the interest payments are less than the initial value of the loan. As the grant element increases, so the loan is said to become 'softer'.

To calculate the 'grant element', 'grant equivalent', or 'aid component' of a loan, the following formula is used:

$$\left[\frac{F - \sum_{t=1}^{T} \frac{Pt}{(1+r)t}}{F} \right] 100$$

where F is the face value of the loan, Pt is the total repayment of principal and interest in year t, T is the maturity of the loan, and r is the discount rate. Thus with a loan of $1,000,000 and a discounted present value of amortization and interest of $750,000 the grant element is 25 per cent. For aid flows that do not have to be repaid the grant element is 100 per cent. On the other hand, for loans that are commercial in all respects the grant element is zero.

As the above formula reveals, the grant element will vary with the rate of interest charged on the loans, the discount rate used, and the maturity of the loan. It will also vary with the so-called grace period, the period of time during which only interest on the loan has to be paid. Assuming a constant rate of discount, the grant element of a loan rises as the interest rate falls, and as the maturity and grace periods lengthen. Although the latter factors exert a crucial impact on the recipients' demand for foreign exchange in particular years and may provide useful ways of improving the recipient's liquidity position, they exert only a relatively minor effect on the grant element, the principal determinant of which is the interest rate relative to the discount rate. Where the discount rate exceeds the interest rate, the grant element is positive. With a given discount rate the grant element varies approximately and inversely in proportion to the interest rate.

In measuring the aid content of financial flows the choice of the discount rate can be seen as being very significant. The question is what rate should be selected? In principle the answer is the social discount rate. In practice, however, this answer gets us little further and one is forced to use some approximation for it, such as the rate of return on investment or the average world interest rate. In the latter case the grant element is then reflected by the difference between what the borrower actually has to pay and what the borrower would have had to pay to raise the loan commercially.[1]

Something that follows on from this discussion is that the grant element as measured by the recipient may differ from that as measured by the donor. In the latter case the grant element represents the extent to which the present value of total receipts falls short of the face value of the loan. Again discounting comes into it. If, however, the donor's discount rate differs from that of the recipient, their estimates of the grant element of the loan will also differ. Where, for instance, the recipient's discount rate exceeds that of the donor, then the aid content as perceived by the recipient will also exceed the donor's perception of it, and in these circumstances the transfer of capital will raise total welfare.

Although the grant element provides a useful insight into the benefits associated with various financial flows and shows some of the factors which influence these – illustrating, for instance, that a reduction in the rate of interest may be offset by a shortening in the maturity of a loan or the grace period – it fails to give the whole picture. What a recipient gains from a loan will also depend on how productively it is used, as well as on the quality of the loan. The former applies to all loans, even purely commercial ones, so does not affect the usefulness of the grant element as a comparative measure. But, through tying, aid is subject to more restrictions on its use than are commercial flows, and for this reason the grant element will tend to overstate the benefits of aid to the recipient.

2.3 Donors and recipients

It is easy to get bogged down in detail when discussing the flow of aid, since a considerable amount of information is fairly easily available. However, in this section we use the accessibility of information elsewhere as an excuse for noting only the broad pattern of aid provision. We also limit the discussion to ODA, and therefore ignore other types of international finance, such as 'other official flows', which include non-concessional public flows, and 'private capital flows', which include private overseas direct investment, export credits, and portfolio investment. The relative importance of these various flows over time is, however, summarized in Table 7.3. It may be seen that ODA has accounted for a declining share of total net financial resource flows to developing countries since 1970.

Table 7.3 also gives a breakdown of ODA by the major donor groups. Notable features are the dominance of the Western economies – co-ordinated through the Development Assistance Committee, which comprises the seventeen largest and most advanced countries within the OECD – the increased contribution of OPEC after 1973 and the low level of aid from Eastern bloc countries (CMEA).

Although the DAC countries are by far the principal donors, the real amount of aid from this source has levelled off since the beginning of the 1980s. While most DAC countries have notionally accepted the UN target set in 1970 for ODA to equal 0·7 per cent of GNP, few have achieved it, and those that have have all been relatively small countries. Of the large contributors, only France has come close to the target, while the United States and Japan, two of the richest countries in the world, have only reached often substantially less than half of the target ratio. For the DAC as a whole, Table 7.4 shows that ODA amounted to 0·38 per cent of GNP in 1982. This compares with a peak of 0·54 per cent in 1961. Given that the figure had already declined to 0·34 per cent by 1970, the unconducive atmosphere created by the oil rise in 1973 and changing political attitudes in the principal donors can only be used to explain the failure of ODA to increase since then, rather than the initial decline from the level achieved at the beginning of the 1960s.

Just as there is considerable variation within the DAC group of countries, Table 7.4 also reveals that the aid record of OPEC as a group of countries conceals great variety. The OPEC current account surplus that so dominated the 1970s was in fact concentrated in very few countries – essentially Saudi Arabia, Kuwait and the United Arab Emirates – whose economies were too small to absorb more than a small proportion of the total revenue accruing from oil sales. It is not surprising to find that these countries are prominent in Table 7.4. Other OPEC members, such as Indonesia and Nigeria, with large populations and high levels of absorptive capacity, have provided insignificant amounts of aid.

Before 1973 OPEC aid was on a relatively small scale. In the following three years it grew rapidly before declining in 1978. This fall reflected in part the decision of the Arab states to terminate assistance to Egypt, previously a major recipient of funds, and the

TABLE 7.3 *Total net resource receipts of developing countries from all sources, 1970–82 – constant prices ($ billion, 1981 prices)*

	1970	*1971*	*1972*	*1973*	*1974*	*1975*	*1976*	*1977*	*1978*	*1979*	*1980*	*1981*	*1982*
I. Official Development Assistance	21.30	22.18	21.48	24.72	29.10	32.03	30.19	28.82	33.53	33.79	36.21	36.62	34.97
1. Bilateral	18.45	19.03	18.47	20.90	24.13	26.16	24.45	22.18	26.36	27.19	28.65	28.70	27.37
DAC countries	14.58	15.31	14.43	13.80	14.51	14.97	14.09	13.85	15.66	17.28	17.56	18.28	18.93
OPEC countries	1.00	1.07	1.44	3.96	7.32	8.69	7.67	5.88	8.23	7.36	8.47	7.61	5.63
CMEA and other donors	2.86	2.65	2.60	3.14	2.29	2.51	2.69	2.46	2.47	2.54	2.62	2.81	2.81
2. Multilateral agencies	2.86	3.16	3.01	3.82	4.97	5.87	5.74	6.63	7.17	6.60	7.56	7.93	(7.61)
II. Grants by private voluntary agencies	2.22	2.21	2.27	2.67	2.15	2.05	2.00	2.04	1.97	2.06	2.24	2.02	2.36
III. Non-concessional flows[1]	28.22	28.71	29.04	38.71	34.94	52.46	51.77	61.21	69.11	61.08	54.71	69.27	(57.84)
1. Official or officially supported	10.20	11.94	8.19	9.47	13.47	16.10	18.78	21.62	22.92	19.81	21.81	22.14	23.12
Private export credits (DAC)	5.39	6.58	3.14	2.26	4.23	6.76	10.00	12.14	11.58	9.37	10.79	11.33	(9.19)
Official export credits (DAC)	1.52	1.75	1.62	2.20	1.41	1.83	2.06	1.98	2.65	1.83	2.39	2.01	(2.50)
Multilateral	1.83	2.23	2.21	2.55	3.19	3.87	3.77	3.70	3.68	4.40	4.70	5.68	6.82
Other official and private flows (DAC)	0.64	0.68	0.98	1.99	1.46	1.15	1.19	0.86	1.62	1.21	2.17	1.96	(3.07)
Other donors[2]	0.82	0.70	0.24	0.47	3.18	2.49	1.76	2.94	3.39	3.01	1.77	1.16	(1.53)

TABLE 7.3—*continued*

	1970	*1971*	*1972*	*1973*	*1974*	*1975*	*1976*	*1977*	*1978*	*1979*	*1980*	*1981*	*1982*
2. Private	18.01	16.77	20.86	29.24	21.46	36.36	32.98	39.59	46.18	41.27	32.90	47.13	34.73
Direct investment	9.51	8.03	9.24	9.20	3.33	17.37	12.33	13.49	13.83	14.20	10.22	16.13	(11.24)
Bank sector[1]	7.73	8.01	10.48	18.91	17.64	18.35	18.84	21.70	27.68	26.35	21.34	29.00	(21.45)
Bond lending	0.77	0.73	1.14	1.13	0.49	0.64	1.81	4.40	4.67	0.72	1.34	2.00	2.04
Total receipts (I+II+III)	51.75	53.11	52.79	66.10	66.19	86.54	83.96	92.07	104.61	96.93	93.16	107.92	95.18
Memorandum items:													
Short-term bank lending	—	—	—	—	—	—	—	21.98	20.29	16.93	25.22	25.00	17.36
IMF purchases, net[3]	0.88	0.12	0.66	0.70	3.07	.95	4.42	−0.59	−1.01	0.55	2.53	6.40	6.86
GNP deflator (1981=100)	38.8	41.2	45.8	51.3	56.7	65.4	67.4	72.8	83.8	94.5	103.1	100.0	97.8

1. Excluding (*i*) bond lending and (*ii*) export credits extended by banks which are included under private export credits. Including loans by branches of OECD banks located in offshore centres, and for 1980, 1981 and 1982 participations of non-OECD banks in international syndicates.
2. Incomplete data for other official flows from OPEC countries, CMEA countries, Luxembourg, Spain, Yugoslavia, India, Israel and Chile.
3. All purchases minus repayments including reserve tranches but excluding loans by the IMF Trust Fund included under multilateral ODA.

SOURCE: *Development Co-operation,* 1983 Review, Paris, OECD.

TABLE 7.4 *ODA as a percentage of GNP, 1970–82 (net disbursements)*

	1970	*1975*	*1978*	*1980*	*1981*	*1982*
DAC countries						
Netherlands	0.61	0.75	0.98	1.03	1.08	1.08
Norway	0.32	0.66	0.93	0.85	0.82	0.99
Sweden	0.38	0.82	0.97	0.79	0.83	1.02
Denmark	0.38	0.58	0.77	0.74	0.73	0.77
France (incl. DOM/TOM)	0.66	0.62	0.60	0.64	0.73	0.75
France (excl. DOM/TOM)	0.42	0.38	0.35	0.38	0.45	0.49
Belgium	0.46	0.59	0.57	0.50	0.59	0.60
Germany	0.33	0.40	0.45	0.44	0.47	0.48
United Kingdom	0.39	0.39	0.52	0.35	0.43	0.37
Canada	0.41	0.54	0.48	0.43	0.43	0.42
Australia	0.62	0.65	0.53	0.48	0.41	0.57
Austria	0.07	0.21	0.19	0.23	0.48	0.53
New Zealand	0.23	0.52	0.33	0.33	0.29	0.28
Japan	0.23	0.23	0.27	0.32	0.28	0.29
Finland	0.06	0.18	0.22	0.22	0.28	0.30
Switzerland	0.15	0.19	0.21	0.24	0.24	0.25
United States	0.32	0.27	0.20	0.27	0.20	0.27
Italy	0.16	0.11	0.08	0.17	0.19	0.24
Total DAC	0.34	0.36	0.35	0.38	0.35	0.38
Other OECD countries	—	(0.03)	0.09	0.09	0.13	0.14
OPEC countries						
Saudi Arabia	5.60	7.76	5.55	5.09	3.58	2.82
Kuwait	6.21	7.40	3.50	3.40	3.55	4.86
UAE	n.a.	11.68	5.09	3.30	2.88	2.06
Iraq	0.13	1.62	2.53	2.39	(0.40)	—
Qatar	n.a.	15.58	6.18	4.03	3.75	(3.80)
Other	0.28	0.66	0.21	0.18	0.15	0.08
Total OPEC	1.18	2.92	1.88	1.84	1.50	1.22
CMEA countries						
USSR	0.16	0.13	0.14	0.15	0.14	0.14
GDR	0.08	0.04	0.18	0.17	0.17	0.15
Eastern Europe, other	0.14	0.08	0.11	0.13	0.13	0.13
Total CMEA	0.15	0.11	0.13	0.15	0.14	0.14

Notes: 1970 and 1975 data exclude administrative costs for all countries with the exception of the United States.

DAC countries are ranked according to their performance vis-à-vis the GNP target in recent years.

SOURCE: *Development Co-operation,* 1983 Review, Paris, OECD.

cessation of virtually all aid from Iran. Subsequently OPEC aid has mirrored quite closely its balance of payments performance; as this has weakened, so the flow of OPEC aid has declined. Although there is a wide dispersion, OPEC as a group has contributed a much higher proportion of GNP to aid than have the DAC countries.

Amongst the centrally planned economies, the USSR is the major contributor, although its relative share has declined and that of China has increased. However, the dominant aspect of CMEA aid is its smallness.

Although most of ODA is bilateral, the proportion channelled through multilateral institutions has increased since the 1960s. Indeed between 1971 and 1976 real multilateral aid from the DAC increased at an annual average rate of over 10 per cent, while bilateral aid declined at ½ per cent per annum. However, in the years 1977–82 the growth of multilateral aid from the DAC fell back to below 3 per cent per annum, while bilateral aid grew at over 5 per cent per annum.

The main international aid institutions are the World Bank and its two affiliates, the International Development Association (IDA) and the International Finance Corporation (IFC); the regional banks related to particular geographical areas, such as Latin America, Asia and Africa; UN and EEC institutions and Arab/OPEC funds; and, to the extent that some of its assistance is concessionary, the IMF. They finance their lending by obtaining capital and other contributions from their member countries as well as, in many cases, from the sale of bonds on the international capital market. Table 7.5 summarises the disbursements made by the main multilateral agencies.

But to which countries does aid go? Given the dominance of bilateral aid, the answer is hardly surprising. In reflection of the large absolute amounts of US aid, Latin America and the Caribbean have historically received the largest share of total ODA.

Most UK and French aid goes to ex-colonies in Africa and Asia, while the overwhelming proportion of OPEC aid goes to countries with which it has cultural or religious ties, such as Syria and Jordan. About half the aid provided by the Soviet Union has gone to Cuba and Vietnam.

As a group, the least developed countries, which are concentrated in two 'poverty belts' in mid-Africa and South-east Asia, usually receive only about 20 per cent of total ODA, even though, because of their strictly limited access to commercial finance, aid remains their principal source of external finance. Measured in per capita terms, ODA to this group of countries falls far below the level directed to

TABLE 7.5 *Loan and grant disbursements by multilateral agencies (net disbursements, $ million)*

Agency	Net							Gross						
	1970	*1977*	*1978*	*1979*	*1980*	*1981*	*1982*	*1970*	*1977*	*1978*	*1979*	*1980*	*1981*	*1982*
	I. CONCESSIONAL FLOWS													
IBRD[1]	—	39	76	107	107	88	58	—	39	76	107	107	88	58
IDA	163	1,132	1,007	1,278	1,543	1,918	2,363	163	1,158	1,038	1,302	1,584	1,963	2,431
IDB	224	299	332	335	326	438	366	245	392	433	461	468	556	518
of which: Grants	—	—	—	—	17	24	33							
African D. Fund	—	26	39	55	96	91	122	—	26	44	57	96	93	124
Asian DB	1	89	161	116	149	146	177	1	100	161	124	159	149	188
of which: Grants	—	8	—	—	8	7	13							
Car. DB	—	12	20	25	43	39	36	—	12	20	25	43	39	36
EEC/EIB[2]	210	549	805	1,124	1,013	1,440	1,143	210	558	815	1,137	1,028	1,453	1,157
of which: Grants	174	473[3]	729[3]	848	900	1,193	895							
IMF Trust Fund	—	175	864	680	1,636	434	—	—	175	864	680	1,636	434	—
IFAD	—	—	—	3	45	75	104	—	—	—	3	45	75	104
United Nations Grants	498	1,404	1,730	2,214	2,487	2,848	2,755	498	1,404	1,730	2,214	2,487	2,848	2,755
Arab OPEC Funds	—	1,107	973	265	293	411	(322)	—	1,107	973	272	302	432	(429)
of which: Grants	—	13	19	19	28	42	44							
Total	1,096	4,832	6,007	6,202	7,738	7,928	7,446	1,117	4,971	6,154	6,382	7,955	8,130	7,800
of which: Grants	672	1,898	2,478	3,081	3,440	4,114	3,740							

TABLE 7.5—*continued*

Agency	Net 1970	Net 1977	Net 1978	Net 1979	Net 1980	Net 1981	Net 1982	Gross 1970	Gross 1977	Gross 1978	Gross 1979	Gross 1980	Gross 1981	Gross 1982
	II. NON-CONCESSIONAL FLOWS													
IBRD	508	1,833	2,104	2,846	3,166	3,603	4,534	810	2,501	2,900	3,786	4,310	5,015	6,363
IDA	—	—	—	—	—	—	—	—	—	—	—	—	—	—
IFC	68	98	58	108	295	510	291	77	174	169	244	465	645	388
IDB	84	388	375	447	567	643	833	150	552	560	613	813	345	1,081
African DB	2	66	83	92	97	70	115	2	73	93	108	117	99	147
Asian DB	15	225	229	278	328	390	473	16	272	294	361	429	518	620
Car. DB	—	11	—	7	13	16	13	—	11	—	7	13	16	13
EEC/EIB[2]	11	49	78	162	257	241	320	(11)	67	104	194	294	275	401
Arab OPEC funds	—	20	157	219	128	212	(100)	—	20	171	292	417	366	(564)
Total	688	2,690	3,084	4,159	4,849	5,685	6,679	1,066	3,670	4,291	5,605	6,858	7,779	9,577

1. Excluding loans transferred to IFC.
2. Excluding funds channelled through other multilateral organisations.
3. Including STABEX.

SOURCE: *Development Co-operation*, 1983 Review, Paris, OECD.

TABLE 7.6 *The distribution of ODA[1] – major aid recipients and their sources, 1980–1 (countries listed in order of absolute volume of aid receipts, gross disbursements)*

	Total ODA $m	Receipts per capita	DAC ODA		OPEC ODA[2]		CMEA ODA		Multilateral ODA	
				$ million		$ million		$ million		$ million
1. India	2,570	4	Egypt	1,217	Syria	1,288	Vietnam	900	India	1,298
2. Egypt	1,472	37	India	1,127	Jordan	942	Cuba	617	Pakistan	379
3. Syria	1,450	161	Bangladesh	986	Morocco	370	Afghanistan	273	Bangladesh	351
4. Bangladesh	1,414	16	Indonesia	970	Lebanon	290	Kampuchea	138	China	234
5. Vietnam	1,140	21	Israel	883	Yemen	279	Laos	90	Egypt	198
6. Pakistan	1,126	14	Turkey	720	Turkey	234	Syria	64	Sudan	179
7. Indonesia	1,122	8	Tanzania	580	Pakistan	218	Pakistan	61	Kampuchea	172
8. Jordan	1,088	335	Pakistan	468	Oman	203	Iraq	49	Somalia	159
9. Turkey	1,035	23	Sudan	360	Sudan	192	Algeria	48	Tanzania	145
10. Israel	883	228	Kenya	336	Bahrain	155	Turkey	46	Ethiopia	136
11. Tanzania	749	41	Thailand	327	Mauritania	119	India	33	Indonesia	130
12. Sudan	736	40	Korea Rep.	317	India	113	Egypt	33	Zaire	103
					Somalia	112	Argentina	23		
				8,291 (46% of DAC bil. ODA)		4,515 (81% of OPEC ODA)[2]		2,375 (92% of CMEA ODA)		3,484 (50% of multilateral ODA)
$14,785 m (45% of total ODA)					$18,665 m (56% of total ODA)					

1. Allocated amounts only.
2. Including flows from Arab multilateral agencies.

SOURCE: *Development Co-operation*, 1983 Review, Paris, OECD

the middle-income countries, which receive approaching 40 per cent of total ODA. Table 7.6 summarizes the destinations of aid.

2.4 Some recent trends

A number of trends in the provision of aid may be observed since 1970. First, aid has accounted for a declining share of total financial flows to developing countries. In the 1970s this reflected the rapid growth in commercial flows and the stagnation in aid. In the early 1980s bank lending stagnated (as reported in the previous chapter) yet aid failed to expand in real terms. As a result of the declining relative importance of aid, financial flows to developing countries have became harder.

Second, a continuously small proportion of aid has been directed towards the least developed countries, even though their problems have become particularly acute and even though a target of at least 0·55 per cent of GNP to these countries has been established. The principal donors have fallen far short of this target. However between 1975 and 1982 the proportion of DAC ODA going to the least developed countries did increase from 20 per cent to almost 22·5 per cent.

Third, with the evolution of the north–south debate, aid has become a political issue of increasing sensitivity.

The basic reasons for aid have become more forcefully questioned by some and at the same time more staunchly defended by others. It is to these basic arguments that we now turn.

2.5 The case for aid

Without a doubt there are numerous reasons why the governments of some countries provide concessionary assistance to others. While these are not mutually exclusive, it is possible to group them under three headings.

2.5.1 Humanitarian

A fundamental motive for aid is the belief that social welfare measures should not be confined to national boundaries and that, as a minimum, all the world's population should have their basic needs met. In terms of per capita income a wide gap exists between the richest and the poorest countries, and the moral argument sees aid as a way of redistributing income at the world level, and of thereby helping to close the development gap and of assisting the poorest people in the world. In proportion to GNP, what the richer countries give up in the form of aid will be far less than what the poorer countries will receive. Furthermore, if the marginal utility of income diminishes, aid will raise world welfare. Advocates argue that there is nothing at all uncommon in using policy to offset the inequality of income distribution. Indeed at a national level it is accepted as one of the central functions of fiscal policy. Aid is viewed merely as a form of global fiscal policy.

2.5.2 Economic

There are basically three economic reasons used in support of foreign aid.

The first argues that economic development is frequently constrained by lack of finance. For growth to occur, investment is needed. Just how much depends on the desired growth rate and on the productivity of investment or the amount of extra output produced by each new piece of capital. Investment is financed through saving. However, it may be that, given the productivity of investment, saving is insufficient to finance the amount of investment required to generate the desired growth in output. Planned investment exceeds planned saving and there is therefore a savings gap. Other things remaining unchanged, this gap may be closed either by an increase in domestic saving or by an inflow of finance from abroad in the form of aid or as a counterpart to a balance of payments surplus.

However, saving may not be the only, or indeed the effective, constraint on growth. Development plans may also be frustrated by a shortage of skills within the domestic work force, or by a shortage of imported goods that are vital for development but which for some reason cannot, at least at present, be produced domestically. If, for example, imports are required in a fixed proportion to output, yet export receipts are only such as to enable a country to buy fewer imports than those needed to achieve the desired level of output, there will be a foreign exchange gap. It could be that, even if it were possible to raise domestic savings, the target rate of growth would be unattainable because of this shortage of foreign exchange. In these circumstances the desired growth rate will not be achieved unless and until this gap is closed. Foreign aid provides one way of closing it. Aid may therefore be seen as playing a dual role in the development process as both a supplement to domestic saving and as a source of scarce foreign exchange.

But how much aid will a country need in order to achieve its growth target? This depends on a number of factors, not least of which is the size of the desired growth rate. However, taking this as given, and assuming that nothing can be done to increase the productivity of investment or foreign exchange earnings, or reduce the import ratio, the amount of foreign aid required will depend on the relative sizes of the two gaps. While, subject to these provisos, the savings gap may be closed either by extra domestic saving or by extra foreign exchange, the foreign exchange gap may only be closed by extra foreign exchange. Thus, the maximum amount of aid required will equal the larger of the two gaps and the minimum amount will equal the excess of the foreign exchange gap over the savings gap.

Dual gap analysis focuses on the benefits of aid for recipients, the second argument put forward in its favour is that it also benefits donors.

Within a national economy redistribution of income may not only be an end but also a means of raising the degree of capacity utilization, of reducing unemployment, and of encouraging economic growth. This analysis hinges on a belief that different groups in society have different propensities to spend out of marginal changes in income. On the assumption that poorer people have a higher marginal propensity to spend than do richer people, redistributing income from rich to poor will raise aggregate expenditure, and if a recession has been caused by a deficiency in demand, then such redistribution will alleviate the situation. If this logic applies equally to the world economy, a transfer of resources from rich to poor countries is in the mutual interests of all countries. Developing countries will benefit from the inflow of financial and real resources while developed countries will benefit from an improvement in their balance of trade, as exports to developing countries rise, and from a fall in unemployment. The argument continues that if developed countries have spare productive capacity, the real costs of the aid in terms of the transfer of resources may be met by additional output.

The third argument is based on the idea that the efficient world allocation of resources requires that capital should go where its marginal productivity is highest. If the productivity of capital is higher in developing than in developed countries, it follows that capital should flow from the latter to the former. If insufficient private financial flows materialize, this may be taken as evidence of market failure and as providing a reason for official intervention via aid to ensure that such flows do occur.

2.5.3 Political, military and historical

Apart from economic considerations, aid is provided as a means of maintaining or increasing political influence and of furthering military objectives. For instance, much US aid clearly has the political objective of preventing the spread of Communism. Of course whether this rationale for aid is regarded as an argument in its favour depends on whether one sympathizes with the political objectives, and whether aid is seen as being an effective way of achieving them.

2.6 The distribution of aid

As the previous section reveals, there are a range of motives lying behind the provision of aid. Before moving on to present the case against aid, it is interesting to consider how these motives are reflected in the actual distribution of aid. The fact of the matter is that research has been singularly unsuccessful in explaining the distribution of either bilateral or multilateral aid in humanitarian or economic terms. It appears that per capita aid does not flow in the main either to those countries with the lowest levels of per capita income, as the equity argument would suggest (indeed, if anything, the relation seems to be the reverse), or to those countries that appear to have the greatest potential for growth as reflected by their absorptive capacity, domestic savings ratio, or rate of return on investment, as the economic argument would suggest.

Instead the evidence seems to suggest that the distribution of aid may be explained much more easily by political, military, security and historical factors, reflecting the foreign policy interests of the donors rather than the economic needs of the recipients. For some donors, such as the United States, it seems as though it is 'power political' and security interests that determine the distribution of their aid. For others, such as the United Kingdom, aid appears to be distributed in an attempt to maintain and further a sphere of influence which is largely defined by former colonial ties. Whatever the precise motivation, the distribution supports the general idea that, with exceptions in the case of some of the small donors, aid is largely determined by foreign policy. Even so, it is still likely to have significant actual and potential economic repercussions.

2.7 The case against aid

The case against aid comprises a wide range of arguments which also touch on the humanitarian, economic and political aspects of it. Broadly speaking, critics of aid maintain that, apart from the activities of charity organisations, it does not assist poor people and fails to fulfil its humanitarian objective; does not bring about economic benefits either for recipients or for donors and indeed may impose costs on them; and does not buy political influence.

Turning firstly to its effects on recipients, critics argue that any increase in the availability of finance from abroad is offset by a reduction in the domestic savings ratio, with the result that there may be no net increase in the amount of development finance. However, not only does the savings ratio fall but so does the productivity of investment as aid encourages the pursuit of grandiose projects. Projects yielding a reasonable rate of return could in any case, so it is argued, attract the necessary commercial finance. As a result recipients become dependent on aid, and this dependency can have an adverse effect on the entire path of their development, not least by influencing the pattern of their trading relations.

Furthermore, aid cushions governments from the full implications of any unsound policies that they may pursue. It may therefore encourage them to maintain an overvalued currency or to over-expand domestic demand, and this will have adverse economic consequences.

As well as encouraging inefficiency in macroeconomic policy, aid-tying causes microeconomic inefficiency since it forces countries to use techniques (particularly capital-intensive ones) that may be inappropriate considering their factor endowments.

As far as the alleviation of poverty is concerned, antagonists argue that aid does not tend to go to the poorest countries. Besides, any benefits to which aid gives rise are usually enjoyed within countries only by the existing elite, and do not trickle down to the poor.

Income inequality is therefore widened both globally and within aid-receiving countries; and a situation may arise where it is poor people living in developed countries who are subsidizing rich people living in developing ones. Indeed, by strengthening the hand of what are quite possibly corrupt regimes, aid may worsen the lot of the poor in the aid-receiving countries.

As for the idea that donors benefit from aid, critics argue that, to the extent that unemployment results from a deficiency of aggregate demand and may be alleviated through additional government spending, this may be more effectively achieved through extra domestic spending rather than extra aid. However, where unemployment is not demand-deficient, additional government expenditure, not least in the form of aid, is likely to be purely inflationary, having no beneficial effect on employment or output. They therefore completely reject the idea that recipients and donors have a mutual self-interest in aid.

Critics further accuse aid of having created political conflict and confrontation, particularly in the guise of the north–south divide, arguing that it is only their aid-receiving status that unites the very dissimilar economies of the south. Donors have certainly gained no prestige or status in the eyes of the recipients as a result of their aid policies.

Finally, it is argued that aid has conspicuously failed to eliminate poverty or to close the development gap. Even after receiving aid over an extended period of time countries that were poor remain poor. Yet at the same time critics argue that international comparisons of living standards conventionally rely too heavily on using exchange rates in order to convert GNPs into a common currency, and do not allow for differences in effective purchasing power.

The end result, so critics argue, is that aid may actually reduce the rate of economic growth below what it would otherwise have been. Economic development does not depend on aid but on internal factors such as the level of domestic saving and the productivity of investment. To the extent that external factors can exert a beneficial influence, it is trade and not aid that is important.

2.8 Evaluating the claims and counter-claims

From this wide-ranging debate about aid let us focus on four issues: the legitimacy of dual gap analysis and of the concept of the foreign exchange constraint; the effects of aid on recipients; the relevance of the mutuality argument; and the considerable area of consensus that in fact exists over aid.

2.8.1 Dual gap analysis

Criticism of dual gap analysis has usually focused on the restrictive assumptions made by it. These include a fixed capital–output ratio for both domestic and imported capital, a fixed import–income ratio, fixed export receipts, and the inability to use excess domestic saving in sectors not requiring imports. The analysis rests basically, however, on the assumption that foreign and domestic resources are not substitutable.

If, on the other hand, greater flexibility is assumed, with a high degree of substitutability between domestic and foreign resources and considerable scope for import substitution and export promotion, both the demand for foreign exchange as well as its supply may be easily modified without damaging growth. In these circumstances a scarcity of foreign exchange hardly constitutes any constraint, since it can be eliminated without difficulty, and savings are left as the only effective constraint on economic growth.

There can be little doubt that in the long run there is scope for import substitution, and for raising the productivity of imports. Similarly, measures which provide an additional incentive to export may be taken. The relevant question is not therefore whether it is possible to imagine a theoretical situation where there is no foreign exchange constraint – the answer is clearly that it is. Indeed it is quite easy to theorize about a situation in which there is no savings constraint either, or no constraint at all. The relevant question is rather which set of assumptions is most realistic from a practical policy point of view.

Since policy has to deal with the short run, and since it is generally accepted that it is more difficult to switch the way in which resources are used in the short run than in the long run, the answer would seem to be that the assumption of perfect substitutability is quite unrealistic. Dual gap analysis therefore survives its critics, and the policy insights it provides remain useful. These are that with a dominant savings constraint measures need to be taken to raise the domestic savings ratio, to substitute foreign exchange for domestic saving and to switch imports towards investment goods, and to increase the productivity of capital. At the same time, with a dominant foreign exchange constraint, policy needs to focus on export promotion and import substitution.

There can be little doubt that applying dual gap analysis to the period since 1973 reveals a dominant foreign exchange gap for non-oil developing countries. While domestic policy can help close this gap, other factors outside the control of these countries will also exert an impact on it. If, for instance, import prices rise relative to export prices, and the demand for exports falls, it seems likely that it will be their growth rates that adjust downwards rather than their foreign exchange that adjusts upwards. Aid then presents itself as one way of protecting the living standards of millions of poor people. But is aid effective?

2.8.2 The effects of aid on its recipients

As an additional source of concessionary capital, aid should in principle increase the rate of economic growth of the recipient, depending on how productively it is used. If the rate of interest on loans exceeds the productivity of the resources, commercial inflows might of course have a negative effect. But with lower interest rates the risks of this happening in the case of aid should be small.

However, the supposition that aid will raise the economic growth rate of recipients rests on the assumption that other things such as the domestic savings ratio and the productivity of capital remain constant, and, as noted in Section 2.7, critics claim that aid causes both of these to fall. Indeed such claims are not without some empirical support. But care needs to be exercised in interpreting such findings. If, for instance, saving is defined as being equal to investment less any inflows of foreign capital, then, unless investment rises by as much as the additional inflow of capital (i.e. unless no part of the capital inflow is consumed), savings will appear to fall. Thus, a situation may arise where the savings ratio falls even though the investment ratio rises, and a rising investment ratio is likely to lead to accelerating growth unless the incremental capital – output ratio (ICOR) rises.

What happens to the ICOR depends on the type of investment undertaken. Investment in construction, which is often financed by aid, has a high ICOR. But before it is concluded that aid is therefore unproductive, the external effects of infrastructure investment need to be remembered. For example, although improving the network of communications may lead to little extra output directly, it is likely to raise the average productivity of capital throughout the economy.

What about the direct evidence on the relation between aid and growth? Does this not resolve the debate over the impact of aid on the recipients? Unfortunately, it does not. On the one hand there is some evidence that aid has a significant positive effect on growth, and, what is more, that it is more productive in generating growth than any other type of foreign capital inflow, or indeed domestic saving. On the other hand, however, evidence has also been presented suggesting that any positive effect of aid on development is short-lived and that in the longer run the effect is negative.

In many ways such evidence raises more questions that it answers. What it probably suggests is that, as noted earlier, there is no one type of capital flow that may be unambiguously and exclusively defined as aid. Different types of aid, such as tied or untied, are likely to have different effects. Findings that aid has had negative effects may be more a criticism of the quality of aid than of aid itself. This is a point which we take up again in a moment.

2.8.3 The mutuality issue

The question of the mutuality of interests and the effects of aid on donors frequently becomes obscured by a debate over the causes of world unemployment. We have already discussed this in Chapter 2, and so can concentrate on other aspects of the issue. First, there are significant two-way trade linkages between the donors of aid and the recipients. If aggregate demand rises in industrial countries, the exports of developing countries will rise, while if aggregate demand rises in developing countries, the exports of industrial countries will rise. It is difficult, if not impossible, therefore, for any country or group of countries to insulate itself from world trends, and to this extent a mutuality of interests undoubtedly exists. Furthermore, if aid is not provided to developing countries facing large payments deficits, they will be forced to deflate demand in order to close the foreign exchange gap, and this will have effects on industrial countries, both via the reduced demand for their exports and the extra risks of debt default.

Second, aid represents a component of government expenditure. Yet the effects of aid will differ from those of other forms of expenditure. Domestic government expenditure will, in most cases, have a more powerful effect than aid on domestic employment or inflation. To this extent a government preoccupied exclusively with reducing domestic unemployment will surely favour domestic expenditure in preference to aid. Moreover, the real resource cost that is associated with aid does not apply to domestic expansion.

However, aid has advantages over domestic expansion as far as the balance of payments is concerned; for while additional domestic government spending by a donor tends to worsen its trade performance, as extra imports are induced, an expansion in aid will tend to improve it through the extra exports that are generated. Where countries are particularly anxious to strengthen exports, aid may be more attractive than increasing domestic government expenditure.

Of course from the recipients' viewpoint even an increase in a donor's domestic expenditure is likely to increase their capacity to earn foreign exchange and thereby alleviate their foreign exchange constraint. This raises the question of whether developing countries would prefer more trade to more aid, a question we discuss briefly in the next sub-section.

2.8.4 Areas of consensus

Much of the recent literature on aid has been presented in a somewhat adversarial way. This is unfortunate, since it conceals what is a considerable area of common ground. Where does this consensus lie? Basically it lies in the fact that it is a mistake to expect either too much or too little from aid.

There would, for example, be a considerable measure of agreement on the following statements. First, developing countries would benefit from easier access to potential export markets, since they acquire much more foreign exchange through trade than through aid, but some types of aid have advantages over exports. Second, there is considerable scope for improving the quality of aid as seen by recipients by, for instance, reducing the extent to which it is tied. Third, the uses made of aid and its administration by recipients could be improved to increase the benefits it has for the poor, and changes in domestic economic management, both at the micro and macro level, could have a beneficial impact on economic development irrespective of what happens to aid. Fourth, aid is not sufficient on its own to ensure that economic development will take place, and in some cases it is not even necessary. But, fifth, the development prospects of the poorest countries, which have little access to private capital, rely heavily on aid. Finally, experiences with aid vary from country to country and it may therefore be unwise to generalize on the basis of specific cases; but at the same time useful insight into the factors determining the success or failure of aid in encouraging economic development may be gained from case studies.

2.9 Policies on aid

Having identified certain areas of consensus concerning aid, we can build on these and come up with an agenda of policies.

If the developed countries were simply to reach the existing UN aid target and at the same time were to raise their GNPs, there would be a significant increase in the size of concessionary financial flows to developing countries; although their significance would be greater when judged against existing flows rather than against the size of the balance of payments deficits that these countries face. However, while the strict control of government expenditure remains the thrust of economic policy in major donors, the prospects for the majority of developing countries of being able to attract substantial additional aid are not good. In any case simply providing more of the same is a somewhat deficient policy.

At least as much attention needs to be focused on ways of improving aid quality and the uses made of aid. Various proposals exist for mitigating the disadvantages for recipients associated with aid-tying without at the same time weakning the balance of payments of donors.[2] Of course the balance of payments costs of untying will be greatest for individual countries if they untie their aid unilaterally. For this reason the best single solution probably remains for donors as a group to agree to reduce their use of tying in the same way that countries have in the past got together to agree on tariff reductions.

The reduction in tying might be most appropriately concentrated on procurement tying, thereby allowing recipients more discretion to choose the lowest cost suppliers. However, modifications to project tying to allow for an appropriate choice of technique, and to permit aid to cover the local currency cost and not just the foreign exchange cost of the project, would also be beneficial. There are also strong arguments for shifting the balance of aid more towards programme lending. Supervision of such lending could be organized under the auspices of the World Bank, as indeed happens with structural adjustment lending. Here it is a range of policies that has to be approved rather than specific projects. We say more about structural adjustment lending and the role of the World Bank in Chapters 9 and 11.

Given the ability of middle and high income developing countries to tap private capital markets, there is an argument for directing a larger proportion of total aid towards low-income countries. Although again many countries have accepted targets for the proportion of GNP that should go as aid to these countries, a significant redistribution would probably call for a move away from bilateral and towards multilateral aid. The benefits that any one unit of aid generates could be increased by improving its administration both on the side of donors and recipients. A suggestion that has been put forward in this context is to take aid out of the hands of governments and put it in the hands of local communities. A related idea is to channel more aid through mechanisms similar to those used by the voluntary aid organisations with the aim of providing more assistance directly to the poor. Indeed joint ventures or cofinancing between governments and these organisations has also been an idea that has been canvassed.

Other schemes worthy of consideration include 'aid-blending', the idea of combining flows which have a high concessional element with those which have a much lower one, enabling a given amount of aid in effect to go further; an expansion in the activities of the IMF; cofinancing between the World Bank and private banks; the use of international monetary reform as a way of directing additional financial flows to developing countries (most notoriously by linking the allocation of SDRs and the provision of development assistance); and the use of debt relief as a form of aid. These are all ideas that are examined in more detail in other chapters and we shall therefore not duplicate the discussion here. However, an important general lesson to be learnt with respect to aid is not to expect miracles; aid, at any level that is politically feasible, is very unlikely to transform economies from low to high rates of growth in a short space of time, or to have a quick and dramatic effect on living standards in the Third World.

8 Debt

1. INTRODUCTION

While the recipients of concessionary and indeed commercial inflows of foreign capital should normally be able to benefit from them in the short run, since they augment the finance that is available via domestic saving, an important question is whether such borrowing creates problems for the future in the form of the related accumulation of debt. The so-called global debt problem has come to dominate much of the discussion of international financial issues in the early 1980s, and the means of solving the problem, or at least of alleviating it, have been high on the agenda of international financial reform.

We begin this chapter by undertaking a brief economic analysis of debt, identifying in the process the factors which determine whether debt constitutes a problem or not. The next section then presents a summary picture of the size and nature of global debt, while the following one looks at the institutional arrangements through which debt problems have been handled. The final section moves on to examine various proposals for reform that have been put forward.

2. THE ECONOMICS OF DEBT

As mentioned above, by relaxing the constraints imposed by domestic saving and foreign exchange, external borrowing allows countries to increase their rate of economic growth. The size and duration of this positive effect depends essentially on how the extra resources are used and on the marginal productivity of capital. However, even if borrowing is used purely to sustain or raise domestic consumption, there will at least be a short-run benefit for the debtor's standard of living.[1]

In the case of grants, i.e. financial inflows with a grant element of 100 per cent, there are no further problems. Although there will be debate over how the money should be used, the question of repaying the debt does not arise.

But most international financial flows are not grants. They are loans that have to be repaid with interest. By borrowing, countries are in effect trading off future domestic absorption, i.e. consumption and investment expenditure, in favour of current absorption. Borrowers are relaxing current constraints at the cost of imposing future ones. Building on the notions of the savings and foreign exchange gaps already developed, borrowing initially allows investment to exceed domestic saving and imports to exceed exports. However, the crux of the debt problem is that in order to repay loans these inequalities have to be reversed to an extent and within a period of time determined by the conditions of the loans. Under normal circumstances loans would not be repaid (gross). Individual country borrowers will merely service them, in which case export earnings have to cover imports and service costs.

In order to avoid a debt problem it is therefore necessary for a borrower to close the savings gap and to go on to generate excess saving. However, since loans normally have to be repaid in foreign exchange rather than in domestic currency, it is also necessary to convert this excess saving into foreign exchange, and to do this exports have to increase relative to imports.

Let us concentrate first of all on savings. If we take the simplest possible savings function, where aggregate saving depends on the average propensity to save and the level of income, we find that savings will increase if either the savings ratio or national income increases. Both changes may occur simultaneously if the marginal propensity to save exceeds the average propensity to save and if the loan causes national income to rise. Assuming for a moment that the repayment of the principal of the loan can be financed by further borrowing, national income will rise provided the marginal productivity of the resources borrowed exceeds the rate of interest on the loan and any depreciation in the borrowers exchange rate.

As regards the foreign exchange aspect of the problem, a borrower's holding of foreign exchange will increse either if exports expand or if there is substitution away from imports. What is required then is a shift of domestic resources into the tradeables sector of the economy. Relevant in this context is a whole range of both demand and supply side factors. Is it possible for the borrower to induce an increase in exports by altering the structure of prices via exchange rate policy or the use of subsidies and taxes, or is there a constraint on export growth imposed by the income elasticity of demand for exports and the growth of income in principal markets? Does the borrower's marginal propensity to import lie below the average propensity to import, in which case the import coefficient will fall with economic growth, or is there scope for encouraging efficient import substitution again through the exchange rate or fiscal system?

It is the interrelation between these various issues that makes debt a complex problem. Generally speaking, however, borrowers with a rising savings ratio, a low and falling incremental capital–output ratio, export growth potential, and paying relatively low interest rates should encounter fewer debt problems than borrowers with falling saving ratios, high and rising ICORs, low export growth, little scope for import substitution other than of the type that adversely affects economic growth, and paying relatively high interest rates. In the latter case difficulties will be compounded by the fact that debtors will find it much more difficult to refinance their existing stock of debt.

A further aspect that complicates debt management relates to the time pattern of repayments. A borrower, while fulfilling the basic solvency criterion that the marginal productivity of the resources borrowed exceeds the rate of interest on the loan, may still encounter liquidity problems in particular years because of temporary shortages of foreign exchange. An additional difficulty here, however, is that what starts off as a liquidity problem may end up as a solvency problem, largely because of its effect on the expectations of lenders, who may become less keen on refinancing debt or may decide to increase the rate of interest charged. In any case it may in practice be difficult to distinguish between the two types of problem. Furthermore, debtors may have to repay the debt in specific foreign currencies, yet their foreign exchange earnings may be in different currencies. Variations in exchange rates can therefore sometimes create debt difficulties if the earning power of exports falls when expressed in the particular currency required, though if trade and debt are invoiced in the same currency, the effect of exchange rate changes on debt is neutralized.

2.1 Why do debt problems arise?

From this discussion it is possible to identify more broadly a number of reasons why debt problems emerge. First, there may be factors that are exogenous to the debtor, such as falling export demand from a world economic recession, rising real world interest rates, or unfavourable changes in exchange rates between third countries. Second, debt may have been poorly managed, with the borrower borrowing more than the economy can repay, failing to choose the most appropriate sources of finance (possibly borrowing over a shorter term and at a higher cost than necessary), and failing to collect adequate information about the debt position. Third, and in addition to poor debt management, the economy itself may have been poorly managed. Failure by governments to undertake measures to increase domestic savings, by, for example, repressing financial markets and preventing domestic real interest rates from rising above very low or even negative levels, or by resisting the opportunity of raising saving compulsorily through the fiscal system, are likely to mean that the savings gap will not be closed. Furthermore, reluctance to reduce exchange rates that are greatly overvalued or to encourage export promotion in other ways will mean that the foreign exchange gap will not be closed.

In practice, of course, any specific country's debt problem will probably have arisen as a result of a combination of these reasons, even though one or other of them may dominate.

Once debt management problems emerge, they frequently become increasingly difficult to control. Failure to service existing debt means that new debts are contracted in order to finance old ones, debt accumulates and the chances of being able to service it recede. Lenders seeing the deteriorating debt position regard the borrowers as less creditworthy and as a result it becomes yet harder for them to refinance.

2.2 Debt capacity

Given the problems associated with overborrowing, the concept of 'debt capacity' is clearly important. Unfortunately, it is a somewhat vague concept, since it can be affected by changes in a number of factors, such as the terms of trade, exchange rates and inflation. However, assuming that these variables do not change, a borrower's rate of debt accumulation will vary negatively with the rate of economic growth, and thus the productivity of capital, and positively with the size of the savings gap and the interest rate on loans, and if an initial savings gap is not closed, or indeed if saving exceeds investment by less than is required to make interest payments on existing loans, new borrowing will be needed if the target growth rate is to be achieved. Indebtedness will therefore increase. If, on the other hand, saving increases so that it exceeds investment by an amount equal to interest payments, then net indebtedness will level off, and if by more, net indebtedness will fall.[2] By trying to calculate the difference between investment and saving in the future borrowers can get some idea of their future capacity to service debt and thereby avoid the slide into further debt.

However, as noted above, such forecasts need to be complemented by considering what may happen to imports and exports, the terms of trade, interest rates and exchange rates. There is therefore no simple formula that allows debt capacity to be estimated with precision and full confidence. And in any case a borrower's capacity to service debt is very closely related to the macroeconomic and microeconomic policies pursued, since many of the relevant variables can be influenced by governmental policy as well as by structural and behavioural change in the economy.

This analysis suggests that evaluating debt capacity is far from simple; each case needs to be examined on its own merits, with many aspects of a country's economic and political structure being taken into account. However, while no doubt recognising this, lenders often find it more convenient to consult a more limited number of indicators of a country's debt position. Most of these indicators are at least loosely based on the analysis of debt capacity outlined above, but, as we shall see, on their own fail to provide a fully rounded picture. What are these indicators and in what ways are they deficient?

2.3 Debt indicators

2.3.1 Outstanding debt

This indicator in fact indicates very little. Not only is there the problem of whether the debt is measured in nominal or real terms, but there is also the point that the measure says nothing about the capacity of economies to repay, and it is really this that creates the problem. Thus one country which has a large amount of outstanding debt may in fact be in a much stronger position than another country which, while having less debt, is less able to repay it. Furthermore, simply looking at the total amount of debt tells us nothing about the structure of the debt. Again a country with a lot of long-term but little short-term debt may be in a stronger position than another country which, while less in total debt, has more short-term debt. The maturity of the debt as well as the interest charge on it will affect the debt service payments (repayment of principal, or amortization, and payment of interest) that have to be made, and it is the size of these in relation to the capacity of the economy to make them that is more important than the total size of the debt.

2.3.2 Debt service ratio

This ratio expresses debt service payments as a proportion of export earnings. While there is always a temptation to select a particular value (say 20 per cent) for the debt service ratio as being some sort of threshold, this is misleading. Again some countries may be able to cope with much higher ratios than others, which are unable to cope with their debt even when the ratio is well below 20 per cent. The explanation of such differences arises from the fact that the debt service ratio is only a narrow measure of the debt problem. For example, it tells us nothing about the structure of debt; the ability to service debt in the long run; the composition, commodity and geographical concentration of exports and the potential for export expansion; the instability of export receipts; the scope for import substitution as a way of increasing the *net* foreign exchange earnings associated with any given level of exports; the scope for balance of payments adjustment; or the level of foreign exchange reserves. On the other hand, the debt service ratio does indicate the degree of rigidity in a country's balance of payments and its vulnerability to problems caused by shortfalls in export receipts. It shows the extent to which there are prior claims on a borrower's foreign exchange earnings. Furthermore, it does have the advantage of relating debt to what is probably the principal variable determining whether the debt can be repaid, namely, export performance. Even so, the debt service ratio may overstate the size of the debt problem and the constraints impinging on debtors, since there may be a chance that borrowers can reschedule or refinance the amortization of outstanding loans.

2.3.3 The ratio of interest payments to export earnings

Where the repayment of principal can be rolled over but interest payments cannot be, it is financing the latter that creates the immediate problem. While the interest payments to exports ratio may indeed provide a more accurate reflection of the liquidity aspect of the debt problem, it needs to be used with care. If, for example, it is possible to finance interest payments from further borrowing, does this mean that there is no debt problem? It would seem that the problem can almost be defined away. The fact is that, as we shall discuss later, further borrowing only defers debt service owed from current income, it does not eliminate servicing difficulties unless in the intervening period the economy's capacity to service debt can be increased. The benefit from a postponement depends on how productively the extra time is used.

One central aspect of the debt problem since the mid-1970s has been the use of floating interest rates on loans. The purpose behind these is to protect lenders from the fall in real interest rates that takes place when, with a given nominal interest rate, the rate of inflation accelerates. A difficulty for borrowers is that their foreign exchange earnings may not fully reflect variations in the global rate of inflation. The prices of different commodities move at different speeds and even in different directions. A situation may therefore arise where a borrower, heavily dependent on one export, experiences a fall in the price of this commodity as well as an increase in nominal interest payments on debt. Even where the export price is rising, the rate of increase may well be below the average rate (for imports) and the country's terms of trade will therefore deteriorate.

Another aspect of floating rates is that since actual interest payments usually include a component reflecting the negative effect of inflation on the real value of the loan, it is amortized at a faster speed in real terms than was agreed when the loan was taken out. This assimilation of some amortization into interest payments can clearly distort the interest payment ratio as a consistent indicator of the size of the debt problem.[3]

2.3.4 The ratio of debt service payments to new disbursements

In a sense this ratio is of more interest to the borrower than the lender, since it basically says in which direction the real resource flow is going. If outgoings on old debt exceed new borrowing, there will be negative net transfer, and the pattern of capital flows will at this time be serving to widen the foreign exchange gap and will therefore be constraining economic development unless domestic saving, exports and the productivity of capital can be increased. While this is clearly of concern to borrowers, it is also of concern to lenders, since, as we have already seen, in the long run it is through economic growth that debts may be repaid. Lenders do not wish to see the countries to which they have lent stagnating – this is an issue to which we shall return later when discussing the role of the Fund and so-called austerity measures in dealing with the debt problem.

2.4 Global aspects of debt

Up to now we have looked at the debt problem from the perspective of the individual borrower, implying thereby that debt problems are in some way self-contained. This is far from the truth. To illustrate the point we consider two possibilities. The first is that, when faced with an unmanageable debt problem, a major borrower decides to default. Given the structure of bank lending, this could easily result in failure for those banks where lending was heavily concentrated in that country. Given that banking systems rely crucially on confidence, a default of this kind would certainly result in a crisis of confidence which would have ramifications for both the countries in which the lenders were located as well as for other borrowers, since the supply of loans would undoubtedly fall. It is difficult to estimate precisely the effects of such defaults but it is clear that the consequences would be global and not country-specific.

The second possibility is that the borrower pursues a programme of economic policies designed to reduce imports and shift the current account of the balance of payments into surplus. But again the outside world would not be unaffected by such measures. A fall in one country's imports means a fall in other countries' exports. Given a simple income expenditure model, this implies a multiplied decline in income in the exporting countries and in turn a fall in imports. There is then a further fall in other countries' exports. World trade shrinks, economic growth slows down, unemployment rises. Again the debt problem is shown to be a global phenomenon. Precisely how significant these trading interrelations are depends on a range of import, export and saving coefficients, and a sophisticated model would be needed to calculate them. However, one estimate made by Morgan Guaranty suggests that a moderate (say 3 per cent) uniform reduction in the real rate of economic growth of developing countries would lower the rate of economic growth in industrial countries by approaching 1 per cent. The closer the trading relations are between countries, say between Mexico and the United States, the more marked the interlinking effect is likely to be.

The conclusion that may be drawn is that there is a mutuality of interest in avoiding severe debt problems. Less severe debt difficulties may of course be more easily handled without the large external effects mentioned above, and may even be strangely helpful in providing the sort of warning necessary to remind participants of the dangers associated with excessive indebtedness.

3. THE SIZE OF THE DEBT PROBLEM: SOME FACTS AND FIGURES

The foregoing discussion identifies a number of variables that might help to indicate the size and nature of the debt problem. Data for some of these and for a number of country groupings are presented in Tables 8.1, 8.2 and 8.3. From our analysis of debt capacity it emerges that the chances of being able to service debt rise with the growth of output and exports. It is to be expected then that in an environment of slow growth and stagnating export performance debt will become more difficult to manage, especially if, at the same time, the terms of lending harden with rising interest rates and falling maturities. However, it also needs to be stressed that mechanically referring to a series of debt indicators can easily lead to misinterpretation, since whether a given debt situation constitutes a problem or not depends crucially on the economic and political circumstances of individual countries. Debt is but one aspect of the much broader problem of economic management and should not be viewed in isolation.

Examination of data on debt reveals a number of developments since the early 1970s. The most important of these can be listed and discussed quite briefly. First, there has been a big increase in the nominal amount of external debt. During 1973–83, for instance, the volume of outstanding debt held by non-oil developing countries increased some five-fold as these countries endeavoured to maintain their rates of economic growth in spite of a deteriorating external environment (see Table 8.1). However, much of this increase reflected the rapid inflation that occurred during the 1970s. Indeed when measured in real terms or in relation to other economic magnitudes such as exports, the debt situation at the end of the 1970s was not substantially different from that at the beginning of the

TABLE 8.1 *Non-oil developing countries: external debt, 1973–83*[1] *(billions of US dollars)*

	1973	*1974*	*1975*	*1976*	*1977*	*1978*	*1979*	*1980*	*1981*	*1982*	*1983*
Total outstanding debt of non-oil developing countries	130.1	160.8	190.8	228.0	278.5	336.3	396.9	474.0	555.0	612.4	664.3
Short-term debt	18.4	22.7	27.3	33.2	42.5	49.7	58.8	85.5	102.2	112.7	92.4
Long-term debt	111.8	138.1	163.5	194.9	235.9	286.6	338.1	388.5	452.8	499.6	571.6
By type of creditor											
Official creditors	51.0	60.1	70.3	82.4	98.7	117.5	133.0	152.9	172.4	193.2	218.7
Governments	37.3	43.4	50.3	57.9	67.6	79.1	87.2	98.7	108.6	120.4	135.3
International institutions	13.7	16.6	20.3	24.8	31.0	38.4	45.8	54.2	63.8	72.8	83.3
Private creditors	60.8	77.9	95.1	114.8	137.3	169.1	205.1	235.6	280.4	306.4	353.0
Unguaranteed debt	29.3	36.0	40.8	45.9	51.4	56.4	67.3	77.5	96.7	103.9	113.7
Guaranteed debt	31.5	42.0	52.4	66.6	85.9	112.7	137.8	158.1	183.7	202.2	239.3
Financial institutions	17.3	25.6	36.7	49.0	59.1	79.5	102.9	121.6	144.5	159.5	193.8
Other private creditors	14.2	16.3	17.6	19.8	26.8	33.2	34.9	36.5	39.2	42.7	45.5
By analytical group											
Net oil exporters	20.4	26.0	34.1	42.4	53.3	61.2	70.5	79.4	96.5	108.1	129.0
Net oil importers	91.4	112.1	129.4	152.5	182.7	225.4	267.6	309.1	356.5	391.5	442.6
Major exporters of manufactures	40.8	51.7	60.9	73.1	85.2	108.1	127.7	145.2	170.6	184.3	212.4
Low-income countries	25.4	29.7	33.2	38.3	46.5	53.1	59.5	67.0	73.0	80.1	90.8
Other net oil importers[2]	25.2	30.6	35.3	41.1	51.0	64.2	80.4	96.9	112.7	127.1	139.4

1. Excludes data for the People's Republic of China before 1977.
2. Middle-income countries that, in general, export mainly primary commodities.

SOURCE: *World Economic Outlook*, Washington, IMF, 1983.

decade (see Table 8.2), but between 1980 and 1982 the debt situation deteriorated. Not only did real debt continue to increase, but even where there was a decline in the rate at which indebtedness was growing, this was more than offset by a reduced rate of export growth. As a result both debt/export and debt service ratios increased significantly for most important debtors (see Table 8.3).

Second, there was a large shift away from public debt towards private debt. Between 1976 and 1981, for instance, about two-thirds of the increase in long-term and medium-term debt was to private banks, mostly as a result of syndicated lending. With short term debt included, the increasing share of the private sector may well have been sharper. Whereas the convention had been to exclude short-term debt from the discussion of debt problems, since it is usually assumed to be trade-related and rolled over automatically, this was no longer the case by the beginning of the 1980s. Many borrowers resorted to short-term borrowing in order to finance longer-term payments deficits, and an implication of this was that the roll over of such short-term credits was no longer automatic. The move towards borrowing from the banks brought with it a hardening in the terms of debt, as the average maturity of the debt shortened and interest payments on it increased. These developments in the structure of debt meant that for any given amount of debt there was a more severe debt problem, especially in terms of illiquidity. The use of floating interest rates and their volatility also meant that the size of the debt problem could suddenly increase as interest rates increased. Between 1980 and 1982 net interest payments more than doubled. Of course where borrowers also hold substantial overseas deposits, there will be a benefit from higher interest rates and the adverse effect on debt will be neutralized.

Third, and largely because banks only lend to countries they deem creditworthy, the shift over to the private sector served to increase the concentration of debt. One's perception of the global debt problem has therefore become increasingly influenced by what happens in a relatively small number of countries. However, debt is not only concentrated on the side of borrowers. The private debts of developing countries have also been quite heavily concentrated in the hands of relatively few banks and this again has increased the fragility of the entire system of international capital flows, although not all banks will respond similarly. If developing country debts are concentrated in the banks whose response is the calmest, this may minimize the destabilizing international financial repercussions.

TABLE 8.2 *Non-oil developing countries: long-term and short-term external debt relative to exports and to GDP, 1973–83*[1] *(per cent)*

	1973	*1974*	*1975*	*1976*	*1977*	*1978*	*1979*	*1980*	*1981*	*1982*	*1983*
Ratio of external debt to exports of goods and services[2]											
All non-oil developing countries	115.4	104.6	122.4	125.5	126.4	130.2	119.2	112.9	124.9	143.3	144.4
By analytical group											
Net oil exporters	154.7	124.9	162.4	169.5	179.3	176.9	144.3	128.4	154.6	179.5	192.2
Net oil importers	109.4	100.9	115.4	117.5	116.8	121.8	114.1	109.5	118.3	135.1	134.3
Major exporters of manufactures	91.7	88.6	103.0	103.3	99.5	101.1	96.9	94.0	100.6	116.2	114.2
Low-income countries	227.9	214.5	226.1	225.1	217.8	226.3	209.8	201.4	231.1	254.1	262.9
Other net oil importers[3]	96.9	84.7	98.3	104.3	111.6	124.8	115.5	110.9	121.9	138.0	136.6
Ratio of external debt to GDP[2]											
All non-oil developing countries	22.4	21.8	23.8	25.7	27.4	28.5	27.5	27.6	31.0	34.7	34.7
By analytical group											
Net oil exporters	26.2	25.5	27.7	32.3	38.5	39.3	37.4	34.0	36.1	44.7	43.5
Net oil importers	21.7	21.2	23.0	24.4	25.4	26.6	25.8	26.3	29.7	32.1	32.7
Major exporters of manufactures	20.2	19.6	22.2	22.7	23.9	25.1	24.6	25.1	29.3	33.2	33.8
Low-income countries	20.1	20.1	20.9	24.4	24.9	24.0	24.4	23.6	24.7	26.2	26.5
Other net oil importers[3]	26.2	25.2	26.2	27.7	28.6	31.5	28.8	30.6	34.1	35.8	35.6
Ratios (including People's Rep. of China)[2]											
To exports:											
All non-oil developing countries					123.6	127.0	116.1	109.4	119.8	136.5	137.7
Low-income countries					169.0	170.0	152.0	137.7	140.0	148.7	155.5

Table 8.2—*continued*

	1973	*1974*	*1975*	*1976*	*1977*	*1978*	*1979*	*1980*	*1981*	*1982*	*1983*
To GDP:											
All non-oil developing countries					23.9	24.6	23.9	24.1	27.3	30.5	30.5
Low-income countries					14.3	13.5	13.4	13.2	14.3	15.1	15.3

1. Excludes data for the People's Republic of China, except where noted.
2. Ratio of year-end debt to exports or GDP for year indicated.
3. Middle-income countries that, in general, export mainly primary commodities.

Source: *World Economic Outlook,* Washington, IMF, 1983.

TABLE 8.3 *Non oil-developing countries: debt service payments on short-term and long-term external debt, 1973–83*[1] *(values in billions of US dollars: ratios in per cent)*

	1973	*1974*	*1975*	*1976*	*1977*	*1978*	*1979*	*1980*	*1981*	*1982*	*1983*
All non-oil developing countries											
Value of debt service payments	17.9	22.1	25.1	27.8	34.7	50.3	65.0	76.2	94.7	107.1	93.2
Interest payments	6.9	9.3	10.5	10.9	13.6	19.4	28.0	40.4	55.1	59.2	55.1
Amortization[2]	11.1	12.8	14.6	16.8	21.1	30.9	36.9	35.8	39.7	47.9	38.1
Debt service ratio[3]	15.9	14.4	16.1	15.3	15.4	19.0	19.0	17.6	20.4	23.9	19.3
Interest payments ratio	6.1	6.1	6.7	6.0	6.0	7.3	8.2	9.3	11.9	13.2	11.4
Amortization ratio[2]	9.8	8.3	9.4	9.3	9.4	11.7	10.8	8.3	8.6	10.7	7.9
By analytical group											
Net oil exporters											
Debt service ratio[3]	29.0	21.1	24.2	24.4	27.0	34.0	32.5	24.7	30.8	37.9	31.5
Interest payments ratio	8.8	7.8	9.3	9.2	9.9	11.4	11.3	12.6	18.2	21.8	20.4
Amortization ratio[2]	20.1	13.3	14.9	15.3	17.2	22.6	21.2	12.0	12.6	16.1	11.1
Major exporters of manufactures											
Debt service ratio[3]	14.5	14.7	16.4	14.2	14.6	16.9	17.6	17.4	19.6	23.7	17.4
Interest payments ratio	5.6	6.1	6.9	5.5	5.4	6.5	7.7	9.0	11.4	12.8	10.8
Amortization ratio[2]	8.9	8.5	9.5	8.7	9.2	10.5	9.9	8.3	8.2	10.9	6.6
Low-income countries											
Debt service ratio[3]	14.6	13.7	14.5	12.8	10.2	10.3	9.7	9.9	10.3	11.8	11.4
Interest payments ratio	6.1	5.4	5.4	4.9	4.1	4.8	4.7	5.0	5.0	4.6	4.1
Amortization ratio	8.5	8.3	9.2	7.8	6.1	5.6	5.0	4.9	5.3	7.2	7.3

TABLE 8.3—*continued*

	1973	*1974*	*1975*	*1976*	*1977*	*1978*	*1979*	*1980*	*1981*	*1982*	*1983*
Other net oil importers[4]											
Debt service ratio[3]	12.7	10.6	11.8	12.9	12.7	18.2	17.3	16.6	19.6	20.5	19.0
Interest payments ratio	5.4	5.2	5.3	5.4	5.8	7.7	8.7	9.5	11.5	12.4	10.5
Amortization ratio[2]	7.2	5.5	6.5	7.4	6.9	10.5	8.6	7.1	8.1	8.1	8.5

1. Excludes data for the People's Republic of China before 1977.
2. On long-term debt only. Estimates for the period up to 1981 reflect actual amortization payments. The estimates for 1982 and 1983 reflect scheduled payments, but are modified to take account of the rescheduling agreements of 1982 and early 1983.
3. Payments (interest, amortization, or both) as percentages of exports of goods and services.
4. Middle-income countries that, in general, export mainly primary commodities.

SOURCE: *World Economic Outlook,* Washington, IMF, 1983.

Fourth, the vicious circle of debt came more into play in the 1980s. Problems of debt management in some countries reduced the confidence of the banks and their willingness to expand lending; indeed, as noted in Chapter 6, net lending actually contracted in 1982 and 1983. At the same time lending from other sources failed to expand to fill the gap that this left. The difficulties of refinancing or rolling over to which this gave rise itself created further debt problems.

One indicator of the deteriorating debt situation is the occurrence of reschedulings: agreements between debtors and creditors to rearrange and effectively postpone debt repayments, particularly repayments of principal but occasionally payments of interest as well. Table 8.4 shows the increasing frequency of debt renegotiations in the 1980s as compared with the 1970s. Note in particular that the column relating to 1983 covers only the first five months of the year, yet even so there had already been more reschedulings than in any previous full year. By the end of 1983 debt was truly a global problem with some thirty LDC and Eastern bloc countries in arrears or renegotiating loans, and with the related threat of default and bank failure affecting creditor countries as well.

Although it is a risky business trying to forecast the evolution of debt–witness the fact that even at the turn of the decade the debt problems of 1982 and 1983 were not being generally predicted – there are a number of pointers that provide little cause for optimism. Not least amongst these is that by 1983 the rate of growth of output in the major borrowing countries had fallen below the rate of interest on loans. Two questions arise. First, how can the debt problem be dealt with in the short run? Second, are there any longer-term or more fundamental reforms that would alleviate it in the not too distant future?

4. SHORT-TERM POLICY: RESCHEDULING[4]

Faced with a large amount of debt that is difficult to manage, there are a number of options open to the debtor. The first, as mentioned earlier, is to default on the loan and simply fail to make payments on it. This is the so called 'market solution'. One advantage of it is that countries that have overborrowed and banks that have overlent learn the folly of their ways. A form of natural selection is allowed to work. Yet it remains a rather extreme and undesirable solution for a series of reasons. For the debtor, default will have a number of consequences, since it will become very unlikely that the debtor country will be able to attract further credit at least for a certain period of time. For the banking system, the failure of banks that might result from default could be very damaging and the knock-on effects on lending countries and other borrowing countries would almost certainly be significant.

Again, as mentioned earlier, the second option is to pursue a programme of demand deflation and import contraction. While this may improve the current account balance of payments in the short run, the costs in terms of economic development are likely to be high and could set off political and social unrest. Furthermore, according to the models of debt capacity the long-term solution to the problem rests on raising output and exports rather than on contracting output and imports. While such deflationary programmes may increase the confidence of lenders in the short run if they are interpreted as suggesting that the borrower is making an effort to solve its problems, they will probably fail to raise confidence in the long run unless the growth of output and exports picks up.

The third option, not open to borrowers themselves, is that creditor and other countries expand their economies. This will improve the external environment in which borrowers find themselves, particularly by increasing the demand for their exports. However, care needs to be exercised with this solution. Expansion in industrial countries will not necessarily have exclusively beneficial effects. It may, for example, be accompanied by rising interest rates which, as we have seen, create an extra debt burden. Furthermore, it may fail to encourage the disciplined economic management that is required if future debt problems are to be avoided.

The fourth option, which Table 8.4 shows has been increasingly adopted, is to reschedule debts. Official debt is usually rescheduled through the Paris Club, which was established in 1956 when a number of European countries met to renegotiate their bilateral loans to Argentina. By the end of 1982 more than sixty multilateral debt renegotiations for at least twenty borrowers had been arranged by it. The Paris Club brings debtors together with their creditors and observers from the IMF, the World Bank, UNCTAD and the OECD. There are no formal rules governing its operations, although certain basic features have emerged over the years. Thus, agreements reached *normally* affect only official or officially guaranteed or insured medium- or long-term debt not previously rescheduled, cover

TABLE 8.4 *Multilateral debt renegotiations, 1974–83*

	1974	*1975*	*1976*	*1977*	*1978*	*1979*	*1980*	*1981*	*1982*	*1983*[1]
Argentina			C							©
Bolivia							C	C		
Brazil										©
Central Afr. Rep.								P		
Chile	P	P								©
Costa Rica										P, ©
Cuba										©
Ecuador										C
Gabon					P					
Ghana	P									
Guyana						C			C	
India	A	A	A	A						
Jamaica						C		C		
Liberia							P	P	C	
Madagascar								P	P	©
Malawi									P, C	
Mexico										©
Nicaragua							C	C	C	
Pakistan	A							A		
Peru			C		P, C		C			
Poland								A	C	©
Romania									P, C	P
Senegal								P	P, C	©
Sierra Leone				P			P			
Sudan						P		C	P	P
Togo						P	C	P		P, ©

TABLE 8.4—*continued*

	1974	*1975*	*1976*	*1977*	*1978*	*1979*	*1980*	*1981*	*1982*	*1983*[1]
Turkey					A	A, C	A		C	
Uganda								P	P	
Yugoslavia										©
Zaïre			P	P		P	C	P		
Zambia										P
	In millions of US dollars									
Total amount:[2]	1,530	375	1,800	240	1,800	6,200	3,750	2,540	10,000	37,000

Notes: This table does not include some cases for which sufficient information was not available.
A=Aid Consortia Renegotiations
C=Commercial bank agreements
©=Under negotiation with commercial banks at the end of May 1983
P=Paris Club agreements

1. As of end-May, 1983.
2. Estimates.

SOURCE: *Finance and Development,* IMF/World Bank, September, 1983.

payments in arrears and those coming due within a specified 12-month period, reschedule 85–90 per cent of this debt, allowing a grace period of up to five years and a further five years to repay, request the debtor not to grant better terms to other creditors, and require the debtor country to negotiate with the IMF and put in place a stabilization programme before the rescheduling is considered.

Rescheduling of commercial debt, which with the move to private borrowing has become increasingly significant, lies outside the scope of the Paris Club and has been handled in a rather more *ad hoc* way. Private debt was rescheduled on at least twenty-four occasions between 1978 and 1982, and fourteen more reschedulings were being negotiated at the beginning of 1983.

In many respects the rescheduling of private debt is more complex than that of official debt, not least because of the sheer number of banks, sometimes as many as 1,200 from different countries. This is not to say that all the lending banks would take part in the negotiations, which are usually conducted by the 'lead banks' and committees representing national groups of creditor banks, but even so it is not surprising that commercial scheduling can take many months to arrange, though it may sometimes take less time to arrange than formal agreements through the Paris Club.

Two basic principles underlie commercial bank rescheduling. First, the banks agree to adopt a common approach. If one bank breaks ranks, then, because of a cross default clause, other banks do not remain bound to the agreement. Second, rescheduling is, with rare exceptions, limited to the principal of the loan. Interest payments continue and in general any arrears in the payment of interest have to be made good before the agreement is signed.

A feature of commercial bank rescheduling is the variety of terms agreed. However, the following terms are typical: limitation of coverage to about 80 per cent of loans coming due within two years, linking of interest rates to LIBOR or the US prime rate, a rescheduling fee, and, since 1978, agreement of a programme of economic stabilization with the IMF.

The main point to grasp about rescheduling is that it provides debtors with time to come up with a solution. Apart from alleviating immediate liquidity problems, it is not a solution in itself. If debtors fail to undertake appropriate action in order to strengthen their balance of payments, or if outside factors do not become more favourable, rescheduling merely postponses the full impact of the debt problem. It is noteworthy that it does not reduce the debt/export ratio, and indeed interest payments may increase. However, the advantages of rescheduling should not be under-estimated. With high discount rates the present value of debt service payments as perceived by debtors may fall. Moreover, there are reasons to believe that a more gradualist approach to balance of payments adjustment will be less costly in terms of its impact on other objectives of domestic economic policy, such as economic growth and employment, than would be shock treatment (an issue to be taken up more fully in Chapter 9). If this is true, rescheduling will permit more cost-efficient solutions to be adopted. Furthermore, by at least temporarily avoiding default, the deleterious effects that this would have on both borrowers and lenders are also avoided. Lenders may also gain from the fact that to compensate for stretching out loans over a longer period than initially planned they usually receive a higher rate of return, since rescheduled loans customarily carry a higher rate of interest than did the original loan.

5. SOLUTIONS TO THE DEBT PROBLEM

While rescheduling offers an expedient way of taking the pressure off, there are a range of other reforms which in principle might provide a better long-term solution. However, reform is not straightforward, largely because it has to offer something to both the debtor countries, primarily concerned about ensuring a continuing inflow of finance, and the lenders, either governments or banks primarily concerned about avoiding default and the associated losses. An appropriate balance needs to be struck between adjustment and financing, with the emphasis falling neither too heavily on adjustment in the debtors nor too heavily on financing by the creditors. It seems most likely that this balance will be reached by a blend of reforms covering the following five basic issues.

5.1 Internal adjustment within the debtor country

The first of these relates to measures that will encourage borrowers to adopt those policies most likely to induce the macroeconomic and structural changes that are needed to reduce the severity of the debt problem. Models of debt capacity reveal clearly the sorts of changes that have to take place: changes to increase saving and the productivity of investment, to economise on inessential imports and expand exports. The threat of default and the jeopardy into which this would put future development provides an incentive for debtors to make such changes, but casual empiricism suggests that outside encouragement under the auspices of the IMF will also be required. The essential thing here is to try and ensure that the programmes the Fund supports are up to the task and have the desired effects.

5.2 External adjustment outside the debtor country

The models of debt capacity also show how sensitive the debt problem is to changes in the demand for exports, the terms of trade and interest rates. Demand expansion in the industrial countries which form the principal market for the exports of the major debtors would reduce the emphasis that would otherwise have to be placed on internal adjustment, and would enable it to take place through expanding output and expanding exports rather than through contracting income and contracting imports. It is hardly coincidental that the debt problem became most pronounced at a time when the world economy was in recession.

5.3 Reforms to support bank lending

At least until more fundamental reforms in the nature of development financing can be arranged, bank lending will remain important. Yet banks have become increasingly reluctant to lend to developing countries. Without going so far as to provide them with a risk-free environment, reforms could be introduced that would at least reduce the degree of uncertainty associated with such lending. These include safety nets, rediscounting, refinancing, guarantees and cofinancing.

The idea behind a safety net is to have some agency that will act as a lender of last resort and prevent the banks from going bankrupt. This could be organised by means of, say, the BIS or the World Bank rediscounting commercial bank credit. The banks would in effect be bought out of their loans. However, the price they would be paid for these assets would not reflect their full value; even so, in some circumstances the banks would probably regard the certainty of something as preferable to the possibility of nothing. The 'price' the borrowers would pay for rediscounting might be in the form of higher interest rates or of having to accept a Fund-approved programme. This 'price' might be more easily exacted by means of refinancing than rediscounting. In fact there is some conflict here, since while refinancing offers a more convenient way of helping the borrower, though in a penalising way, rediscounting offers a more convenient way of helping yet also penalizing the lenders. With refinancing the lenders are more likely to escape penalty whereas with rediscounting it is the borrowers who are more likely to escape it.

In a way of course the opportunity for banks to rediscount loans or countries to refinance debt provides a guarantee. However, these could also be arranged in a number of other ways. One alternative relative to new lending rather than the conversion of existing debt would be for either lenders or borrowers to take out a form of insurance cover for which they would pay a premium. They would pay into a fund that would be used to finance bad debts. Certainly it would be unwise to provide guarantees gratuitously through an official agency such as the Fund, since this would create a 'moral hazard' inasmuch as the supposed solution would contribute to causing the very problem with which it is designed to deal. Banks might become less careful in analysing risk and overlend, and borrowers become less concerned about taking on too much debt and fail to pursue the domestic policies necessary to ensure that loans can be repaid. Both lenders and borrowers should therefore be asked to give up something in exchange for the provision of guarantees; in the case of borrowers this again could be their independence in the formulation of economic policy. The benefit to borrowers would come from the larger flow of finance that guarantees would induce and the lower rate of interest that they would have to pay. The hope would of course be that guarantees would not be called upon since it would be their existence rather than their use that would raise confidence.

Cofinancing with the World Bank has also been used as a way of encouraging the banks to continue lending. The specifics of cofinancing vary. Until 1983 the World Bank and the commercial banks entered into separate loan agreements with borrowing countries, but since then there has been some joint participation in loans, with the Bank deferring the repayment of its principal until after commercial banks have been repaid, financing any balance of principal left at the end of the scheduled term of commercial loans resulting from higher than anticipated interest rates – thereby allowing borrowers' annual debt service payments to be fixed and the maturity of the loan extended, and, in effect, guaranteeing the repayment of the later part of loans in which it did not initially participate. There may be scope for extending such arrangements by means of the conditionality that the Bank can bring to bear via structural adjustment lending and raising the degree of control over the way in which borrowed resources are used. Similarly, there is scope for improving the organization of commercial rescheduling and for increasing the degree of co-operation between the banks, the multilateral institutions such as the Fund and the World Bank, and the governments of both lenders and borrowers.

Although all the above schemes involve some degree of official intervention, proposals have also been put forward which rely more on creating a private secondary market in debt. However, the object of such ideas remains that of providing banks with the opportunity of selling off the debt they are owed, at a discount, which, in this case, would be determined by market forces.

5.4 A shift away from bank lending

While in the short run the debt position would be made more acute by the banks pulling out of balance of payments financing, the deficiencies of short-term bank lending argue for reducing its relative contribution in the longer run. Crucial aspects of the debt position relate to the maturity of the debt and unexpected changes in interest rates and exchange rates. There is then a case for moving towards longer-term lending in the form of bonds denominated in SDRs (representing the average value of a number of currencies) and carrying a rate of interest which is fixed in real terms by being index-linked to inflation, or even Consols. However, the question remains of whether a potential market exists for such instruments.

Other plans of this genre also involve trying to change the basic nature of the instruments through which creditors lend to debtors. They include equity investments which would give lenders a 'stake' in a borrower's future economic performance, and the indexing of repayments to the capacity of the borrower to repay as measured, say, by export growth.

5.5 Other forms of debt relief

While the reforms discussed in Sub-sections (5.3) and (5.4) above relate to banks and the private sector, there are a range of other, sometimes rather more radical, proposals for solving the debt problem which apply primarily to official debt. These include most simply a general moratorium on debt service payments, or even debt cancellation. More subtle are proposals for reciprocal tying, interest rate subsidies, deferred repayment or extra creation of SDRs.

With reciprocal tying debtors repay creditors in local currency, thereby effectively tying the repayments to purchases of exports from the debtor. Although having a certain appeal, particularly when one considers donors' proclivities to tie aid, there are a number of weaknesses with the scheme, not least of which is that donors would find it unattractive, since it limits their choice of imported commodities and sources of supply.

Interest rate subsidies could be used to alleviate that aspect of the debt problem associated with high and rising interest rates. Subsidization could be offered in a number of ways. Donors could, for instance, provide assistance by paying a subsidy direct to commercial lenders. This would maintain the lenders' interest receipts, avoid any burden on the donor's balance of payments, and reduce the demand for foreign exchange in the borrowing countries, since interest payments would be lowered. Alternatively, donors could pay in contributions to an internationally organized subsidy fund.[5] Payments out of the fund could then be made on a discretionary basis or on the basis of some agreed formula which estimated the deviation of interest rates from their expected trend.[6]

The deferral of repayment could be achieved by debtors making payments in local currency to a multilateral institution which would then on-lend the money to another developing country to buy exports from the initial debtor. This country would in effect take over the debt with the initial creditor. The debt would gradually be paid off as it came into the hands of countries with surplus foreign exchange. It would probably not be paid off in one go by one country. In the interim the debt would have served to encourage export expansion amongst developing countries. While attractive as a way of encouraging intra-south trade, such a scheme suffers from a number of weaknesses. First, it includes an element of tying, and most developing countries would probably prefer to buy goods from industrial countries than from other developing countries. Second, although the original debtors do not default, the creditors would not know when they would be repaid. Since also the distribution of aid is highly political and this scheme spreads the benefits of aid around amongst a number of developing countries, creditors are unlikely to accept it.

An extra creation of SDRs and a modification to the formula on which they are distributed could be used to provide debtors with access to additional foreign exchange and thus alleviate their liquidity problems. Although using SDRs means paying a rate of interest equivalent to the market rate, they provide a permanent source of credit for the user. Since they do not have to be repaid, the cost of using them is initially cheaper than the cost of an equivalent loan, which has to be amortized. The SDRs can be repurchased at any time chosen freely by the user. There is therefore no problem arising from maturity structure.

6. CRITICISMS OF PROPOSED 'SOLUTIONS'

Just as there is no shortage of proposals for dealing with the debt problem there is also no shortage of criticisms of such proposals. However these tend to fall into two categories. The first is that the size of the debt problem has been overestimated, and that by using existing techniques for rescheduling, backed up by adjustment programmes supported by the IMF, the problem may be satisfactorily managed. Of course adopting this attitude involves a high risk. What if things do not turn out this way? The costs of being wrong could be very significant.

The second criticism is that schemes for rediscounting and for setting up safety nets would themselves encounter problems. By reducing the expected return on loans and by effectively writing down the value of bank capital the incentive for banks to make new loans would be reduced: at present banks may be encouraged to make new loans merely to secure their outstanding ones. However new loans are vitally important to debtor countries. Rediscounting schemes would, so critics maintain, thereby create precisely the crisis they are supposed to help avoid. Moreover to set up such schemes would require more public capital than seems likely to be made available given other official capital flows. Furthermore the schemes involve a 'moral hazard' problem since they would encourage debtor countries to get into situations where they warrant relief. They would discourage debtors from trying to deal domestically with their difficulties via appropriate adjustment measures. Schemes for debt relief therefore need to avoid simply condoning excesses by borrowers, or indeed by lenders. They also need to avoid implicitly accepting the historical pattern of international financial assistance.

7. CONCLUDING REMARKS

Although it is not the purpose of this chapter to provide yet another proposal for handling debt, but rather to provide a succinct summary of the main issues involved in understanding international debt, it may be worthwhile to draw out a few conclusions from the above discussion.

Although current arrangements involving rescheduling and the IMF may have the advantage of producing an environment that is not risk free for the banks (and of not permitting the banks to get a 'free ride' on the back of the IMF) and yet of not giving debtors a soft option, it is unsatisfactory on a number of counts. Most significantly the uncertainty it involves in terms of the risk of default, the emphasis on coercion, and the short term nature of rescue packages is destabilising for the international financial system. There is a case for trying to devise a better and more structured system for handling international debt. Debt is a complex issue and proposals which treat it as if it was one dimensional are unlikely to be fully satisfactory. Undoubtedly there are problems in striking a balance between what is offered to creditors and to debtors. Critics are therefore right to point to the potential problems associated with many proposals that have been put forward for solving the debt problem. However this is no reason to abandon any attempt at reform, it simply makes the problem more challenging. Three issues need to be examined in any reform exercise. The first relates to the ways by which the capacity of debtors to service their existing debts may be increased. The second relates to the ways in which illiquidity crises – temporary mismatches between receipts and payments – may be handled while causing minimum economic and political disturbance. And the third relates to the ways in which the likelihood of such crises occurring in the future may be reduced.

With regards the first issue the role of the IMF, and to a lesser extent the World Bank, as adjustment institutions is central. What form should conditionality take? Should this continue to be based on short term financially based programmes or should longer term, more structurally oriented programmes be accommodated?

The second issue involves modifying rescheduling to allow for the stretching out of existing debt, possibly to involve interest payments as well as principal. However debt problems of the illiquidity type may be dealt with not only by reducing current payments, which rescheduling attempts to achieve, but also by increasing short term financial inflows. A question here is how such additional flows may be best achieved.

The third issue involves measures to deal with the overhang of relatively short term debt. It is here that proposals for rediscounting either through official agencies or private secondary markets become relevant, even with their various problems. However it is not simply a matter of dealing with accumulated debt but also of ensuring that new financial flows continue. It is in this context that insurance schemes and guarantees become relevant. Yet the arguments for moving away from the heavy reliance that has been placed on short term lending by the banks remain strong. This raises questions relating to the instruments through which creditors may lend to debtors and the appropriate division of functions between the banks and the international agencies.

Unless relatively rapid and sustained economic growth in the major industrial countries comes along to alleviate the situation all these issues are likely to receive considerable attention in the rest of the 1980s.

Because debt problems have external implications for others than borrower and lender, there is a reason for taking measures to relieve the situation. However, providing help for those debtors that have captured the headlines in the financial press, such as some of the Eastern European and Latin American countries, should not exclude consideration being given to ways of assisting the low-income countries which have had less opportunity to borrow commercially. These distributional issues, as well as ways in which international financial reform may be used to deal with them, are taken up again in Chapter 11.

Part III
Balance of Payments Adjustment

9 The Need for and Means of Balance of Payments Adjustment

1. INTRODUCTION

There are two basic policy problems associated with the balance of payments. The first is to determine the circumstances under which policy action (as opposed to inaction) is needed. The second is to determine what form this action should take. Related to both these questions is the further one of how balance of payments difficulties arise in the first place.

This chapter examines each of these issues. In addition, it briefly discusses the role of the IMF as an adjustment institution and looks at the problem of assessing the nature and impact of balance of payments policy. Although such assessments usually focus on individual countries, this chapter also considers adjustment as a global phenomenon and looks at the problem of international consistency between the adjustment strategies pursued by individual countries. Very little space in the chapter is devoted to discussing the balance of payments in an accounting sense, although there is a brief discussion of definitions.

2. WHAT IS THE BALANCE OF PAYMENTS?

Broadly speaking, the balance of payments of any particular country is a statement of all transactions, receipts and payments between that country and the rest of the world during a certain period of time. Since international transactions are carried through by the exchange of currencies on the foreign exchange market, a country's balance of payments position is reflected by the demand for and supply of its currency in this market. Where demand equals supply, there is so-called balance of payments equilibrium (though as will be argued in a moment this is a rather restrictive definition). Where the demand for a country's currency exceeds its supply, the country has a balance of payments surplus, and where supply exceeds demand, there is a balance of payments deficit.

These terms require further clarification. Balance of payments accounts may be presented using various levels of disaggregation. As an absolute minimum the distinction is made between, first, the current account, which covers both 'visible' trade in goods and 'invisible' trade in services, as well as non-governmental and sometimes governmental transfer payments; and, second, the capital account, within which an attempt is usually made to distinguish between long-term and short-term flows. The precise way in which balance of payments data are presented varies between countries. But irrespective of the details, and because as a result of double-entry book-keeping the complete accounts sum to zero, a balance of payments deficit refers only to a sub-total or partial balance. The three most frequently used sub-totals are the balance on current account, the basic balance (the current account, plus official transfers and long-term capital movements), and the overall balance (which also includes short-term capital movements, errors and omissions, and is the balance which in an accounting sense must be matched by an equivalent change in official foreign exchange reserves).

2.1 What constitutes a balance of payments problem?

As well as being quite a fundamental question, this is a difficult one to answer. The difficulties may be illustrated by starting off with the definition often implied by lay discussion of the balance of payments, namely that there is a deficit on the current account, with imports exceeding exports. But is it in fact the case that a country has a problem every time the current account moves into deficit? It is not.

First, the deficit may be temporary and self-reversing. A deficit may have been preceded by or may be followed by an equivalent surplus. The problem, inasmuch as there is one, is then simply that receipts and payments are not synchronized through time even though in the long run they are equal. In principle the country concerned merely has to ensure that a sufficient proportion of any surplus is retained as additional reserves in order to finance the ensuing deficit. Alternatively, it may borrow to finance the deficit and pay back the loan with the excess revenue associated with a future surplus. In such circumstances the balance of payments will only become a problem if the country over-consumes in response to a surplus or is unable to attract credit. This latter aspect of the problem highlights the ambiguity of the word 'temporary' used above. Even temporary difficulties may create problems if the turn-round does not occur quickly enough, given the capacity of the economy to finance the deficit.

Second, even though the current account is in deficit, there may be an equivalent net inflow of capital to offset it. As a result the basic balance may be in equilibrium. Certainly in assessing the size and nature of a country's balance of payments problem capital flows need to be considered. A developing country receiving a fairly constant and perpetual inflow of aid will be able to run an equivalent current account deficit without encountering too many difficulties. Here a small current account deficit represents balance of payments equilibrium inasmuch as it is sustainable without anything else having to change.

However, this will not always be the case. Where the loan has to be repaid and interest has to be paid on it, a current account surplus will at least eventually be required to earn the necessary foreign exchange. In these circumstances a zero basic balance can give an overly optimistic impression of the strength of the balance of payments.

This will also be the case if a zero current account or basic balance is maintained only by pursuing domestic policies which reduce the demand for imports either by deflating domestic demand, resulting in high levels of unemployment, spare productive capacity and low rates of economic growth, or by imposing import controls, which may also have deleterious effects (to be examined later). Here a balance of payments problem exists but is suppressed or concealed. Directly domestic demand is increased in an attempt to reduce unemployment or increase the rate of economic growth, or import controls are lifted, the current account moves into deficit. Where the simultaneous realization of both internal and external targets is not possible, it may be argued that there is a fundamental disequilibrium.

What emerges so far is that merely looking at balance of payments data can provide an imperfect or misleading guide to the existence of a balance of payments problem. A deficit on the current account, if sustainable, or even in the basic balance, if temporary, does not necessarily mean that there is a problem. Similarly, the lack of a deficit does not necessarily mean that there is no problem if the associated cost is an undesirably high level of unemployment or low rate of economic growth.

The above discussion suggests that a balance of payments problem arises where current performance is unsustainable in the long run. The idea of sustainability is important partly because, from one point of view, a deficit is a highly desirable state of affairs. After all, positive net imports mean that a country is able to enjoy a current standard of living above the level warranted by current domestic production. The problem the country faces arises precisely from the fact that such a situation will not be sustainable in the long run, unless the country concerned can finance the net imports by the additional creation of its own currency that is then willingly held by the rest of the world, and this option is available to very few countries.

However, while being useful, the notion of sustainability can give a rather narrow interpretation of a balance of payments problem, since it implies that a surplus (which is often quite sustainable) does not constitute a problem. In fact, it may well do, not only from the point of view of the individual surplus country but also from that of the world economy.

For individual countries there is the opportunity cost of acquiring reserves by running surpluses. Welfare gains might be higher if the money were used to buy imported goods and services. For the world as a whole it is important to remember that surpluses and deficits cancel each other out. If there are deficits in one part of the world, they will be matched by equivalent surpluses elsewhere. Although attention tends to focus on deficit countries, for it is they which run out of reserves or which have to borrow, the real problem may in some cases be more appropriately judged to exist in the surplus countries. For example, any account of the world's balance of payments difficulties in the period since 1973 which ignored the part played by the OPEC surplus would be seriously lacking.

3. THE CAUSES OF BALANCE OF PAYMENTS DISEQUILIBRIA

In order to assess the appropriateness of alternative policy measures it is important for policy-makers to know something about the causes of payments problems. This is not to argue that policies unrelated to the basic causes will always fail to work in the narrow sense of strengthening the balance of payments, but rather that it seems reasonable to presume that policies directed at the causes will bring about the improvement in the most efficient manner, doing minimum damage to other domestic policy objectives. For example, following a long-lasting adverse movement in the terms of trade, domestic demand deflation will almost certainly improve the current account by reducing the demand for imports, but it will also tend to increase unemployment and reduce economic growth. On the other hand, policies directed more specifically towards making traded goods more competitive may induce a similar improvement but at higher levels of output by encouraging export growth rather than by relying on import contraction.

Payments disequilibria may of course be caused by a range of factors, and in any one case more than one factor is likely to be at work. However, for presentational reasons it is convenient, at least to begin with, to classify the causes of payments problems under three headings: structural, absorption, and monetary.

3.1 Structural causes

3.1.1 'Wrong' goods: low income elasticity of demand for exports

The first structural cause is where a country produces the 'wrong' sorts of goods, by which is meant goods having a relatively low income elasticity of demand. In this case the demand for its exports will over time rise less rapidly than the demand for its imports, and there will be a secular deterioration in its balance of payments.

Given the low income elasticity of demand for primary products and the high degree of export concentration on them, it is not surprising that this explanation is most commonly offered in the context of payments difficulties in developing countries. But it is a mistake to think that it is only relevant in such countries. Industrial countries which do not adapt to changing demands can easily find themselves suffering in a similar way.

Apart from the direct effect on the balance of payments, differing income elasticities of demand for exports and imports may also mean that the terms of trade, i.e. the relative price of exports and imports, change adversely. Assuming similar supply conditions and an expansion in demand, goods with a relatively high income elasticity of demand will experience a bigger price increase than those where the elasticity is low. Countries exporting goods with low income elasticities and importing goods with high income elasticities will therefore also tend to encounter a deterioration in their terms of trade. If price elasticities of demand are low, this will be translated into a deterioration in their balance of payments.

In addition, goods possessing low price elasticities of both demand and supply will tend to have unstable prices if variations occur in supply and demand as a result of factors other than price changing. Countries concentrating on the export of such commodities will then face unstable export receipts. Although instability is another dimension of the structural cause of payments difficulties relating to the sorts of goods being produced, *per se* it need not necessarily constitute a severe problem for reasons noted in the previous section. In the long run it is trend movements that are more important than instabilities about the trend.

3.1.2 Market problems

A second structural cause of payments problems relates to the markets in which exports are being sold. It is not enough for a country to produce goods with high income elasticities of demand if these goods are then sold only in markets where income is rising slowly. The geographical pattern of trade as well as the pattern of production may then exert a significant influence on the balance of payments. Success rests not only on identifying the right goods but also the right markets.

3.1.3 Economic inefficiency

Economic inefficiency is the third principal structural cause of payments problems. It may be that a country is producing goods which have a high income elasticity of demand, and is selling them in markets where income is growing rapidly, but that it is producing the goods less efficiently than others. Higher costs will either be reflected in higher prices, meaning that less goods will be sold, or lower profits, meaning that future cost-reducing investment is less likely.

Inefficiency is of course in itself only an intermediate explanation of balance of payments problems. It is the causes of the inefficiency which provide the ultimate explanation, and these may span trades union restrictive practices and monopoly practices, incompetent management, inappropriate government economic policy with respect to the fiscal system and industrial policy, and various other socio–economic factors. Whatever its causes, until the underlying inefficiency is eliminated, the balance of payments is unlikely to improve for long. Given the dynamics of the situation, namely that inefficiency is frequently self-perpetuating, policies not directly oriented towards raising relative efficiency and reducing unit costs are likely to have at best only a transient effect.

Recognizing the importance of efficiency also highlights the fact that it is a mistake to take too narrow a view of balance of payments policy, since policies which at first sight do not appear to be primarily directed towards eliminating payments problems may have a fundamental role to play.

3.2 Domestic absorption

The absorption approach to explaining balance of payments deficits uses the basic Keynesian income expenditure equation. At the end of the day the resources absorbed by an economy will equal the claims on them. Resources are made up of domestically produced goods Y and imported goods M. Claims arise from consumption C, investment I, government expenditure G and foreign demand or exports X. It follows that:

$$Y+M=C+I+G+X$$

This equation may be expressed in a slightly different form,

$$X-M=Y-(C+I+G)$$

where $X-M$ measures the balance of payments, Y again measures domestic production and $(C+I+G)$ measures domestic absorption. The equation reveals that if domestic absorption exceeds domestic production, a balance of payments deficit of equivalent size will result, with imports exceeding exports. The balance of payments depends on the relative sizes of domestic output and domestic absorption. While in a closed economy excess demand will generate inflation, in an open economy it will generate balance of payments problems.

An important question arising from the above discussion relates to the way in which excess demand is financed, and leads us on to the third potential cause of payments disequilibria.

3.3 Monetary causes

The monetary approach explains payments problems exclusively in terms of domestic monetary disequilibrium. By comparison with the absorption approach, which is usually presented in real terms but to which monetary aspects may be appended, the monetary approach views money as the essence of the matter.

Presented on the assumption of fixed exchange rates, the monetary approach assumes that the nominal demand for money is a stable and linearly homogeneous function of nominal income. It goes on to point out that the nominal supply of money is the product of the money multiplier and the monetary base, with the latter comprising a domestic component consisting of domestic credit created by the monetary authorities and an international component consisting of the domestic holdings of international reserves. Given a tendency toward equilibrium in the monetary sector of the economy, and assuming a constant money multiplier, it follows that changes in reserves (taken as the measure of the state of the balance of payments) strictly reflect any imbalance between the change in the domestic demand for money and the change in the supply of domestic credit. Excess demand for money will be met by a net inflow of reserves, i.e. a surplus, while excess creation of domestic credit will be reflected by a deficit. It is the change in reserves which in the long run restores monetary equilibrium.

Notationally the basics of the monetary approach may be simply shown by the following group of equations:

$$M^d = k\ PY$$
$$M^s = D + R$$
$$M^d = M^s$$
$$R = M^d - D$$

and $\Delta R = \Delta M^d - \Delta D$

where M^d is the demand for money, M^s is the supply of money (or monetary base), D is domestic credit creation, R is reserves and ΔR the change in reserves or the money inflow from abroad, PY is nominal national income and k is the income elasticity of demand for money. It may be seen from these equations that if there is no change in the demand for money, then any change in domestic credit creation will be fully reflected by an equivalent change in reserves, with an increase in credit creation causing an equivalent fall in reserves or an equivalent balance of payments deficit. Excessive domestic credit creation has no long-term effect on output or employment but is completely offset by the loss of reserves.

The basic point is that under fixed exchange rates and with capital mobility the domestic money supply is independent of domestic credit policy. The domestic demand for money may be met either by domestic credit creation or by inflows of money from abroad. Under the monetary approach it is the latter, as shown by changes in reserves, which adjusts to accommodate any discrepancy between changes in the domestic demand for money and changes in the domestic component of the money supply.

Another important aspect of the monetary approach is that, provided the authorities do not sterilize the effects of changes in reserves by compensating changes in domestic credit creation, balance of payments problems are essentially transitory. The balance of payments will eventually return to equilibrium; once stock equilibrium has been restored, the flow of reserves will cease. However, the improvement implies reduced net importation of goods and services and therefore reduced domestic absorption.

Having established that the monetary approach maintains that there is a close correlation (of unity) between domestic credit expansion and the balance of payments, we must ask how the former affects the latter. What is the transmission mechanism? In principle there are a number of avenues through which the effects may be felt.

Starting from a situation of monetary equilibrium, the creation of credit at a rate in excess of the growth in demand for money will have the immediate effect of creating excess real cash balances; the implications of this situation will depend on the ways in which individuals and firms attempt to dispose of their excess holdings. The options are to spend them on domestic and/or foreign, real and/or financial assets. Spending them on foreign assets will have a direct impact on the balance of payments either on the current account, when expenditure is on real assets, or on the capital account, when expenditure is on financial assets. Spending on domestic real assets will either raise real output where there is spare capacity or will raise the domestic price level. In the latter case there will be an adverse effect on the current account (assuming a fixed exchange rate). Spending excess holdings on domestic financial assets will, in the short run at least, tend to reduce interest rates, which will have an adverse effect on the capital account and perhaps on the current account as well. The monetary approach conventionally concentrates on the direct impact on imports and plays down any lasting influence on real output and employment.

3.4 Synthesizing the causes

In the literature on the balance of payments there is a tendency for advocates to state their views on causation in the most extreme fashion, often offering their own explanation as an exclusive one. This is unfortunate because there is a considerable degree of overlap between the various approaches discussed above. Indeed in many respects they are very closely interrelated. Furthermore, it is most unlikely that the assumption of unicausality is realistic. Yet the tendency remains understandable simply because a wide-ranging explanation is more difficult to cope with analytically and may be seen as providing less precise policy advice. However, reality is likely to be complex.

Having stated some potential causes in the previous sections, we may usefully show ways in which they can be synthesized. First, for example, structural factors may be important in explaining why domestic output is relatively low or domestic absorption relatively high. Structural explanations do not therefore conflict with the absorption approach. Second, the absorption approach does not deny that excess credit creation may cause excess aggregate monetary demand and balance of payments deficits; it is therefore consistent with the fundamentals of the monetary approach. Even the broad nature of the transmission mechanism is not in dispute. Third, the monetary approach, although emphasizing credit creation, does not explain what factors lead to over-rapid expansion; credit creation is treated as exogenous. The structural and absorption approaches can, on the other hand, be used to look behind credit creation at its causes. They are therefore complementary to the monetary approach. Furthermore 'over-expansion' is a relative and not an absolute concept. The capacity of an economy to meet, in real terms, a given increase in nominal demand without causing payments difficulties will vary according to a range of structural factors. A specific rate of credit creation which at one time does not represent over-expansion may do so at another time because structural changes have reduced aggregate supply.

Of course if there is so much common ground and complementarity between the various approaches, the question arises as to whether there is any point in distinguishing between them. If, for example, the monetary approach is merely suggesting that rapid credit creation results in payments deficits and that financial discipline is necessary to avoid payments problems, is it really adding much to the absorption approach? Perhaps the novelty of the monetary approach lies in its rather more extreme claims that excess domestic credit creation is perfectly mirrored by a weakening in the balance of payments and that no policy action, other than the control of credit, is needed. However, it is precisely here that the approach is at its weakest, since these claims rest on a number of restrictive assumptions. These include the following: policy-makers are able to wait for the long run to come round, they are largely indifferent to the composition of the balance of payments (the monetary approach argues that the distinction between the current and capital accounts is largely irrelevant), capital is perfectly mobile and capital assets and goods and services in different countries are perfectly substitutable, the demand for money is stable and predictable, full employment may be assumed to exist, and sterilization policies will not be pursued. If these assumptions are unrealistic, the novelty of the monetary approach all but disappears.

In explaining payments problems one is then forced to examine a range of structural, real, and financial variables. In some cases one factor or a small number or factors may dominate; in other cases a broader collection of causes may have been at work.

Before moving on to apply some of this analysis of the causes of payments problems to recent payments disequilibria, it is worth noting that the analysis changes its focus of attention under a regime of flexible exchange rates. Under such a regime the exchange rate moves to maintain balance of payments equilibrium. What have to be explained, then, are not variations in the balance of payments but variations in the exchange rate. These are analysed more fully in Chapter 10.

3.5 The sources of payments deficits after 1973

One way of looking at the causes of deficits in practice is to undertake a series of case studies on the sources of payments problems in individual countries and to then go on, where possible, to draw general conclusions; even if the only conclusion is that circumstances vary widely between countries. A second way is to take a more aggregated look at a number of global factors and endeavour to see the extent to which observed deficits can be explained by these factors. Where they cannot be so explained, then clearly other influences are important. This latter approach suggests a distinction between external and internal causes. External factors include deteriorating terms of trade, falling export demand caused by stagnating economic activity in principal markets, and increasing real interest rates. Internal factors involve some form of domestic economic mismanagement, and include, at the macroeconomic level, large fiscal deficits, rapid credit creation, and appreciating real effective exchange rates induced by inflation which is unmatched by currency depreciation.

Empirical evidence from the non-oil developing countries – the main group of deficit countries in the period 1973–83 – reveals that they were indeed buffeted by a deteriorating external environment. Partly as a result of the increase in the price of oil their terms of trade deteriorated, economic growth in industrial countries declined to a very low rate by the early 1980s, and, having been negative for most of the 1970s, real interest rates became significantly positive in the 1980s. Although to some extent non-oil developing countries were able to minimize the impact of these changes on their balance of payments by, for example, active and aggressive marketing of their exports, enabling them to capture a larger share of declining industrial country markets and to exploit the growing demand in oil exporting countries, it has to be accepted that external factors were a principal cause of payments deficits during the period 1973–83. From amongst these external factors, and over the period as a whole, deteriorating terms of trade seem to have had the single most significant impact.

Yet external factors do not provide the complete explanation. Deficits have generally been rather larger than might have been suggested by external factors alone. Domestic influences have also been at work, perhaps most significantly the pursuit of policies by governments which result in levels of aggregate demand that the economy is unable to meet in real terms. Fiscal deficits, particularly when financed by additional domestic credit creation, are likely to weaken the balance of payments, either directly by spilling over into additional demand for imports, or by causing inflation which leads to an appreciation in the real effective exchange rate unless matched by an equivalent depreciation in the nominal exchange rate.

Again evidence confirms that over 1973–83 and for non-oil developing countries as a group government expenditure exceeded tax revenue, and that the size of fiscal deficits increased. Not unrelated to this, inflation accelerated significantly, while changes in nominal exchange rates failed to offset the impact of inflation on real exchange rates. As a result, relative prices changed in such a way that imports were encouraged and exports discouraged. In the case of those exports where prices are fixed in world markets the effect of price changes on domestic supply, causing costs to increase and profits to fall, is more important than that on foreign demand.

The above discussion implicitly illustrates some of the difficulties in identifying the primary causes of payments problems and in distinguishing between domestic and external influences; for while evidence may suggest that the real exchange rate has appreciated because of inflation, this alone does not allow a conclusion to be reached on the cause of the inflation. It may result from fiscal imbalance but it may also result from deteriorating terms of trade and increasing import prices, which push up the domestic price level. More likely perhaps it results from a combination of the two.

Even though it is difficult to quantify precisely the contribution of different factors to payments disequilibria, it is important to try and reach some conclusions on the matter for two basic reasons. First, it is helpful for policy-makers to know whether the disequilibria are likely to be temporary or longer lasting, since, along with other factors, this will determine the need for an active adjustment policy and the relevant blend between adjustment and financing. Second, knowledge of the causes of non-temporary payments disequilibria will help in designing appropriate adjustment policy, ensuring that balance of payments correction is achieved in the most efficient fashion. There will be a range of policies which might be expected to strengthen the balance of payments, and policy-makers need to make a choice as to which policy or combination of policies are to be adopted. Knowing the causes of the problem makes choosing easier.

4. THE CHOICE BETWEEN FINANCING AND ADJUSTMENT

In principle, a payments deficit may initially be financed by running down international reserves and by international borrowing, or it may be corrected through the pursuit of adjustment policies, or be repressed by controls. While financing is appropriate when the deficit is transitory, it is inappropriate as an exclusive policy when the deficit is persistent and reflects fundamental disequilibrium; in these circumstances financing constitutes only a short-term palliative and some combination of financing and adjustment will be required. The greater the degree of financing, the less rapid is the required rate of adjustment.

The optimum combination of financing and adjustment will be achieved where the marginal rate of substitution between current and future expenditure equals their marginal rate of transformation. Given a deficit of similar size, this may not lead to the same combination of policies in a developing country (LDC) as it would in a developed one. Since LDCs encounter relatively high financing costs, they will be encouraged to make relatively greater use of adjustment. On the other hand, if the social marginal productivity of resources is higher in LDCs, this will encourage them to make relatively greater use of financing; as will also be the case if they possess a relatively strong preference for current as opposed to future expenditure. Furthermore, since the capacity for short-run adjustment is probably lower in LDCs than in industrial countries and the costs of adjustment higher, it might be expected that for these reasons LDCs will be more inclined to try to finance a deficit than correct it. However, they may be precluded from using the theoretically optimum combination of financing and adjustment by the constrained availability of finance and they may therefore be forced to adjust more rapidly than they would wish. In addition, the rudimentary nature of financial systems and the large perceived uncertainty in most LDCs do not facilitate monetary policy as a means of inducing capital inflows to offset current account deficits.

As events in the 1970s and 1980s have aptly shown, in practice the choice, though constrained, between adjustment and financing is very much more difficult than the above discussion suggests. The main source of this difficulty, as mentioned earlier in the chapter, arises from the practical problem of distinguishing between temporary and permanent disequilibria. The crux of this problem is that whereas temporary disequilibria may only be unambiguously identified *after* time has elapsed, balance of payments policy has to be determined *at* the time. What happens, for example, where a country encounters what it anticipates as being a temporary deterioration in its terms of trade? It may respond by borrowing to finance the deficit, expecting to be able to pay back the loans when the terms of trade improve. But what if they do not improve and the deterioration turns out to be fairly permanent? The country will be left with an unmanageable volume of debt which eventually forces it to take draconian corrective measures. With more accurate information about future movements in its terms of trade the country might well have adopted a far different adjustment and financing strategy. While it is easy to be wise after the event, policy-makers have to operate without the benefit of hindsight. They may make forecasts, but forecasting is a notoriously imprecise activity. In choosing to finance a deficit the authorities are therefore taking a risk, and their willingness to borrow or run down reserves implicitly reveals something about their risk preferences.

Unfortunately for policy-makers, putting more emphasis on adjustment is also risky, since they cannot be certain that the policies they adopt will work, or will work as quickly as necessary, or that the costs of adjustment will be politically acceptable. The policy-makers' dilemma is that, faced with a payments deficit, they have to do something in circumstances where they would prefer not to have to do anything.

5. WHAT ADJUSTMENT HAS TO ACHIEVE: EXPENDITURE REDUCING AND SWITCHING EFFECTS

The desire to do nothing arises from the inescapable fact that when real domestic output cannot be increased the correction of a current account deficit entails a reduction in domestic absorption, i.e. consumption and/or investment. This will be the case even if the demand by foreigners for domestic output rises, since this demand may be met, in conditions of low short-run supply elasticity, only if the resources demanded by foreigners are freed by residents. Greater absorption of domestic and foreign output by foreigners clearly means lower absorption of domestic and foreign output by residents. Irrespective of whether the initial impact of any policy is to reduce domestic expenditure or to switch expenditure from abroad, correction of the deficit will be achieved only if there is a reduction in real domestic expenditure. If this reduction is not achieved, the deficit will not be corrected. Thus, unless domestic output can be increased, it is misguided to imagine that the correction of a balance of payments deficit may in some sense be costless. However, the more output may be increased, the less expenditure need fall in absolute terms.

A reduction in domestic expenditure may be achieved by pursuing a range of 'expenditure reducing' policies, such as contractionary monetary and fiscal policy, which, by lowering domestic income, serve to reduce expenditure on all goods, traded and non-traded. The greater the income elasticity of demand for traded goods, the smaller will be the fall in income necessary to bring about the required fall in payments to foreigners. Expenditure-reducing policies, inasmuch as they reduce the demand for imports, can be sufficient on their own to correct a deficit. In addition, because expenditure-reducing policies may also induce a fall in the price of domestically produced goods, they can encourage a switch in domestic and foreign expenditure away from foreign output and towards domestic output. The resources necessary to meet this extra demand for domestic output will have been freed by the reduction in domestic expenditure, provided that the expenditure reductions affect traded goods and not exclusively non-traded goods. Where the pattern of domestic absorption does not match that of exports, the process of adjustment will be slower, since the pattern of output will have to change towards producing more export goods.

However, a transfer of expenditure from residents to foreigners is more conventionally engineered by means of 'expenditure-switching' policies such as devaluation, which are designed to lower the incentive for residents to buy foreign goods and raise the incentive for both residents and foreigners to buy domestic goods. Such a switch in real expenditure may be encouraged by changing the price of domestic output relative to that of foreign output. Unlike expenditure-reducing policies, however, expenditure-switching policies on their own may be insufficient to correct a deficit. Although, where there is spare capacity in the relevant sectors, the additional demand for exports and import substitutes induced by a fall in the relative price of domestic output may be met in real terms, in conditions of full capacity utilization any extra demand created by the expenditure-switching policies will simply generate inflation, unless action is simultaneously taken to free the resources needed to meet the extra demand. However, as will be seen later, expenditure-switching policies may themselves be demand-deflationary. Furthermore, in the context of developing countries the impact of devaluation on supply, through raising the incentive to produce exports, is more important than the demand switching effect that devaluation theory conventionally emphasizes.

According to the monetary approach, a payments deficit will be corrected only if the monetary disequilibrium associated with it is also corrected. This necessitates either a reduction in the real supply of money or a rise in the real demand for money. A fall in the real supply of money may be brought about either by a fall in the nominal supply of money or by a rise in the general price level. A rise in the real demand for money may be brought about through a rise in the level of real income or through a strengthening in any preference for money vis-à-vis other assets.

The monetary approach thus concurs with the absorption approach that unless real income is rising fast enough to induce an adequate increase in the demand for money, the deflationary implications of a deficit will have to be accepted if the balance of payments is to be improved. It emerges that any government setting out to achieve payments adjustment at zero costs is likely to be thwarted in all but limited circumstances. The more appropriate objective for policy-makers is to achieve a specific improvement in the balance of payments at minimum cost and with an acceptable distribution of this cost. It is not enough that policies should be effective in the narrow sense of reducing the deficit; they should also be cost-effective in terms of doing the least possible damage to economic growth, employment and income distribution. From this point of view policies designed to induce adjustment by increasing output rather than reducing expenditure will be favoured. The problem is how to raise output without also raising domestic expenditure, which then negates the impact on the balance of payments.

Let us now move on to examine the range of policies available to policy-makers before returning to this question.

6. THE SPECIFICS OF POLICY

Having identified the objectives of adjustment policy, let us look at a number of specific policies that may help to realize them. This does not imply that governments will use exclusively one balance of payments tool. It is much more likely that they will adopt a package of policies. However, for presentational reasons it is convenient to examine the basic instruments individually.

6.1 Varying the exchange rate

There are a number of methods by which a government may try to ensure that the country's currency does not become overvalued (or indeed undervalued). The real exchange rate can be altered either by altering the domestic rate of inflation in relation to the foreign inflation rate or by altering the nominal exchange rate. In the latter case the exchange rate can be changed by a relatively large amount at one particular moment in time, i.e. a devaluation or revaluation. Alternatively, it can be changed by smaller amounts over a more protracted period of time. We return to the pros and cons of the various techniques when we come on to talk about policy choice. To begin with, however, we concentrate on devaluation, since an examination of this reveals most of the principal issues associated with using the exchange rate as an instrument of balance of payments policy.

6.1.1 Devaluation – the relevance of elasticities to its effects on the current account

Devaluation has conventionally been presented as an expenditure-switching policy. In circumstances where devaluation fails to strengthen the balance of payments it is therefore often assumed that other expenditure-switching policies will not work either. Care needs to be exercised in drawing such conclusions, since some policies may be more (or less) successful in inducing the relative price changes which cause expenditure to be switched.

Devaluation operates by either increasing the domestic currency price, or reducing the foreign currency price, of exports. It generates price incentives which tend to lower domestic demand for imports expressed in foreign exchange, to raise domestic demand for and supply of import substitutes, to increase foreign demand for exports, and/or to lower the domestic demand for and increase the production of exportables. The responses to these price changes depend on a range of demand and supply elasticities.

The significance of the different elasticities varies between countries. For countries where major exports are priced on the world market in foreign currency, devaluation will fail to reduce the world price, and the export elasticity of demand is largely irrelevant; but in these circumstances devaluation will raise the domestic currency price and the profitability of exporting, thereby emphasizing the importance of elasticity of supply. Of course if a country is a major world producer of a particular commodity, then the world price may not be taken as given, and devaluation, through its impact on world supply, may eventually reduce the world price even if this is expressed in foreign currency. For countries whose exports are priced in domestic currency, devaluation will cause the equivalent foreign currency price to fall and it will be the response to this price reduction that will be important in determining the impact of devaluation on exports.

As regards imports, most countries exert little impact on the foreign currency price of their imports, since their demand will represent only a small part of total world demand. In these circumstances devaluation will raise the domestic currency price of imports, since each unit of domestic currency will now buy less foreign currency. Of course domestic prices need not rise to the full exent of devaluation if it is accompanied by the removal of import controls. Nor need exporting become more profitable when expressed in domestic currency if the authorities introduce schemes that effectively tax extra profits. Here it will be government revenue rather than export profitability that rises.

However, assuming that relative prices do change, the success of devaluation in strengthening the current account of the balance of payments depends on the demand and supply response to these changes. To be successful, devaluation needs to reduce the demand for foreign exchange and/or increase its supply. The impact on the demand for foreign exchange depends on the domestic price elasticity of demand for imports, while the impact on the supply of foreign exchange depends on either the elasticity of supply with respect to increased profits in the export sector (where the world price is given) or on the foreign price elasticity of demand for exports (where it is not).

But what values do these elasticities need to have in order to ensure that devaluation will strengthen the current account? Unfortunately, no absolutely clear and unambiguous answer can be given. It all depends on the type of country being examined.

For small countries that can sell as much as they wish at the current world price two elasticities are crucial. On the export supply side the price elasticity must exceed zero if the supply of foreign exchange is to increase. On the import demand side the price elasticity must again exceed zero in order to reduce the demand for foreign exchange. Taking export supply and import demand together, devaluation will improve the current account, provided only that the sum of the price elasticities of export supply and import demand exceeds zero.

If, however, the small country assumptions are not met, then some modifications to this analysis are required. Where a country is not a price-taker for its exports, the supply of foreign exchange will only rise following devaluation if the elasticity of export demand exceeds one. Even if it is less than one, the current account may still improve if the demand for foreign exchange falls by more than the supply. In principle, it is possible that if the demand for imports is very inelastic, then the demand for foreign exchange will fall less than the supply and the current account will deteriorate. Pessimism over the values of foreign trade elasticities has cast some doubt over whether devaluation will always be an effective balance of payments instrument.

However, in practice there seems to be only rather isolated cases where elasticities are sufficiently low for the perverse effects of devaluation to operate. In most countries foreign trade elasticities appear adequate to ensure that devaluation which causes the real exchange rate to depreciate will strengthen the current account. The fact that countries do not revalue to improve their payments position, something that they should do if foreign trade elasticities are very low, and that when real exchange rates are allowed to become overvalued, payments deficits and not surpluses are the result, gives grounds for general optimism.

A more relevant concern is whether nominal devaluation will actually cause the real exchange rate to depreciate. If it merely causes an offsetting acceleration in domestic cost inflation, any relative price changes will quickly evaporate and the elasticities, even if high enough, will simply not be exploited.

6.1.2 Devaluation – implications for absorption and the monetary sector

Whereas the analysis of devaluation based on elasticities stresses its expenditure- and resource-switching aspects, its effects on the level of real expenditure should not be ignored.

If export and import demand elasticities are relatively high, devaluation may have an expansionary impact by increasing the demand for exports and import substitutes. Provided supply is not inelastic, this extra demand may be met, at least partially, by additional real domestic output. However if the demand elasticities are low, devaluation is more likely to reduce real expenditure.

First, a demand-deflationary influence may emanate from the

trading sector. Where domestic currency expenditure on imports increases because of inelastic demand, there will be a net reduction in aggregate demand for domestic output. The higher the average propensity to import and the lower the price elasticity of demand for imports, the greater will be this deflationary impact of devaluation.

Second, devaluation has redistributive effects on income between the trading and non-trading sectors, and the factors of production. Its precise results depend on a range of variables and may change over time. The key variables include the response of money wages in the trading and non-trading sectors to the extra profitability which devaluation induces in the trading sector, the import content of traded and non-traded goods, the response in the non-trading sector to higher wage and import costs, the factor intensitites in and ownership of the various sectors, and the degree of factor mobility. A number of scenarios may be imagined. Since wage and profit recipients may differ in their marginal propensities to spend, different scenarios will have different impacts on domestic expenditure. If, for instance, money wages in both the trading and non-trading sectors rise less than the general price level, perhaps because of money illusion, real wages will fall; and if there is a lower propensity to spend out of profits than out of wages, domestic expenditure will fall.

The durability of the effects of devaluation on expenditure via income redistribution clearly depends on the permanence of the redistribution. This, in turn, will depend on whether those experiencing a relative loss recognize what has happened and have the power to reverse it. If all factor rewards are quickly restored to their pre-devaluation real levels, then devaluation will fail to exert a long-run effect on the level of expenditure. If the impact effect perseveres, then so will the expenditure-reducing effect.

Third, if there are *ad valorem* taxes on exports and imports, devaluation will redistribute income from the private sector to the government, and, if the government has a higher saving propensity, aggregate demand will again fall in the short run. However, it is difficult to be precise about the fiscal effects of devaluation, partly because the fiscal outcome depends significantly on what other policies are simultaneously pursued. For instance, is devaluation accompanied by changes in tariffs, quotas and subsidies? Also important are the effects of devaluation on output, income, domestic expenditure, employment, and inflation, as well as on the underlying structure of government taxation and expenditure.

A fourth potential, and increasingly significant, source of demand deflation which might be induced by devaluation arises from debt-servicing. Devaluation will raise the domestic-currency costs of servicing external obligations expressed in foreign currency and will therefore bring about a reduction in domestic expenditure.

The monetary approach sees the monetary implications of devaluation as crucial, though it also sees devaluation as unnecessary, provided enough time, i.e. financing, is available for automatic correction to occur. According to this approach, devaluation affects the balance of payments by raising the domestic price level, thereby increasing the demand for nominal money balances. The real supply of domestic credit is reduced and monetary-sector equilibrium is maintained by an inflow of reserves. To the extent that devaluation induces a payments surplus it may lead to problems with inflation via its effect on the money supply, but, in theory, once stock equilibrium has been achieved, this inflow ceases. As a result, the effect of devaluation is purely transitory. Relative price changes play no significant role in the monetary approach, and the domestic prices of traded goods are assumed to rise by the full extent of the devaluation. The monetary approach might therefore appear to contrast sharply with the elasticities approach.

However, the differences can be exaggerated, since the increase in the relative price of traded goods encourages demand to switch towards non-traded goods and supply to switch towards traded goods, with the result that exports rise and imports fall. It emerges, then, that certain underlying relations are consistent with any one of the basic theoretical approaches to payments adjustment, i.e. elasticities, absorption, or monetary.

6.1.3 Devaluation – consequences for the capital account

The monetary approach to the balance of payments puts little emphasis on the distinction between the current and capital accounts. However, there are reasons to believe that devaluation will affect the latter as well as the former. This partly results from the restoration of confidence which it may bring about – it may be seen as a means of enhancing a county's current account prospects or at least of showing that a government is prepared to take unpopular decisions designed to strengthen trade performance. To the extent that it eliminates expected depreciation, and possibly raises the chance of appreciation in the future, demand for the currency may increase. Furthermore, if devaluation is accompanied by rising interest rates as the nominal demand for money increases, then a capital inflow may be induced.

6.2 Alternative techniques for switching expenditure

Devaluation is not the only way of bringing about relative price changes, and it has been criticized for being insufficiently selective in its effects. There are other switching policies which can, in principle, exploit the potential gains from price discrimination arising from differential elasticities. These include tariffs and multiple exchange rates, as well as domestic taxes and subsidies, i.e. the fiscal system.

From one point of view such policies have considerable appeal, since they are advocated on the reasonable assumption that similar elasticities do not exist across all sectors and all industries. Thus, even for a country where price elasticities are in general very low – ruling out devaluation – some form of effective multiple exchange practice may strengthen the balance of payments. Furthermore, it might be expected that selective measures would be more effective as a means of moving resources into sectors with high growth potential as reflected by income elasticity of demand.

With formal multiple exchange rates, for example, in circumstances where the price elasticity of demand for a particular import is low, a relatively high exchange rate would be applied. Conversely, for import transactions for which the price elasticity of demand is high, the exchange rate would be relatively low. Where the foreign price of a commodity is fixed, a relatively high exchange rate would be applied to transactions in commodities which possess low supply elasticities with respect to the domestic currency price, and a relatively low exchange rate would be applied to transactions in commodities which possess high supply elasticities.

The alternative is to achieve a greater degree of discrimination through the fiscal system. However, where incentives for import substitution and export promotion are provided in this way, the effect on the fiscal balance must be considered. If the budget deficit increases, this may cause inflation to accelerate and the beneficial effects on the balance of payments to be lost. What happens to the fiscal balance depends on the precise configuration of subsidies and taxes and the costs of operating the scheme. Even if the scheme initially involves net expenditure on subsidies, this may be offset by future tax revenue if export-led growth is encouraged.

However, various criticisms of multiple rate schemes may be made. First, there is the problem of identifying the optimum number and level of rates, or taxes and subsidies. Second, there are the administrative costs of implementing the schemes. Furthermore, doubts about whether fiscal incentives will be retained in the future may reduce the impact that changes in taxes and subsidies have on investment. Third, the use of multiple rates, including the use of taxes and subsidies, can provide opportunities for corruption, evasion, and misuse.

Generally speaking, these difficulties make the fiscal simulation of devaluation or the use of multiple rates inferior alternatives to overt devaluation. However, in principle, they remain useful instruments, since they may be directed towards dealing with the basic problem of switching resources into tradeables. As such, and where practicable, they are valuable, especially in circumstances where devaluation is for some reason unlikely to be politically acceptable, or where a significant number of the relevant elasticities are very low.

6.3 Exchange and import controls

The debate over exchange controls ultimately hinges on the efficiency of the market mechanism and raises the whole range of issues associated with government intervention. Those who believe in the superior allocative efficiency of the price system oppose controls and prefer market-related policies, while those who emphasize market failures in the areas of monopoly, externalities and income distribution are more likely to favour them.

More specifically, exchange controls are seen by their advocates as having a number of advantages over such policies as devaluation or demand deflation, of which the following are the most significant. First, they exert a prompt, direct and predictable effect on imports; they do not rely on the intermediation of a price change and therefore on the size of price elasticities to improve the balance of payments. Second, they may in principle be imposed selectively, allowing the authorities to discriminate between imports and make the most effective use of scarce foreign exchange. Third, unlike demand deflation, controls do not rely on a fall in national income to induce a fall in imports. Furthermore, the allocation of import licences may be used to ensure that a given improvement in the balance of payments has the minimum adverse effect on the poor.

Against this apparently strong case a number of counter-arguments may be presented. First, in many countries there may be little scope for cutting down on 'inessentials' – a frequent target of controls – even if it were possible to identify what imports are inessential. Second, controls increase the degree of monopoly enjoyed by domestic producers, and although this may be advantageous to them, domestic consumers may lose from the higher prices they have to pay and the inefficient import substitution that controls encourage. Third, controls imply a complex administrative system which, even if it works as intended, will be expensive in resource costs. But there is the danger that it will not work as intended and that in practice 'national objectives' will not be served. Part of the problem here is that the system encourages corruption and the provision of inaccurate information. Furthermore, it will tend to lengthen the time-lag between a need for particular imports arising and their delivery. Such delays will cause shortages and the under-utilization of capital. The latter may also result if controls encourage firms to build larger than optimum scale plants in order to obtain extra allocations of foreign exchange.

The most fundamental criticism of controls is that they suppress rather than cure payments problems. An implication of this is that, should the controls be removed, the problem will reappear. Even if there is an underlying improvement in the balance of payments, due, say, to an improvement in the terms of trade, their retention is encouraged by such other factors as the protection of local industry or the continuation of the benefits which controls may generate for powerful interest groups. The situation will be worse still if controls, far from improving the underlying payments position, actually lead to a deterioration. The chief purpose of controls is to reduce imports below what they would otherwise have been at a given exchange rate and thereby reduce the effective demand for foreign exchange. This effect is achieved not by reducing the incentive to import but by frustrating it. In addition, controls do nothing to raise the incentive to export. Indeed, because controls serve to defend on over-valued exchange rate, they discriminate against exports by keeping the profitability of exporting, expressed in domestic currency, below what it would be with a lower exchange rate. Although, in principle, the adverse effect on export performance might be neutralized through a system of export subsidies, these are themselves problematical, not least because they may discriminate in favour of high cost and relatively inefficient exports and against more efficient (traditional) exports.

Bearing in mind both the allocational and practical problems associated with exchange controls, it seems reasonable to conclude that, while they may in some cases provide a useful short-run tourniquet in an emergency, they do not generally offer a cost-effective means of correcting deficits in the long run.

6.4 Structural policies

It is difficult to discuss structural policies at all succinctly, since there are a myriad of policies which might be described as 'structural'. Moreover, they can be seen in the context of any of the basic analyses of payments problems. For instance, they may be seen as altering the basic pattern of production and trade or the efficiency of production; raising, in the absorption framework, output relative to expenditure; or increasing, in the monetary framework, the demand for money.

With the emphasis certainly being on increasing aggregate supply or on altering the composition of aggregate demand rather than on reducing the level of aggregate demand, structural policies are usually concerned with modifying the ownership of factors of production, factor mobility, wage bargaining, the degree of competition and monopoly, the activities of multinationals, or the distribution of output between consumption and investment. The policies tend to be microeconomic rather than macroeconomic, and relate to individual sectors of the economy where supply bottlenecks are seen as a major cause of disequilibrium. They may rely on changing relative prices or be based on planning. In the former sense devaluation may be seen as a structural policy.

A central problem with many structural policies is that they exert their main beneficial impact on the balance of payments only in the long run. Their short-run effect may indeed be adverse, with the result that balance of payments 'crises' requiring fairly drastic action on demand prevent the long-run benefits from ever being realized. Structural policies directed towards supply are undoubtedly more difficult to devise and implement than policies directed towards demand. Yet the fact remains that where deficits are caused by underlying structural deficiencies, the long-run solution to payments problems rests on structural adaptation.

6.5 Demand management: monetary and fiscal policy

Whereas devaluation may have coincidental expenditure-reducing effects, the main macroeconomic purpose of monetary and fiscal policy as a tool of payments adjustment is to deflate domestic demand. The idea is to reduce imports to a level consistent with a given level of exports. Since it is demand that is reduced, and since interest rates are likely to rise, demand management policies may be accompanied by falling output as well as by falling domestic expenditure.

Fairly clearly such policies fit into the framework of both the absorption and monetary approaches. In the latter case a reduction in the rate of domestic credit creation means that excess demand for money will be met by an inflow of reserves. The ways in which a deceleration in the rate of credit creation is transmitted into an improvement in the balance of payments mirrors the earlier discussion of monetary causation. They include the direct impact on the demand for imports, the indirect effect on imports and exports resulting from any reduction in the rate of inflation, and the effect on capital flows as domestic interest rates rise.

While monetary analysis concentrates on credit creation, this cannot be disassociated from the state of the fiscal balance and the related levels of government expenditure and taxation. The means by which a fiscal deficit is financed will have implications for the balance of payments. Where it is financed by borrowing, the domestic rate of interest will rise. The expansionary effects of the deficit will therefore be neutralized to some extent and the level of imports will be lower than would have been the case had the fiscal deficit been financed by credit creation. Moreover, with a rising interest rate induced by a bond-financed fiscal deficit the capital account will tend to be in surplus, whereas with a fiscal deficit financed by credit creation the domestic interest rate will not rise and may even fall with capital flowing out of the country.

Although the main thrust of demand-management policies is to reduce expenditure, they may also switch the pattern of expenditure if, as mentioned before, they serve to reduce the rate of inflation. However, there are the counter-arguments that, first, any induced accumulation of reserves will be inflationary, and, second, that rising interest rates will themselves induce cost inflation.

Furthermore, the extent to which restricting credit creation will strengthen the balance of payments depends on the stability of the demand for money and its interest rate elasticity. If the demand for money is highly elastic with respect to the rate of interest, the effect of financial contraction on the balance of payments will be relatively small, while if the demand is unstable, it will be unpredictable.

7. THE CHOICE OF ADJUSTMENT POLICY

In choosing a balance of payments policy it may be assumed that governments will be guided either consciously or subconsciously by a number of criteria. In this section we list the criteria and examine how the various policies discussed above perform when judged against them. Let it be recalled, however, that, in the absence of improvements in the terms of trade or increases in tradeable output, balance of payments adjustment is often a painful experience, implying as it does reduced domestic absorption. Governments would in this sense prefer to avoid it altogether. The problem is that postponing adjustment may make the eventual outcome worse than it need otherwise have been. Policy-makers are, however, notoriously myopic.

7.1 Effectiveness

The question here is whether the conditions necessary for a particular policy to be effective exist. In the case of exchange-rate depreciation, for example, the relevant issues are whether the foreign trade elasticities are high enough and whether the resultant inflationary impulse is likely to be sufficiently small. As for demand deflation, one might imagine that there would ultimately be a level of aggregate demand at which a balance of payments deficit would be eliminated. However, this rests on the assumption that exports may be treated as given and that imports are compressible. If exports are in fact positively correlated to the level of domestic demand, there is no guarantee that deflationary policies will be effective; they may merely result in lower output, lower domestic absorption and a deterioration in the balance of payments. Basically no policy can automatically be assumed to be effective.

7.2 Cost-efficiency

Governments have other policy objectives apart from balance of payments equilibrium. In selecting adjustment policy they will endeavour to do minimum damage to these other policies. Ideally they will select payments policies which reduce unemployment and expand output, but they will attempt at least to achieve payments equilibrium at the highest possible level of economic activity. Generally speaking, in deficit situations this argues in favour of exchange rate depreciation as opposed to the contraction of domestic demand. On the other hand, while devaluation tends to cause inflation, monetary contraction may reduce it. It follows that the choice between devaluation and monetary contraction depends on the current rates of unemployment and inflation and the government's priorities between them.

7.3 Resource efficiency

The question here is whether the policy results in an efficient use of scarce resources? Import controls may, for example, improve the current account by encouraging inefficient and high-cost import substitution, whereas it might be more efficient to finance more imported goods by expanding efficient low-cost exports. Demand deflation may result in resource inefficiency by causing underutilization of capacity.

7.4 Relation with the causes of the problem

As shown by the earlier section on the sources of payments deficits, an important cause since 1973 has been the deterioration in the terms of trade of primary product producing countries. Assuming that this is permanent, countries need to induce structural changes if they wish to strengthen their balance of payments by transferring resources into the traded goods sector and perhaps by export diversification. A question is whether policies will induce such shifts. While exchange rate depreciation may normally be expected to encourage resource reallocation and export growth, a reduction in the supply of credit is less likely to change relative prices and is therefore less likely to induce the required structural changes. Structural change may still occur, however, if the reliance on bank credit varies across firms and sectors, with the increasing cost of credit and its reduced availability adversely affecting those that rely on it. But if the worst affected firms are infant manufacturing ones, then the structural changes induced by credit contraction may be undesirable.

In other circumstances, where, for example, payments deficits have been caused by large fiscal deficits, restrictionary demand management policies may be more appropriate and structural change may not be necessary. Indeed policies causing structural change may be misplaced.

A more awkward policy problem may arise when there are multiple causes, since policies which reduce the pressure of demand may discourage required changes on the supply side. Meanwhile, some structurally oriented policies may cause fiscal deficits to increase. It is illegitimate to regard aggregate supply and aggregate demand as unrelated; the two interact upon each other.

Even where the principal thrust of adjustment policy is to raise aggregate supply, policy-makers will be unwise to ignore the demand side. The success of a supply-orientated adjustment strategy may easily be sabotaged if it is accompanied by financial profligacy.

7.5 Distributional considerations

Different balance of payments policies will have different distributional affects. If governments have defined distributional objectives, motivated either by the pursuit of greater equity or by that of re-election, they will be unfavourably disposed to policies conflicting with these objectives. Devaluation may be expected to increase the profitability of the export sector but to reduce at least some real wages. Since it also changes the internal terms of trade in favour of tradeables, those employed in the non-tradeable sector but consuming tradeables may lose. Yet if devaluation succeeds in reducing unemployment and increasing output, the distributional consequences become more difficult to disentangle.

7.6 Political and technical feasibility

This will not be unrelated to the question of distributional effects, but certainly some policies will be more easily implemented than others and less politically sensitive. For example, if the consequences of devaluation for real wages and income distribution are not well understood, it may prove a more acceptable policy than monetary contraction, which emphasizes a fall in the nominal money supply and money wages and which, in certain cases, may be difficult to operate because of imperfect control over the rate of domestic credit creation by the monetary authorities.

7.7 The time profile of effects

Individual adjustment policies may each have advantages and disadvantages. The above discussion suggests that governments will try to maximize the net advantages, though, depending on their preferences, it may also be rational for them to minimize the absolute disadvantages. However, the timing of the benefits and costs associated with different policies will also be significant. If politicians are primarily concerned with the short run, they may favour a policy which has large short-run benefits and low short-run costs even though in the long run the costs are significant. Related to this is the debate over shock versus gradualist policies. On the basis of the above discussion governments may be predisposed towards gradualism, where the costs of adjustment are spread over a lengthy time period. Yet circumstances may exist where governments feel that short sharp shock treatment will be more easily carried through and may be showing significant beneficial effects long before a gradualist strategy would. In any case care has to be exercised in distinguishing between shock treatment and gradualism, since shock policies such as a large discrete devaluation may have gradual effects on the current account as well as immediate ones on the capital account, whereas the announcement of gradual policies such as a reduction in the future rate of growth of credit may have significant immediate (as well as longer-term) effects as expectations are changed.

Of course the freedom of governments to select the optimum time profile on the basis of domestic considerations may be strictly constrained. In crisis conditions where financing is unavailable, or available only with conditions attached, they may be forced to select policies that strengthen the balance of payments as quickly as possible, irrespective of the costs.

7.8 The blend of policies and their specifics

Governments are likely to try and solve payments problems by a blend of policies. Apart from the fact that in conditions of uncertainty it is unwise for risk-averters to rely on just one policy, there are quite reasonable economic arguments for doing so. For example, where it is felt that devaluation will fail to depreciate the real exchange rate because of induced cost inflation, it may be combined with an incomes policy designed to prevent real wages from rising to their previous level; or where the expansionary effects of devaluation will only be felt after a lapse of time, monetary policy may be modified to be relatively more restrictive in the long run than in the short run. However, the blend of policies will not always be the same; the short-run impact of devaluation may not always be contractionary and accompanying monetary policy will need to compensate for this.

Up to now the discussion has placed insufficient emphasis on the variety of policy. Financial policy may include limiting credit to the government or to the private sector. It may also discriminate between various components of expenditure. Fiscal policy can clearly incorporate a wide range of tax and expenditure measures, while exchange rates may be altered infrequently by large discrete amounts (devaluations and revaluations) or frequently and by smaller amounts (crawling rates). Although crawling is inappropriate where there are large disequilibria, it offers a way of altering exchange rates that is less disruptive both politically and economically than is devaluation. Small frequent changes will generally cause less speculation, lead to less inflation, and have less effect on income distribution than will a large devaluation (see also Chapter 10).

In addition, it is important to see all aspects of balance of payments policy in a dynamic setting. For example, once an equilibrium real exchange rate has been achieved, it is important to monitor changes in the rate and be prepared to make further changes in the nominal rate should the real rate become overvalued again.

8. JUDGING THE SUCCESS OF A BALANCE OF PAYMENTS POLICY

Having designed and implemented a programme of balance of payments policies, it is important to know how successful they have been. The problem here is to devise criteria upon which success may be evaluated.

As a starter one might look and see whether or not the balance of payments has been strengthened. However, there are numerous difficulties associated with this apparently straightforward idea. What is meant by the phrase a 'strengthening in the balance of payments'? Does it refer to the current account or the capital account? Does it simply look at statistically observed payments performance or does it look at the underlying situation? Does it require some movement in the direction of eliminating what were the causes of payments disequilibria? It is possible to think of situations where there may be a statistical improvement in a country's balance of payments at the same time as there is no change in the underlying situation. For example, a policy of demand deflation or import controls may reduce imports but may do little to bring about the structural changes that are needed.

Leading on from this, it is also important to examine not only the effectiveness of payments policies in terms of eliminating disequilibria but also to look at their cost-efficiency. Policies that induce external balance by sacrificing internal objectives such as full employment and growth are only successful in a very restricted sense.

Another problem is that observed changes in the balance of payments may have little to do with the policies that have been pursued. For example, a country may experience an improvement in its balance of payments exclusively because of a changing global environment and improving terms of trade. In these circumstances it is hardly the policies that have been successful unless they were devised specifically on the assumption of such changes. On the other hand, policies may have been successful in terms of making the balance of payments stronger than it would otherwise have been even where recorded balance of payments performance has deteriorated. Ideally, then, one needs to have an idea of what the position would have been had no policy change been made or indeed had other policies been adopted. This is ultimately a matter of guesswork, and makes the *ex post* evaluation of payments policies that much more difficult and imprecise.

A further possible approach is to compare what has happened with what the policies were designed to achieve. A problem here is that aspirations may have been unrealistic. Policies which do not realize their targets may, with the benefit of hindsight, still be seen as having been largely successful. While on the question of defining targets, it is important to stress again that it may be inappropriate to target the elimination of, say, a balance of payments deficit. In many countries a more appropriate target may be the reduction in the size of a current acount deficit to a level that may be sustained by capital inflows.

In any case balance of payments policies are likely to be multi-faceted in their impact. It is therefore unwise to use too narrow a definition of success or failure. The time dimension is one important facet. The effects of policies will be spread over time. A package of policies that over, say, three or five years strengthens the balance of payments may actually make it worse to begin with. Similarly, policies which maximize the short-term beneficial effect may have adverse consequences in the long run.

We must conclude that the evaluation of balance of payments policies is complex. Where simple techniques are used, their deficiencies need to be clearly kept in mind.

9. THE ROLE OF THE IMF AS AN ADJUSTMENT INSTITUTION

The problem of assessing the impact of payments policies has been, and continues to be, an important issue in discussions about the role of the IMF as an adjustment institution. Although the Fund publicly claims some measure of success for the programmes it supports, outside observers have argued that they have very little effect one way or the other on either the balance of payments or other macroeconomic variables. The Fund's input into adjustment in individual countries comes partly from a reasonably continuous process of consultation but mainly from the fact that relatively large amounts of Fund finance are only made available after a detailed programme has been negotiated between a potential borrower and the Fund (and then implemented).

Although the Fund acknowledges the increasing importance of external factors in causing many of the payments deficits experienced in the period since 1973, it still believes that more often than not over-expansionary demand management policies are the principal cause. Not surprisingly, therefore, ceilings on the rate of domestic credit creation often form the centrepiece of Fund-supported programmes. This does not necessarily imply that the Fund is 'monetarist', as some critics claim; indeed the use of devaluation as a tool for changing relative prices, concern over the current account and over the short-run, advocacy on occasions of incomes or wages policy, and a general interventionist flavour to Fund thinking, cast doubt over such a claim. Rather it suggests that the Fund sees credit as something that can be measured objectively by readily available data, something that can be used to monitor economic progress more broadly, and something that can be controlled by the authorities. These assumptions may themselves be challenged, and there may be some scope for improving balance of payments adjustment policy within countries by modifying the nature of Fund conditionality. This is an issue to which we return in Chapter 12.

10. GLOBAL ASPECTS OF ADJUSTMENT

Up to now we have concentrated on balance of payments policy in the context of individual countries. The implicit assumption is that other things, such as the level of aggregate demand in major markets, the level of protectionism, and the prices of other currencies, remain constant.

However this may not always be a reasonable assumption. If a significant number of deficit countries are simultaneously pursuing similar policies, the effectiveness of the policies for any one country is likely to diminish. If all deficit countries deflate domestic demand, then, although their imports may fall, so will their exports, and the balance of payments may therefore fail to improve. Similarly, if a group of competing deficit countries all depreciate their exchange rates at the same time, none of them will gain a competitive advantage *vis-à-vis* each other. Or again if all deficit countries adopt a more aggressive approach to export promotion, it will become progressively less easy for any one country to expand exports.

There may well be an element of the fallacy of composition in balance of payments adjustment. What looks to be effective policy from the viewpoint of an individual country in isolation may not look so effective where a significant number of countries are pursuing similar policies. The issue comes down to the zero sum nature of global disequilibria and their distribution. If one country is to reduce its deficit, this means that other countries will have to accept larger deficits or smaller surpluses. The desire of deficit countries as a group to move out of deficit can only be achieved if surplus countries are prepared to accommodate it. If they are not, the current international financial system has little way of putting pressure on them. The 'scarce currency' clause within the Fund, which was designed to allow discrimination against countries running persistent surpluses, has never been used and has in effect been ruled out, whereas Fund surveillance and advice carries much less weight when it is not given against a background in which countries need to borrow.

These observations lead to an interesting reversal of the earlier division between adjustment and financing; for, if the assumption is made that surplus countries will not choose and cannot be persuaded to reduce their surpluses, it follows that the equivalent deficits cannot be eliminated. Adjustment at the global level will not take place. Furthermore, attempts to adjust will merely result in a globally deflationary bias. In these circumstances and in principle there may be a case for simply providing additional finance to deficit countries through the recycling of surpluses or the creation of new reserves, or for at least putting more emphasis on global financing until global adjustment becomes more attainable. The problem is that in circumstances where surplus countries are reluctant to countenance a reduction in their surpluses they may also be reluctant to agree to measures that channel more finance to deficit countries.

10 Exchange Rates: Systems and Policies

Discussion of exchange rates ties in closely with the analysis of the balance of payments in the previous chapter. Under a system of fixed exchange rates it is volumes that alter, with payments disequilibria resulting in changes in reserve holdings. Under flexible exchange rates it is the price variable, i.e. the exchange rate, that changes in response to disequilibria. In principle the level of reserves does not change. As these remarks suggest it is the way in which disequilibria are revealed rather than their basic causes that differentiates fixed rate and flexible rate systems.

This having been said, the introduction of generalized floating in 1973 has resulted in a great deal of extra attention being paid to the analysis of exchange rates, and a voluminous literature has quickly accumulated attempting to explain their behaviour – the principal theories are reviewed in Section 6 of this chapter. As exchange rates have moved to front stage, so liquidity issues have moved to the back. As explained in Chapter 5, the logic of this is that the question of reserve adequacy loses much of its relevance under flexible exchange rates. If the exchange rate is automatically bearing most of the brunt of adjustment, the need for financing is that much less.

However, the experience with floating rates has been far from problem-free, and has led to a number of questions being asked about their operation. First, does the experience match what was expected? If not, in what ways have expectations been unfulfilled and why? Second, what determines exchange rates? If there is a model that explains them, can this be used to predict what future rates will be? Third, and from a policy point of view, should exchange rates be left alone to be determined purely by unfettered market forces or should governments intervene in order to manage them? In other words should floating be 'clean' or 'dirty'? If dirty, just how dirty should it be? The very use of the word dirty suggests that governments may in some rather disreputable way be gaining a competitive advantage. But is the management of exchange rates always disreputable? If governments are to intervene in foreign exchange markets, how should they? Is it possible to devise a code of good practice for exchange rate management? Fourth, but leading on from this, is it possible to reach any conclusions about the relative desirability of different exchange rate systems? This question does not require us to find a system that is perfect in all respects but merely to identify one system that on balance seems to have more to be said for it and less to be said against it than the alternatives.

This chapter discusses each of these questions and tries where possible to suggest some tentative answers to them. However, it needs to be emphasized that our knowledge of exchange rates is far from satisfactory, and much of the work that has been done on them has gone to show how little they are truly understood.

1. DEFINITIONS

Before moving on to examine some of the central issues listed above, we shall try and define what is being discussed. This is particularly important with exchange rates, because different concepts exist. According to one definition the exchange rate may be moving in one direction, but according to another it may be moving in precisely the opposite one. This can clearly result in confusion.

1.1 Nominal exchange rates (NERs)

The NER expresses the price of one national currency in terms of another. It tells us the number of units of one currency that must be paid to buy one unit of another currency. The NER is, therefore, a bilateral rate between two individual currencies.

However, even this apparently simple definition conceals the seeds of confusion, and care has to be exercised in interpreting information about NERs. For example, take the NER between pounds sterling and US dollars. In principle this can be expressed either in terms of dollars per pound (say $1·50 per £1) or pounds per dollar (in this case £0·66 per $1·0). The problem is that a depreciation of sterling implies a *fall* in the $/£ rate (say to $1·40 per £1) but a *rise* in the £/$ rate (in this case to £0·714 per $1·0). Furthermore, the percentage changes differ in the two cases. This example makes apparent the ambiguity of phrases such as 'a fall in the exchange rate'.

A further possible confusion arises from the fact that whereas under a fixed rate system nominal exchange rates will be the administered official 'par' or 'central' values, with floating rates NERs will be market-determined.

In contrast to NERs, which can be observed, there are fundamental equilibrium rates (FERs), which cannot. The FER is essentially the rate that would exist on the basis of so-called economic fundamentals. It is the rate that would simultaneously give both internal and external balance. At any one time it may happen to coincide with the nominal rate but, as will be seen later, there is no presumption that it will. FERs will tend to change because of changes in capital flows, changes in the pattern of demand for and supply conditions of traded goods, because of the discovery of new resources, or because of long-lasting exogenous changes in the terms of trade. The existence of a FER is quite consistent with there being a current account deficit in the balance of payments, provided that this may be sustained on a long-run basis by capital inflows.

1.2 Effective exchange rates (EERs)

Individual countries will have bilateral NERs with many countries, but these may be changing by different amounts and even in different directions. A summary measure of exchange rate movements is therefore needed. This is derived by taking a weighted average of NER movements. The weighting reflects the importance in trade and financial flows of particular foreign currencies. The resulting measure is what is normally known as the effective exchange rate (EER).

However, there is an alternative way in which the concept of an effective exchange rate is used. In some countries governments may not allow traders to swap domestic currency for foreign currencies at the nominal rate. Depending on the circumstances, more or less advantageous rates of exchange will be offered. In these cases the 'effective rate' needs to be distinguished from the nominal rate. Clearly it is important to identify the way in which the word effective is being used. Potential confusion is increased by the fact that the two definitions are not mutually exclusive. The EER as derived by the first method may not be an accurate summary of the rates *actually* used by traders.

1.3 Real exchange rates (RERs)

While the NER says how many units of one currency can be bought with one unit of another currency, a remaining question relates to the rate at which real goods and services in one country may be swapped for real goods and services in another. This depends not only on the NER but also on the relative price levels in the two countries. The real exchange rate endeavours to answer this question of 'real' exchange by modifying the NER (or EER) to allow for differences in price levels.
Thus:

$$\text{RER} = \text{NER}. \frac{pd}{pf}$$

where *pd* is the domestic price level and *pf* is the foreign price level. According to the above formula, a country's RER will appreciate as its NER appreciates or as its price level rises relative to that abroad. In turn this suggests that policies can affect the RER either by working on the NER or on the domestic price level.

Of course if all countries had similar rates of inflation, movements in NERs or EERs would stand as close proxies for those in RERs. It is when inflation rates diverge that the separate measurement of RERs becomes important, not least because it helps indicate changes in countries' competitiveness. An appreciation in an RER generally means that the country in question has become less competitive, though things may not be that straightforward. A problem arises in measuring 'the' price level. For example, imagine that domestic prices have on average risen, but that this average conceals the fact that it is the prices of non-traded goods that have risen much more than those of traded goods. Indeed the prices of traded goods may have risen less rapidly than those of traded goods abroad. While, according to our earlier measure, the country's RER has appreciated, the output of its traded goods sectors has actually become *more* competitive. This is very much what happened in Japan in the 1960s. As a result, while Japan had faster rates of inflation than most other industrial countries, its balance of payments still continued to run persistent and increasing surpluses.

Yet, subject to such complexities, distinguishing RERs from NERs remains very important from a policy point of view. Movements in NERs may not have the anticipated effects simply because they are not reflected by equivalent movements in RERs.

2. FIXED EXCHANGE RATE SYSTEMS

Although in principle the Bretton Woods system was based on adjustable pegs, in practice it operated with essentially fixed rates. These were only occasionally altered and then in a last ditch attempt to correct payments disequilibria and often in an environment of international financial 'crisis'. Par values were, however, clearly established and defended for protracted periods.

2.1 Advantages

The principal appeal of fixed exchange rates is that they appear to yield many of the benefits associated with unified currencies. It is widely accepted as being advantageous to have only one currency circulating inside a nation state, because it encourages specialization, trade and inter-temporal transactions, and eliminates the uncertainties that would exist if different monies were used. While it may be unrealistic to expect the world to adopt one unified currency, the same sort of certainty may in principle be achieved by pegging nominal exchange rates between currencies. Traders in one country can calculate with certainty the value of their own currency in terms of foreign currencies and can then determine what is for them a utility-maximizing pattern of trade. Given the usual assumptions of trade theory, the world as a whole benefits from minimizing the impediments to trade. Superficially of course the evidence of the 1950s and 1960s – a time of rapid growth in world trade – seemed to support this argument, though the causal interrelation between the trade growth of the Bretton Woods era and its underlying exchange rate regime is very much more complex than this simple correlation may seem to suggest.

A second advantage claimed for fixed rates is that they provide a centrally agreed focus for the conduct and co-ordination of national economic policies. Under the gold standard, for example, domestic money supplies respond directly and automatically to disequilibria in the balance of payments. Even in less extreme forms of fixed exchange rate system reserve losses still tend to have deflationary consequences, both directly and indirectly, via induced policy changes, while reserve gains may have a not necessarily symmetrical expansionary influence. The acceptance of fixed rates is seen as imposing a beneficial discipline on the way in which economies are managed, and as ensuring that national policies are globally consistent.

2.2 Disadvantages

Perhaps the principal problem with fixed exchange rates is that in practice they do not endure. As observed earlier, even in the case of the Bretton Woods system occasional large alterations were made in exchange rates. As soon as such alterations are accepted as legitimate, much of the certainty associated with the system disappears, as therefore do the advantages associated with certainty. Indeed, with such large infrequent exchange rate changes, uncertainty and speculation are heightened.

Yet even if there were to be confidence in the retention of fixed rates, problems still exist. Indeed these other problems become more significant precisely because fixed rates are maintained. The main one arises when the officially fixed rate is not the same as the free market rate or the fundamental equilibrium rate. Trading will then be conducted at a disequilibrium set of relative prices. The wrong price signals are given to consumers and producers and the pattern of demand and production adapts in ways that do not make the best use of scarce global resources, i.e. inefficiency is the outcome. But is this likely to be the case? The answer must be that it is. Even if authorities were initially able to identify accurately what the equilibrium set of exchange rates were at a particular point in time, these rates are unlikely to remain equilibrium ones for long. As there are changes in the pattern of global demand; changes in national supply conditions associated, for instance, with differing rates of productivity growth and unit production costs; differing rates of inflation, even though inflation rates do tend to diverge less under fixed exchange rates; and changes in savings and investment trends; so balance of payments disequilibria will develop, with some countries running persistent deficits and others persistent surpluses at the old set of fixed rates.

Even where countries have similar structural trends and similar trade-offs between, say, inflation and unemployment, different governments are likely to have different policy priorities, and these will be reflected in the balance of payments. A country whose government puts top priority on reducing unemployment is likely to end up with a payments deficit, while another whose government is rather more anxious to reduce the rate of inflation is likely to push the balance of payments into surplus. Fixed exchange rates should not then be accepted on the belief that payments disequilibria are unlikely to arise.

However, the existence of such disquilibria does not in itself irrevocably damage the case for fixed rates. First of all they may be salvaged if capital flows are so organized as to offset the current account disequilibria. Fixed rates may prove sustainable if surplus countries stand perpetually prepared to finance the deficit ones by transferring purchasing power to them. This happens in the context of unified currency systems where not all (or even any) regions will be in payments equilibrium and richer regions effectively subsidize poorer ones. But subsidization which is accepted within nation states may not be so easily accepted between them, though regional policy within the European Economic Community has similar implications. A key question with any fixed exchange rate system is whether there are enough reserves and official liquidity in the system to support it and keep confidence in fixed rates. It was in part the inadequacy of 'official' liquidity relative to private capital flows in the Bretton Woods system that led to its collapse.

However, even if the perpetual financing of deficits is not an option that is available, fixed exchange rate systems may still survive if other adjustment policies which are both effective and efficient can be used to eliminate disequilibria, either by changing relative prices or by changing the relative levels of output and expenditure.

By adopting fixed exchange rates, governments are in effect reducing their policy instruments by one and yet are retaining all their policy targets. Indeed, to the extent that fixed rates mean that governments lose control over the domestic money supply, they may be seen as sacrificing more than just one instrument.

Using our earlier definitions of the exchange rate, we must ask whether, and at what cost, a country's authorities can induce changes in the real exchange rate while holding a fixed nominal exchange rate. This depends on the extent to which they can control the domestic inflation rate through (1) the management of demand, (2) incomes policy, or (3) supply side policies designed to expand output. Furthermore, how appropriate such policies are will in turn depend on the initial causes of payments disequilibria. Where, for example, the principal cause has been over-expansionary demand policy, then some contraction in demand will be an effective and an efficient policy. However, in circumstances where the principal causes are structural, demand deflation is likely to be an inefficient and costly method of eliminating a payments deficit, especially if the interest rate elasticity of the demand for money and the income elasticity of the demand for imports are both low, and if inflation does not respond to reduced aggregate demand. If expenditure-switching and output-increasing policies are required, demand deflation will only adjust the deficit away to the extent that it depreciates the real exchange rate. If it does not achieve this, it will only be effective in eliminating deficits at a fixed exchange rate by suppressing the disequilibrium through sacrificing internal policy objectives such as full employment and economic growth.

More generally currency misalignment may force governments to accept a combination of inflation and employment that they would have preferred to avoid. Over-valuation may, for instance, imply a higher level of unemployment, as traded goods industries facing reduced demand shed labour, and a lower price level, as the prices of imported goods are kept below what they would have been with a depreciated exchange rate.

Where governments are reluctant to make such sacrifices, they may be tempted to introduce tariffs, quotas, and exchange controls. While such measures may reduce the size of the deficit associated with an over-valued exchange rate, they are hardly consistent with the trade-creating advantages that fixed exchange rates are claimed to possess, and may be inefficient in a number of other ways.

To the extent that it is demand management that bears the brunt of compensating for disequilibrium rates and to the extent that exchange rates are altered infrequently and in large amounts, uncertainty about exchange rates is simply replaced by uncertainty about the level of domestic demand. Moreover, the variability in consumption associated with fluctuations in the level of domestic demand may be another source of welfare loss if it is argued, as many theories of the consumption function do, that consumers prefer to have a sustainable level of consumption and actively seek to avoid fluctuations.

Furthermore, if under a fixed exchange rate system the burden of adjustment is asymmetrically placed on deficit countries, the whole system will take on a deflationary bias. Given the greater immediacy of the difficulties associated with reserve losses than with reserve gains, asymmetrical adjustment is likely to be a feature of fixed rate systems.

3. FLEXIBLE EXCHANGE RATE SYSTEMS: THE ARGUMENTS FOR AND AGAINST

Against these disadvantages of fixed exchange rates, which became more widely recognized in the later years of the Bretton Woods system, there was a growing body of opinion in favour of greater exchange rate flexibility, although there was some disagreement over the precise type of flexibility that should be adopted. Some advocates favoured free floating while others opted for managed floating.

3.1 Advantages

In presenting their case advocates claimed a series of advantages for flexible exchange rates.

First and foremost it was argued that flexibility in nominal rates would allow fundamental equilibrium rates to be maintained and the costs of misalignment to be avoided. Nominal rates were envisaged as being likely to respond quickly and automatically to fundamental disequilibria, which would thereby be eliminated. No policy decisions would be needed with regard to the exchange rate and crises of confidence would be avoided. Exchange rates would move in a smooth fashion, in stark contrast to the sudden erratic jumps that came to be a feature of the Bretton Woods system.

It was recognized by advocates that current account and capital account disequilibria might persist in certain countries even with flexible rates, but it was argued that the pattern of such disequilibria would simply reflect the pattern of saving and investment throughout the world, with some countries being net exporters and others net importers of capital.

A second argument put forward in favour of flexible rates was that they would overcome the problem of asymmetrical adjustment, since not only would over-valued currencies depreciate but under-valued ones would appreciate. The deflationary bias in the world economy would thereby disappear.

Third, emphasis on the role of exchange rates in correcting payments disequilibria would reduce or remove the need for other payments policies, such as demand management and protectionism. Full employment of the world's resources as well as their efficient use would result. At the same time, there would be a not insignificant resource saving from governments being able to avoid intervention in foreign exchange markets. Furthermore, since countries would need to hold fewer reserves as a buffer against balance of payments deficits, the opportunity costs of holding these reserves could be avoided.

Fourth, advocates argued that speculation, rather than destabilizing the system as it had in the case of the Bretton Woods fixed rate regime, would fulfil a stabilizing role by preventing exchange rates from overshooting their fundamental equilibrium values. Over-valued currencies would be sold, thus reducing their value, and under-valued currencies would be bought, thus pushing up their value. In any case flexible rates would eliminate what had been the principal cause of speculation, i.e. large delayed discrete changes in exchange rates.

Finally, and again in stark contrast to the Bretton Woods system, flexible exchange rates were seen as offering a way in which countries could insulate their economies from destabilizing influences initiated abroad. Countries would be able to pursue their own independent policies. The greater consistency that this would permit in the conduct of domestic policy was seen as likely to lead to higher levels of real output in the long run.

Clearly an apparently compelling case for floating rates was mustered. Their basic appeal lay in the claim that the free market would efficiently achieve what exchange rate fixing had failed to achieve. Yet it needs to be recognized even at this juncture that flexible rates do not offer a costless way of correcting payments deficits. Where these have been caused by excess domestic absorption relative to domestic output and where domestic output cannot be increased, correction relies on reducing domestic absorption. In turn this means that consumption, investment, and/or government expenditure will have to be reduced, and such cuts imply real sacrifices. It is only if flexible exchange rates enable deficits to be corrected by inducing an increase in domestic output that the costs of adjustment in terms of reduced absorption may be avoided. However, even in these circumstances the fact remains that with a given level of output an economy will be enjoying a temporarily higher, real standard of living with a deficit than it would be without it.

3.2 Disadvantages

Although there were many grounds for believing that flexible exchange rates offered a superior alternative to fixed rates, their introduction in 1973 did not reflect a triumph of reasoning. Rather the fixed rate system had clearly become unsustainable and flexible rates were an expedient answer. Indeed, even accepting the deficiencies of fixed rates, some reservations about the operation of a flexible rate system existed.

First, there was the question of whether they would smoothly eliminate payments disequilibria. Much of the case for flexible rates had been made on the basis of their supposed impact on current account disequilibria. However, if foreign trade elasticities are low, large movements in exchange rates will be needed to correct disequilibria, and these may then have undesirable side effects, such as generating a more rapid rate of inflation in countries whose currencies depreciate; with elasticities less than one, disequilibria will not be corrected whatever the size of the exchange rate movement. Indeed one concern was that flexibility in nominal rates would not necessarily bring with it flexibility in real rates, since rates of inflation would modify to offset changes in nominal exchange rates. Furthermore, if trade elasticities are lower in the short run than in the long run, adjustment will be 'sticky'. Initially therefore exchange rates will 'overshoot' their longer run equilibrium values.

Although such overshooting could in principal be dampened by capital movements, a second reservation about flexible rates was that speculation would in fact be destabilizing rather than stabilizing. The fear here was that speculators would be poorly informed about long-run equilibrium exchange rates and would instead take a movement in any exchange rate in one direction as an indication that there would be a further movement in the same direction. In these circumstances profit-maximising speculators would sell depreciating currencies, thus making them depreciate even more, and would buy appreciating currencies, thus accentuating the appreciation. Far from a flexible rate system performing a useful smoothing function, it would lead, it was feared, to short-term capital movements making market rates extremely volatile. An implication of this view was that there was no presumption that market exchange rates would be any closer to their fundamental equilibrium values than official rates had been under the Bretton Woods system. The costs of currency misalignment might therefore persist under a flexible rate system whose principal advantage had been presented as their elimination.

Third, a further concern was that the uncertainty that would be associated with exchange rate volatility would have adverse effects on the growth of world trade. Traders would be encouraged to switch more of their business towards the home market. More generally, the traded sector of economies would be discriminated against and the non-traded sector would be relatively advantaged. Of course to some extent the risks of dealing in foreign currencies may be reduced by making use of the forward market, which enables the details of a deal to be fixed in advance. A trader due to receive a currency which may depreciate in value can sell it forward. However, risk cannot be offloaded at zero cost. Apart from the transactions cost, the forward price of a currency under the threat of depreciation will be below its current spot price, i.e. there will be a forward discount. Even with forward cover, then, there is an additional cost which may discriminate against trade. Of course not all traders throughout the world have access to forward markets; and for some deals the transactions costs may be prohibitive. For them the risk element associated with flexible exchange rates remains.

A fourth reservation about flexible rates was that the discipline on domestic economic management imposed by reserve losses would disappear. Unconstrained by the balance of payments, governments would pursue over-expansionary policies that would lead to an increase in the world rate of inflation. Apart from the acceleration in the global rate of inflation, the scope for a more independent approach to macroeconomic management would mean more variation in inflation rates throughout the world, reflecting the different policy priorities of governments. Dispersion in inflation rates would again mean that nominal exchange rates would be far from static but would move to reflect the differing rates of inflation. For this reason it was again argued that a flexible exchange rate system would be rather unstable.

A final concern was that governments would not be prepared to allow market forces to work. Instead it was felt that they would be seduced into managing exchange rates in an aggressive way in order to achieve competitive advantages. This in turn suggested that a code of practice would be needed as a basis for foreign exchange market intervention. Sceptics argued that while such guidelines might be required, there was little hope of them being successfully negotiated.

Given the debate over flexible exchange rates, it is clearly relevant to ask how the various arguments have stood up to experience. What lessons can be learnt from the period since 1973 during which a flexible rate system has been in operation?

4. EVALUATING THE EXPERIENCE WITH FLEXIBLE EXCHANGE RATES

An important point to underline at the outset is that the world's experience with flexible exchange rates since 1973 does not permit easy conclusions to be drawn. To make a meaningful comparison between fixed and flexible rate systems we would ideally like to find periods of time that were identical in all key respects other than the nature of the exchange rate regime. Differing economic performance could then be attributed to differences in the exchange rate system. Unfortunately, in the real world such comparisons never seem to present themselves.

The pitfall to avoid is to assume implicitly that 'other things' remain constant. For example, it is superficially appealing simply to examine world economic performance during the period 1962–72, when the Bretton Woods system of essentially fixed exchange rates operated, and compare this period with performance since 1973, when exchange rates have been flexible. What one discovers from such an exercise is that economic performance has been almost unambiguously inferior under the regime of flexible rates. Inflation and unemployment have been higher, the rate of economic growth and trade growth have been lower (if not negative in some years), and even the size of balance of payments disequilibria has been greater. Does this experience not condemn flexible exchange rates? The answer has to be not necessarily. There is no necessary reason to believe that economic performance would have been worse during 1962–72 had flexible rates been operating nor that it would have been better after 1973 had fixed rates remained. Indeed the limitations of the fixed rate system were clearly revealed by its inability to cope with the problems of the early 1970s and its eventual collapse. It is difficult to see how fixed rates could have survived beyond 1973. This observation suggests that exchange rate systems may be as much if not more a function of world economic performance than a cause of them. Correlation is not the same thing as causation.

Things after 1973 clearly did not remain as they had been beforehand. Rates of growth in some key economies were already beginning to decline, rates of inflation had begun to accelerate in the late 1960s and early 1970s, and with their increased openness economies had become more exposed to instability through both trade and speculative capital flows. Furthermore, technological advances in communications and growing financial sophistication meant that capital became more mobile. Add to this the implications of the large increases in oil prices, and the emergence of the newly industrializing countries as significant producers of manufactures, and it is clearly invalid to explain world economic performance since 1973 purely in terms of the exchange rate regime – though, as will be noted a little later, this may have contributed to it.

Some aspects of the post-1973 experience with flexible rates can be less ambiguously established. On any measure nominal exchange rates have been very volatile, and large short-run variations in exchange rates have occurred. By comparison with the average situation during the era of the Bretton Woods system, the exchange rates of the major industrial countries since 1973 have been almost ten times as variable. In addition to their increased volatility it is also generally accepted that exchange rate movements have been difficult to predict. The stability and predictability that some advocates claimed for floating rates have therefore not materialized.

The statistically observed volatility of exchange rates could imply two things. It might mean that fundamental equilibrium rates are themselves volatile and that nominal rates have moved quickly to validate such changes. On the other hand, it might mean that while fundamental equilibrium rates are relatively stable, for much of the time nominal rates do not equal fundamental equilibrium rates. Generally speaking, the factors determining fundamental equilibrium exchange rates, such as productivity growth, terms of trade movements, changes in savings, investment, and natural resource endowments, do not normally alter quickly and dramatically. While these factors may explain slow movements in exchange rates or even occasional large movements in a particular direction, it is difficult to see how they could explain a high degree of volatility. The conclusion which follows is that for much of the time since 1973 there has been considerable misalignment of currencies.

It is the failure of the market to find fundamental equilibrium exchange rates that is perhaps of more concern than this volatility itself, since, in addition to the costs of misalignment discussed earlier, there are other costs which may be specifically associated with misalignment under a flexible exchange rate system. These arise from the fact that currencies may be misaligned in different directions over quite a short period of time. The principal cost is that rather than having a constant set of inappropriate relative prices there will be ever-changing sets of inappropriate relative prices. People do not then know to which set they should respond. An extra element of uncertainty is created.

What are likely to be the implications of this uncertainty? The main one is that there is likely to be an under-utilization of resources rather than simply a misallocation of resources. The temptation will be to defer decisions until it is established whether exchange rate movements are temporary or permanent, and to shift resources into sectors where the uncertainty is less, namely, the non-traded goods sector. Such a shift of resources will have a number of macroeconomic implications. For example, evidence generally suggests that productivity growth is slower in the non-traded goods sector than in the traded goods sector. A reduced rate of productivity growth may in turn lead to reduced economic growth, an increased rate of inflation, and increased unemployment. Furthermore, it is likely to have an affect on the balance of payments and the future exchange rate. Even where the allocation of resources does change in response to changing price signals, reallocation will not be costless; indeed the costs are likely to be significant in capital, human, and social terms.

Moreover, responses to fundamental disequilibrium rates may be asymmetrical. Faced with an over-valued rate, de-industrialization may take place as exporters find difficulty in selling goods abroad and have difficulty in covering their variable costs of production. However, if the rate subsequently becomes under-valued, re-industrialization cannot be guaranteed, since at this stage fixed costs need to be taken into account by those setting up in business. Industrial decline associated with exchange over-valuation will not necessarily be replaced by industrial regeneration when the exchange rate falls. There will then be a downward ratchet effect and the industrial base may contract as the exchange rate fluctuates. There may also be a ratchet effect on inflation, with over-valuation of an exchange rate leading to subsequent depreciation, and an increase in the price level and possibly the rate of inflation, but undervaluation and subsequent appreciation not having an equivalent disinflationary impact, since expectations have adjusted to the more rapid inflation.

As noted above, the fact that trade growth has been much less rapid since flexible exchange rates were introduced does not in itself prove the argument that flexibility will adversely affect trade because of the uncertainty that results. However, neither does it seem to support the view that flexible rates remove the need for deflationary and protectionist policies. The issue here may again be that flexible rates have in practice failed to eradicate over- and under-valuation of currencies. Where a rate is over-valued, there will be pressures from home producers of tradeable goods for protection from foreign competition. However, if protectionist measures are introduced, there is no presumption that these will be removed when the exchange rate subsequently depreciates. Indeed under-valuation may simply encourage an expansion in the traded goods sector which is ill-founded in the long run and which merely results in further protectionism when the exchange rate rises again. For these reasons the co-existence of exchange instability, constrained trade growth, and increasing protection may be unsurprising. While the conventional uncertainty argument would clearly be consistent with slow trade growth, it does not directly explain the simultaneous rise in protectionism that occurred during the 1970s and 1980s.

Experience since 1973 also allows us to say something more about the debate over whether exchange rate flexibility will remove the deflationary bias in the world economy or cause an upsurge in global inflation. Yet again only somewhat tentative conclusions can be drawn. Flexible rates were initially accompanied by a rapid acceleration in inflation, but after the mid-1970s inflation began to decline. This would seem to suggest that factors other than the exchange rate regime are the principal determinants of inflation. Evidence drawn from the 1980s shows that there is no necessary reason why a flexible exchange rate system will be more inflationary than a fixed rate one.

It has already been mentioned that exchange rate volatility may have a demand-deflationary effect. Furthermore, some governments have given a high priority to avoiding inflation. They have therefore been anxious to avoid the inflationary implications of exchange rate depreciation. Indeed, inasmuch as flexible exchange rates tend to prevent domestic inflationary impulses from leaking abroad via increased imports, the desire to avoid domestic inflation will in one way imply a more deflationary bias under a flexible rate than under a fixed rate system. Certainly governments have shown themselves to be not indifferent about exchange rates, and the removal of fixed rates has not brought with it an expansionary free for all.

Although the desire to avoid inflation could in principle provide a reason for government intervention in foreign exchange markets, and although market forces have not always been left to operate freely, experience since 1973 is not consistent with the view that governments find it impossible to resist the temptation to play 'dirty' and continue aggressively to manipulate exchange rates. Intervention has in practice been much more passive and has usually only attempted to 'lean against the wind' and thereby moderate the exchange rate movements that would have otherwise occurred. Intervention has not generally set out to alter the direction in which exchange rates are moving but merely to alter the speed at which they move in any one direction.

Finally the evidence since 1973 does not support the claim that economies become more independent of and insulated from one another under flexible exchange rates. Nominal exchange rates have not moved in a way that fully compensates for differences in inflation rates, suggesting that inflationary pressures have continued to spread between countries and have not been completely neutralized by exchange rate changes. Furthermore, the economic performance of countries in terms of output, economic growth and employment has been quite closely correlated, suggesting interdependence.

In retrospect, there are logical reasons for anticipating that income trends will be correlated between countries even with floating rates. Demand may be more responsive over the short run to income changes than to price changes. The effects of an increase in domestic demand in one country on its imports – and thereby on the exports of other countries and their levels of aggregate demand – may take some time to be offset via exchange rate depreciation. Furthermore, if income changes are seen as temporary and not as a change in the trend, speculation will tend to keep the market exchange rate close to the trend. The deviations of income from trend may therefore be greater than the deviations of the exchange rate from its trend, with the result that income deviations will be transmitted abroad via the foreign trade sector. Business cycles will therefore still be synchronized.

It emerges from this review of experience that flexible exchange rates have not conclusively proved either their advocates or their critics to have been completely right. While the Bretton Woods exchange rate system would have been unable to cope with the economic disequilibria that were a feature of the post-1973 period, flexible rates have, for the reasons discussed above, failed to provide a perfect solution either. Market exchange rates have moved in a volatile, erratic, and largely unpredictable fashion, and have not always kept close to their fundamental equilibrium values. At the same time, the broad indicators of world economic performance have not behaved in the way that advocates had claimed they would. Where does this leave us with regard to the future choice of exchange rate system?

5. THE FUTURE EXCHANGE RATE SYSTEM: THE POLICY OPTIONS

There are numerous types of exchange rate regime that could in principle be adopted, ranging from universally and completely fixed rates at one end of the scale to universally and completely flexible rates at the other. Although the gold standard version of fixed rates still retains an appeal in some quarters, largely because of the supposed automaticity with which adjustment occurs, the fixed exchange rate system has been discredited in most eyes both in theory and practice. In theory there is little point in modifying a range of real variables such as output, employment and trade merely to ensure consistency with a random set of relative prices. In practice the rigidity of fixed rate systems in a setting of a dynamic world economy have meant that they have eventually had to be abandoned. Yet while the fixity of exchange rates may be a mistaken objective, their stability is not.

It is largely the instability and volatility of rates that has discredited the flexible exchange rate system. Certainly this has not provided an all-embracing answer to the world's balance of payments problems, as some of its most outspoken advocates had suggested it would. As the system has operated, it is clear that just as with the fixed rate system market rates can depart from their fundamental equilibrium values for protracted periods of time. Nor has the system been free from the destabilizing influences of speculation.

Of course it may quite simply be unrealistic to hanker after a perfect system. The community of nations may ultimately have to choose between systems that are imperfect in various ways, opting for the one that yields the greatest benefits or the lowest costs. However, there is no clear reason to believe that such a system must be based on either fixed or flexible rates. There are a number of alternatives which lie between these two extremes. Indeed, as noted earlier, even with the general agreement that the Bretton Woods system was too inflexible, there has been considerable disagreement about just how flexible exchange rates should be. If fixed rates are rejected, and yet at the same time it is felt that a free foreign exchange market in some way fails to generate a satisfactory solution, is there a case for a more conscious form of constrained or managed floating which attempts to avoid the problems associated with the other two systems?

5.1 Managed floating

The idea behind managed floating is to provide flexibility for exchange rates to change in response to 'economic fundamentals' and at the same time avoid some of the costs of a free foreign exchange market. As might be imagined, discussion of managed floating is essentially a debate over the pros and cons of market intervention by governments. The basic case for exchange rate management is that the authorities know better than private speculators what the appropriate exchange rate is. The exchange rate is seen as being too significant an economic variable to be left to the whims of the market because of the crucial effects it has on the real economy. However, critics argue that governments are unlikely to be better informed about fundamental equilibrium exchange rates than private speculators, and are therefore just as likely to intervene in a way that prevents these from being achieved. Managed floating is seen by critics as suffering from essentially the same shortcomings as does a fixed rate system.

Certainly the central issue with managed floating relates to the problem of estimating a set of fundamental equilibrium rates or, at least, 'target zones' around them. Once this has been done, intervention can relatively easily be used to keep the market rate inside the target zone, though a secondary problem is that of reaching general agreement on a set of rates between countries and of persuading governments to orientate their intervention towards moving market rates towards their equilibrium values. This will call for a more aggressive intervention policy than the more commonly used and passive one of simply 'leaning against the wind', i.e. moderating market excesses. Problems will clearly arise if different governments have different views about what is the fundamental equilibrium exchange rate between their currencies. Here intervention could become competitive, with one government trying to force the rate down and the other trying to force it up.

More generally, since the idea behind managed floating is to limit the degree of flexibility, to avoid excessive instability, and to avoid currency over- and under-valuation, it implies a need for some co-ordination of macroeconomic policies between countries. Constraining the flexibility of exchange rates itself constrains the range of other macroeconomic policies that will be consistent with balance of payments equilibria.[1] Since differential inflation rates are an important, though not exclusive, cause of nominal exchange rate movements, managed floating not least implies that governments need to control inflation.

Of course differential inflation is likely to persist to some extent under a system of managed floating and may indeed be used as one way of estimating the movements in nominal rates required to maintain fundamental equilibrium rates. However, factors other than differences in inflation rates will affect such rates. These factors include changes in the distribution of saving and investment throughout the world, which will influence the size and pattern of capital flows; changes in the terms of trade between product groups; and changes in the pressure of demand in different countries. Given information on all these variables, supporters of managed floating claim that it is not beyond the powers of the authorities to estimate a set of exchange rates that would enable countries to have a consistent set of balance of payments performances. Critics remain sceptical, pointing to the inability of authorities to identify fundamental equilibrium exchange rates in the past. However, the fact remains that governments do intervene in foreign exchange markets, or certainly would intervene in certain circumstances. Informally or subconsciously therefore they are working on the basis of target zones. Schemes for managed floating are merely attempting to formalize such procedures and to ensure that more rigorous thought is given to estimating fundamental equilibrium rates.

A related problem is that fundamental equilibrium exchange rates will not be static, they will change over time. Authorities will then need to monitor the situation continuously and modify target zones in the light of changes in economic fundamentals. Should the market rate become out of line with the fundamental equilibrium rate, a question arises as to how rapidly the authorities should try to eliminate the disequilibrium. Clearly there is an argument for rapid elimination, thus minimizing the amount of time during which trade takes place at 'false' prices. On the other hand, intervention by the authorities on a relatively large scale, and the associated rapid movements in exchange rates, may have destabilizing effects on confidence and on private speculation, and may adversely affect expectations. For example, a rapid depreciation may be more inflationary and generally more disruptive than a more gradual and measured slide would be.

The effects of private speculation within the context of a managed floating system are extremely significant. They depend on how speculators respond to official intervention. If they have confidence in the authorities' assessment of fundamental rates, they will act in a way that endorses the official view, and the need for and size of official intervention will to that extent be reduced. If, however, their view is that the authorities have miscalculated the fundamental equilibrium rate, their activities will compete with official intervention policy. Should the authorities lose such a competition because they possess fewer resources to back up their view than do private speculators, this will adversely affect future confidence in the system. Experience suggests that it is unrealistic to assume simply that speculation will be stabilizing. The implication of this is that if a system of managed floating is to be introduced, it needs to be supported by sufficient official liquidity. It would be a mistake to ignore the implications that changing the exchange rate regime has on the demand for reserves.

5.2 Sliding parties or crawling pegs

While exchange rate management attempts to constrain the volatility of exchange rates within the context of basically floating rates, sliding parity or crawling peg regimes attempt to increase the flexibility of exchange rates within the context of basically fixed rates. Under a crawling peg system there is an official rate, even though this may be changed quite frequently.

Although there are a number of variants of the crawling peg system, the general idea behind all of them is that exchange rates change slowly and gradually, such that speculative disturbances – primarily associated with large infrequent changes – are minimized. Exchange rates would change at a speed of say 0.15 per cent per month. Losses incurred by holding a depreciating currency would then be offset by offering holders of the currency a positive interest rate differential. Crawling could occur automatically, with official rates being based on a moving average of market rates or on the level of reserve holdings; alternatively, discretionary changes could be made with no agreed formula being used.

However, although offering more flexibility than does a fixed rate system, crawling pegs mean that the authorities have to direct domestic monetary policy towards achieving interest rates that will prevent capital outflows by compensating for expected exchange rate depreciation in conditions where they will not have full control over the domestic money supply. Even if they can control the domestic money supply, they have to be prepared to use monetary policy to achieve external rather than internal objectives – though the exchange rate will have repercussions for the domestic economy. Furthermore, if the speed at which exchange rates crawl is less than the speed at which disequilibria arise, confidence in the system will falter. Crawling pegs are more attractive if introduced at a time when fundamental equilibrium exchange rates exist and if disequilibria only arise at a crawling rate. They do not provide a means of dealing with large disequilibria or disequilibria that are highly unstable.

5.3 Wider bands

Another scheme for providing more flexibility within the context of a fixed rate system is to widen the margins around the par or central value within which currencies can move, thereby essentially internalizing flexibility within the band. In principle wider bands can provide considerable scope for the value of one currency to move relative to that of another, as one currency moves from the top of its band to the bottom and the other currency moves from the bottom of its band to the top. The increased flexibility in exchange rates would enable countries to pursue domestic policies more independently. For example, a country would be able to push its interest rate below the world level for domestic reasons; the exchange rate would depreciate to the bottom of the band and investors from abroad would be compensated by the resulting expected appreciation. Indeed advocates of the scheme maintained that it would encourage stabilizing speculation. Speculators seeing a currency's value arrive at the bottom of its band would expect an appreciation and would therefore buy up the currency, and this in turn would cause the expectation to be fulfilled. Indeed then introduction of wider bands has often been presented as a means of increasing the incentive to speculate in a stabilizing way by increasing the profits from such activity and at the same time increasing the losses for destabilizing speculation. However, this stabilizing effect depends crucially on speculators being persuaded about the long-term viability of the central value. If instead they expect not an appreciation but a devaluation of the central value, they will continue to sell rather than to buy the currency. Here the authorities will have to run down reserves at least in the short run and will effectively have to compete against the private speculators, hoping ultimately to alter their view of likely exchange rate movements.

Although one's assessment of wider bands depends to some extent on how wide the bands are, the experience with their use as part of the Smithsonian Agreement provides little reason for believing that they are likely to provide any fundamental improvement in the operation of a fixed rate regime.

There have also been proposals for combining wider bands and sliding parities, and thus for having sliding bands.

5.4 Joint floating and monetary integration

Rather than all countries adopting flexible rates or all countries adopting fixed rates there may be some circumstances under which a group of countries agrees to maintain relatively fixed rates between themselves but a flexible rate with the rest of the world. The countries in the group will use some form of 'monetary integration'. This is a conceptually weak term, since it can mean different things. It normally incorporates some form of exchange rate union and free convertibility. Monetary union may in turn include the establishment of a new reference (or even a common) currency, a reserve fund to provide member countries with balance of payments finance, and a high degree of policy co-ordination, with ultimately, perhaps, only one set of monetary and fiscal authorities. As a first step, on the other hand, it may merely constitute a commitment to peg exchange rates.

Having defined monetary integration, we must now identify the features that characterize a group of countries between which it might occur. This reduces to listing the factors that define optimum currency areas.

5.4.1 Optimum currency areas

A general guideline here is that an optimum currency area will exist between countries which are either unlikely to have to adjust or may easily and at relatively little cost adjust by means other than altering exchange rates. Over the years a number of criteria for demarcating optimum currency areas have been suggested.

The first relates to the degree of factor mobility. Countries between which there is considerable mobility of both capital and labour are candidates for exchange rate union, since factor mobility substitutes for exchange rate flexibility. For example, if in a two-country world one country has a trade deficit and excess labour supply and the other country has a trade surplus and excess labour demand, labour migrates from the first to the second country. This both alleviates the labour market disequilibria in the two countries and corrects the balance of trade disequilibria, since what was formerly home demand in the first country now becomes export demand and what was formerly export demand in the second country now becomes home demand. Clearly there are a number of implicit assumptions here, including the assumption that labour is homogeneous and may equally well be employed in either country to produce any good, and also that labour is demanded in a fixed proportion to output, i.e. that there are fixed technical coefficients. But if these assumptions are valid, then the need to alter the exchange rate between the two countries to induce a change in the pattern of expenditure can be avoided.

With well developed and integrated capital markets, capital may also move rather than exchange rates. Trade deficits are offset by capital inflows, which may ultimately result in a changing level and pattern of output in the capital-importing and capital-exporting countries eliminating the trade deficit and surplus.

A second criterion for delineating optimum currency areas relates to the openness of the economies concerned. With open economies which possess high propensities to import, the less will be the amount of demand deflation required to correct a deficit or demand expansion required to correct a deficit; the more will be the impact of exchange rate variations on the domestic price level, and possibly on the rate of inflation; and the greater will be the number of transactions to which exchange rate uncertainty will apply. The greater will therefore be the incentive to adopt a fixed exchange rate. Furthermore, the higher the degree of trade inter-penetration between the countries, the greater will be the advantages from a fixed exchange rate, since the benefits from certainty will apply to a larger proportion of the total trade of the countries concerned.

A third criterion relates to the commodity and geographical diversification of trade. Where there is a significant diversity in the range of products a country produces, the law of large numbers will operate to reduce the likelihood that adjustment, and therefore exchange rate changes, will be required. Or again, if a country's trade is geographically diversified with other countries in the group, it will be protected from shocks emanating from trading partners, and exchange rate changes are less likely to be required. Indeed to the extent that random shocks within the union offset one another, the common exchange rate – vis-à-vis the rest of the world will be relatively stable, and this will make the price level inside the union more stable than it might otherwise be.

A fourth criterion relates to the similarity of governmental priorities between key macroeconomic policy objectives. If a group of countries face similar trade-offs between, say, inflation and unemployment, and left to themselves individual governments would choose a similar location on this trade-off, then similar inflation rates will result and the policies will be consistent from a balance of payments point of view. But if different countries face different trade-offs or if they select different combinations of inflation and unemployment, then initially their policies will result in payments disequilibria. The financial flows generated by such disequilibria under fixed exchange rates will eventually tend to eliminate the divergences, but this means that countries will have to be prepared to accept rates of inflation and levels of unemployment that they do not regard as optimal. In order to comply with external constraints they will be sacrificing internal objectives.[2] The problems created by trying to pursue divergent policies within a group of countries with fixed exchange rates provides an argument for monetary and fiscal harmonization, but this may be difficult to arrange. Of course the need to eliminate deficits and surpluses will be less marked if a fairly permanent redistribution of income from surplus to deficit countries within the group is accepted. But such regional assistance is usually less acceptable between countries than within them. One implication is that the asymmetry of adjustment associated with fixed rate systems may be internalized within the monetary union, and a deflationary bias result.

Finally, but more generally, the more effective and cost-efficient exchange rate variations are at correcting balance of payments disequilibria, the more reluctant will countries be to give up this policy instrument. On the other hand, in circumstances where exchange rate changes are ineffective, because of low trade elasticities perhaps or a high degree of real wage resistance, or inefficient, because disequilibria have perhaps arisen from domestic financial mismanagement, countries may be more prepared to engage in monetary integration.

The world has some experience with monetary integration in the form of the European Monetary System established in 1979 and its predecessor the so-called 'snake'. The basic idea within the EMS is to sell over-valued currencies in order to buy under-valued ones and thereby maintain a system of essentially fixed rates between the members of the EMS.

Unfortunately, the experience with the EMS is not unambiguous. On the one hand, its admirers claim that it has stabilized exchange rates amongst the member countries as compared with what would otherwise have happened. By constraining exchange rate volatility the EMS is claimed to have reduced inflation and unemployment and to have provided a better environment for trade growth amongst its members. The relatively poor performance of the UK economy by comparison with other European countries is attributed to the fact that the UK did not join the EMS.

On the other hand, critics see the experience as supporting their claims that the EMS is subject to the same deficiencies as any fixed rate system. The fact that some of the initial exchange rates have had to be altered is taken as illustrating the view that countries will not be prepared to subjugate domestic policy objectives simply in order to maintain a particular exchange rate. Once it is recognized within the member countries that exchange rates can and will be altered, critics argue, any benefits that the EMS might have had will be lost. While admirers therefore see the EMS as the shape of things to come, critics see it as facing impending collapse.

Of course, given the continuing debate over fixed and flexible rate systems, it is hardly surprising that the EMS generates this ambivalent response. In practice it is very difficult to try and avoid simultaneously both the costs of fixed rates as well as the costs of flexible rates. Any compromise based on some form of limited flexibility is likely to be open to the accusations that it is either too flexible or too fixed.

5.5 Optimal pegs

Before leaving this review of exchange rate options, we should note that the move over to generalized floating amongst the industrial countries of the world in 1973 created a particular problem for developing countries in terms of their own exchange rate policy. If developing countries reject a floating rate because their capital and foreign exchange markets are small and poorly developed, then they clearly opt to peg their exchange rates. But to what should they peg the value of their currencies?

Under a generalized fixed rate regime this does not matter too much, since by pegging to one major currency they are in effect pegging to all the others. But this is not the case with generalized floating. If a developing country pegs to one currency which then depreciates, the country has effectively also depreciated against all the other principal world currencies. A fixed nominal rate in terms of one currency does not now imply that the effective exchange rate will be fixed unless all foreign trade dealings are in that one currency. Where trade is diversified, the effective exchange rate will depreciate. The depreciation may not be called for from the viewpoint of the developing country and may merely destabilize the economy. Rather than peg one nominal rate, therefore, the country may be better advised to try and peg its effective exchange rate to a basket of currencies or to the SDR, whose value represents the weighted average value of the five principal world currencies. In these circumstances the effects of exchange rate changes amongst the major currencies on the developing country will tend to cancel one another out. However, the cost of gaining a greater degree of macroeconomic stability through pegging to a basket of currencies is the loss of stability in any one nominal exchange rate. To what extent the benefits outweigh the costs depends very much on the pattern and concentration of the developing country's trade and its future trading plans.

6. EXCHANGE RATE DETERMINATION: A POSTSCRIPT

Our main focus in this chapter is on the merits and demerits of different exchange rate *systems*. However, one of the main implications of moving over to flexible rates has been that a great deal of attention has been focused on trying to find out what factors determine exchange rates under free markets. Ideas have evolved at a rapid rate, with different models making different assumptions and reaching different conclusions. From the range of theories available there is beginning to emerge an attempt to provide a synthesis of ideas, although the search for a general theory of exchange rate determination remains to be finished. Unfortunately, the empirical testing of the various theories has been of only limited assistance. In the main it has performed only the negative function of casting doubt on many of the ideas that have been put forward. However, as will be seen at the end of this section, which may be regarded as an appendix to the rest of the chapter, it is possible to draw some positive policy conclusions even from largely negative empirical results.

Of course at a superficial level it is very easy to 'explain' how exchange rates are determined. After all, they are simply the relative prices of different currencies and as such result from the interplay of demand and supply in foreign exchange markets which, because of arbitrage, can be treated as one market. Starting from a situation of equilibrium in the foreign exchange market, excess demand or excess supply of a currency arises, disequilibrium exists at the old exchange rate and the exchange rate appreciates or depreciates. The change in the exchange rate continues and modifies the demand for and supply of currencies until equilibrium is restored. Just as with any market model, the sign of the exchange rate change depends on the source of the original disturbance, whether it affects the demand for or the supply of the currency, and the size of the change depends on the price elasticity of the demand and supply schedules.

The problem of explaining how exchange rates are determined does not, then, come from a difficulty in finding a satisfactory basic analytical framework. Instead it comes from trying to explain what factors influence the demand and supply of currencies in the foreign exchange market, and in estimating the various coefficients which relate changes in demand and supply to changes in these determinants.

Although some models of the exchange rate become rather complex, the basic approaches to analysing the balance of payments, i.e. structural, absorption and monetary, may equally well be applied to analysing the exchange rate, since disequilibriating forces are now reflected not by payments disequilibria but by movements in exchange rates.

6.1 Structural and absorption approaches

The structural explanation focuses on the changing pattern of demand and supply of goods in different countries resulting from, for example, changing tastes, different or varying income elasticities of demand, changing costs of production and technological progress, and resource discoveries. This approach therefore identifies 'real' factors and current account disequilibria as being the principal sources of exchange rate changes. However, if the approach is re-interpreted as looking at the differing patterns of saving and investment across countries, then it clearly has a corollary in the capital account, through which excess saving in some countries is transmitted to other countries with excess investment.

The absorption approach also focuses on the real economy and real variables. Here excess domestic absorption relative to domestic output results in exchange depreciation, and excess output relative to absorption results in appreciation. Again the emphasis is on the flow of goods and services and therefore on the current account as the main source of exchange rate changes. The capital account can be incorporated into such an approach, since disequilibrium in the real sector of the economy will have implications for the financial sector and for interest rates, and changes in these will affect capital flows. For example, whereas an increase in government expenditure which is financed by borrowing will increase the interest rate and induce a capital inflow, an increase financed by extra credit creation will not.

However, while the capital account can be integrated into the absorption approach, capital movements are viewed as being only a secondary influence on the exchange rate. Furthermore, they are treated as flows which will continue for as long as there is an incentive in the form of an interest rate differential. The current account remains the centre of attention.

What predictions about the behaviour of exchange rates follow on from such explanations of their determination? First, the impact of shifts in currency demand or supply schedules on the exchange rate will depend on a range of foreign trade elasticities. If these are low, a shift in one of the schedules may clearly be associated with a significant movement in the exchange rate. If elasticities are relatively high, however, smaller changes in exchange rates will be needed to restore balance of payments equilibrium. Moreover, if elasticities are lower in the short run than they are in the long run, an exchange rate may initially 'overshoot' on its path towards its new long-run equilibrium. Such overshooting may make rates appear rather volatile. Second, however, the structural and absorption approaches to exchange rate determination do not predict extreme volatility, largely because the factors that are viewed as causing the underlying changes in the demand for and supply of goods and services themselves only change slowly. Furthermore, analysis of changes in demand- and supply-side determinants and of foreign trade elasticities would allow both the direction and size of exchange rate changes to be anticipated.

Yet, as observed earlier in this chapter, key aspects of exchange rate movements since 1973 have been their volatility and unpredictability. Approaches based exclusively on the real sectors of economies and on the current account may therefore leave something to be desired.

6.2 The monetary approach

Mirroring the monetary approach to the balance of payments, a monetary explanation of exchange rate changes has also evolved. This approach incorporates a number of features.

First, an exchange rate is seen as the relative price of two monies. From this observation it follows that exchange rate changes can be explained by changes in the relative demand and supply of monies. Let us take the sterling/dollar exchange rate as an example. If the supply of sterling is increased relative to the demand for it at the same time as monetary sector equilibrium is maintained in the United States, then the price of sterling in terms of dollars will fall, i.e. sterling will depreciate against the dollar.

Second, exchange rate changes are seen as arising from *stock* disequilibria in the monetary sector, even though these stock disequilibria may be translated into an excess *flow* demand or *flow* supply of goods and services.

Third, the effects of excess domestic money supply growth on domestic prices is brought in via the concept of purchasing power parity (PPP). This claims that nominal exchange rates alter in response to differential rates of inflation in order to maintain real exchange rates. Prices in one country will equal those in another country when expressed in a common currency, i.e. the purchasing power of different currencies will be equalized. Thus, if a particular good costs £1 in the UK and \$1.50 in the US, the nominal exchange rate between sterling and dollars will settle at \$1.50 per £1 or £0.66 per \$1.

The various elements of the monetary approach may be illustrated by the following set of equations, where letters with the superscript * refer to values in the USA and letters without superscripts refer to values in the UK. The demand for money coefficient k is assumed to be the same in both countries. Then,

$$M = kPY$$
$$M^* = kP^*Y^*$$
$$P^* = E\,P \text{ and } E = \frac{P^*}{P}$$

$$\text{therefore E} = \frac{M^*/kY^*}{M/kY}$$

$$= \frac{M^*kY}{MkY^*}$$

It follows that, starting from a given exchange rate, an increase in the UK money supply will result in a sterling depreciation which completely offsets the effect that the induced increase in the UK price level has on both the UK and US balance of payments. There is no import leakage with floating rates and no change in reserves.

As with monetary explanations of many economic phenomena, perhaps the principal appeal of this approach is its apparent simplicity. It seems to offer an unambiguous and unicausal explanation of exchange rate changes. But appearances can be deceptive. As with the monetary approach to the balance of payments, it rests on a number of restrictive assumptions about the exogeneity of the money supply, the stability of the demand for money and the invariance of output. Furthermore, the PPP doctrine has a number of deficiencies. First, not all goods are tradeable and where there is a significant non-tradeable sector, price levels may not be equalized. Second, it does not say anything specifically about causation; is it differential inflation rates which cause exchange rate movements or exchange rate movements which cause differential inflation? Third, it implies that nominal rates will change only in response to differences in inflation rates. This in turn means that fundamental equilibrium real exchange rates do not change through time as a result of other influences, which seems rather unlikely. Fourth, it implies perfect arbitrage. Fifth, most of the empirical evidence is inconsistent with PPP, although, as will be seen in a moment, there is a counter-claim that PPP is a long-run phenomenon, and that it is therefore not surprising to find little evidence of it holding in the short run.

Although the monetary approach emphasizes the key role of the stock of money, it is still consistent with a largely current account explanation of exchange rate changes, with an excess supply of money being reflected in an excess demand for goods. However, money may be demanded as an asset as well as a medium of exchange. Focusing on the asset demand for money shifts attention towards the capital account as the source of exchange rate changes.

6.3 The asset market approach

In a sense the asset market approach to exchange rate determination is an extension and sophistication of the monetary approach. It suggests that it is the interaction between the stocks of monies as assets and the preferences of asset-holders that dominates the determination of exchange rates.

The principal factors influencing the demand for different monies as assets are, first, relative interest rates, and, second, expected movements in exchange rates. Demand for any particular currency will strengthen as the interest rate differential in its favour widens and as the size of the expected appreciation increases.

Given these determinants and that in equilibrium the world's stock of monies has to be willingly held, what condition will ensure such asset – stock equilibrium? Assuming that holders regard assets in different countries as perfect substitutes the condition is that:

$$ER^e - ER^a = i^* - i$$

where ER^e is the expected exchange rate, ER^a is the actual exchange rate, i^* is the foreign interest rate and i is the home interest rate.

In other words, the expected exchange rate change equals the interest rate differential. If the interest rate in one country is below that on offer abroad, holders of the currency will need to feel that the value of the currency will rise sufficiently to compensate them for the interest rate disadvantage to which they are exposed. The system will always tend towards this condition, even if it does not initially hold. If the anticipated appreciation does not compensate for the interest rate disadvantage, the currency will be sold and the actual exchange rate ER^a will depreciate until the difference between this rate and the expected future rate ER^e, i.e. the expected appreciation, is big enough.

In the context of the asset market approach, changing the stock of different assets affects interest rate differentials and thereby expected exchange rate changes. But what is the relation between expected future movements in exchange rates and current movements in the spot rate? If the rate is expected to appreciate in the future, this will increase the current demand for the currency and the spot rate will therefore rise. It will continue to rise for as long as appreciation is expected. The spot rate will therefore rise by the full extent of the expected appreciation.

6.3.1 Expectations and exchange rates

Expectations are then a central part of the asset market approach. But how are they formed? This is a question of some general interest not only with respect to the analysis of exchange rates. There are a number of possibilities. First, it may simply be expected that the current rate will persist. Second, past changes in the exchange rate may lead to the expectation that future changes in the same direction will occur either at the same rate or at a faster or slower rate. Third, dealers may have a notion of what is the 'normal' rate and will expect the rise to move towards it. They would then expect any movement away from the normal rate to be reversed.

The first two methods by which expectations are formed rely exclusively on examining the past performance of the exchange rate. But is this rational? An alternative assumption is that the market will use all the information that is available to it at the time that the expectation is formed. This will include not only historical information but also current and anticipated future developments. Since news is continually becoming available, expectations will be continually modified in the light of fresh information. Moreover, if news is unpredictable and volatile, so will be exchange rates. To argue that exchange rates are determined by expectations and that exchange rate volatility reflects the volatility of expectations may be accurate but gets us no further in providing an explanation upon which predictions can be based.

6.3.2 Overshooting

One attempt to provide a more formal explanation of exchange rate volatility, and of the fact that PPP does not appear to hold, suggests that different prices adjust to disequilibria at different speeds. More specifically it is suggested that while asset prices adjust instantaneously, goods prices adjust only slowly.

Having made this key assumption, let us further assume that an economy is in equilibrium in terms of the asset-stock equilibrium condition discussed earlier. Now assume that there is an unforeseen increase in the domestic money supply. This results in an immediate fall in the domestic rate of interest (since asset prices rise instantaneously) and a *gradual* increase in the price level (since goods prices rise only slowly). However, since a rise in the price level will be expected, so will be the exchange depreciation required to restore purchasing power parity. The combination of low interest rates and expected exchange rate depreciation will lead to an immediate capital outflow and an immediate depreciation. In order to restore asset–stock equilibrium in circumstances where the domestic interest rate is below the world level an expected exchange rate appreciation is necessary. But since the new long-run nominal equilibrium exchange rate is lower than it was before the money supply was increased, it follows that such an expectation will only be formed if the exchange rate initially falls below, or overshoots, its new long-run equilibrium.

As goods prices gradually rise and nominal income rises, the nominal demand for money will rise, as will the nominal interest rate. The negative interest rate differential will close and the required expected exchange rate appreciation will therefore be less. Eventually, and with no further shocks to the system, the new set of equilibrium values will be reached, with the ultimate fall in the nominal exchange rate just offsetting the increase in prices. For a time during the adjustment process the interest rate, prices and the exchange rate will all be rising – a combination inconsistent with many other models of exchange rate determination, including PPP. In this model of exchange rate overshooting, PPP holds only in the long run.

6.3.3 Forward markets

The asset market approach to exchange rate determination has some interesting implications for the relation between the spot market and the forward market. Forward markets in foreign exchange enable traders and investors to sell the risk associated with exchange rate variations. They can therefore fix the parameters of any deal by covering forward and securing a 'closed' rather than an 'open' position. However, they will get a poorer rate of exchange in the forward market than they would do in the current spot market; there will be a forward discount. Eliminating their risk is not costless.

Arbitrage will tend to ensure that the forward discount on a currency's exchange rate equals the interest rate differential between the two countries concerned, a state of affairs called closed or covered interest rate parity. Thus, and again looking at it on the basis of the asset market approach, if interest rates are higher in the US than in the UK, UK investors will be tempted to switch sterling into dollars and to make loans in the US rather than in the UK, entering into future contracts to sell a specified amount of dollars in exchange for sterling at the forward exchange rate, which will give a lower sterling price for dollars than the current spot rate. Making loans in the US will be preferred for as long as the forward discount on dollars does not offset the interest rate advantage in the US. But the impact of the transactions will be to lower US interest rates, raise UK interest rates, and cause the price of dollars on the forward market to depreciate until interest rate parity is achieved.

The interesting thing is that the condition for asset–stock equilibrium states that the expected change in the exchange rate equals the interest rate differential. It follows therefore that the forward discount (or premium) on a currency equals the expected spot market depreciation (or appreciation), or, what comes to the same thing, the forward rate is equal to the expected future spot rate. Expectations may of course not be fulfilled and the spot rate in three months' time may not actually equal the value predicted on the basis of the forward rate, since extra news which will affect the spot rate will become available in the intervening time.

In circumstances where investors do not regard assets in different countries as perfect substitutes for one another, i.e. where there is imperfect capital mobility, or where there are significant transactions costs, neither interest rate parity nor the asset–stock equilibrium condition will hold.

Of course if one group of transactors is selling risk in the forward foreign exchange market, another group must be taking it on. These are the 'speculators' who set out to make profits through variations in the spot price of currencies. If they sell a currency forward, their hope is that they will be able to buy it in three months' time (or whatever the length of the forward contract is) more cheaply. Speculation requires holding an open or uncovered position. As more traders wish to sell a currency forward, so the forward rate will drop. The forward discount is the incentive needed to persuade speculators to take on the risk of buying the currency forward. Where the forward discount required to clear the forward market exceeds the interest rate differential, speculators are in effect being offered a 'risk premium', and the forward rate may not indicate the expected future spot rate.

6.4 Synthesising the approaches: some tentative conclusions

So what does determine exchange rates? Although the asset market approach undoubtedly provides certain insights by drawing attention to the importance of the capital account, stock adjustments and expectations, it has a number of limitations. First, assets in different countries are surely unlikely to be regarded as perfect substitutes. Expected exchange rate changes will not therefore correspond exactly to interest rate differentials, interest parity will not hold and currencies will carry risk premia (portfolio balance models of the exchange rate which attempt to deal with this weakness have been developed). Second, asset prices may not adjust instantaneously; instead they themselves may be sticky. Third, goods prices may adjust more rapidly than is assumed by the theory, or there may be asymmetries in the speed of adjustment, with prices moving more quickly upwards than downwards. Fourth, if goods prices do not respond to financial stock disequilibria, it may be that real output does. It may therefore be real income that changes rather than prices. Recognising the possibility that output may change brings into consideration a whole range of 'real' factors affecting the level of capacity utilization and aggregate supply as potential determinants of exchange rates – the real economy has been too readily ignored in recent exchange rate models. Again leading on from this, and fifth, it seems unwise to ignore either the current or the capital account, not least because the two are interrelated. For example, an increase in investment which influences domestic absorption and the current account will increase the volume of assets in an economy and may therefore affect the capital account via the asset market mechanism. Or again an increase in government expenditure – another component of domestic absorption – unmatched by increased taxation leads to an increase in assets and liabilities. The implications for expenditure depend on the responses of those acquiring the extra assets and liabilities. These may not be symmetrical.

What one is left with is a feeling that monetary models of the exchange rate beg as many questions as they answer. Indeed they may be seen as failing to answer the really fundamental questions or as providing at best only an approximate answer. What is needed is an explanation which accomodates all the various real and financial variables likely to exert some influence over the exchange rate. In the absence of such a model it is unwise to base exchange rate policy exclusively on any one of the existing models, which both in terms of their theoretical underpinning and empirical support seem to be incomplete.

The basics of such a synthesizing model might be as follows. Exchange rate changes are caused by something disturbing what is an initial state of macroequilibrium. The disturbance may emanate from the demand side or the supply side of the economy, or from outside the economy, and it may reflect financial or real changes, i.e. it may occur as a result of a change in any factor that helped to determine the initial equilibrium. The response to disequilibrium may be reflected by changes not only in the exchange rate but in other macroeconomic variables as well, but these are likely to interact with the exchange rate. Short-run changes in the variables affected may differ from long-run changes if, as seems likely, they adjust at different speeds. Adjustment speeds and indeed the scope for adjustment in particular macroeconomic variables may differ both within and between countries – for example, there may be more real wage resistance in some countries than in others. Furthermore, the level of capacity utilization will be important; full employment cannot simply be assumed. The extent to which different variables change will depend on a range of supply factors as well as demand factors, such as price and income elasticities and elasticities of substitution between money, goods and assets. In what ways, for instance, will people choose to dispose of excess cash balances, and what will influence their choice?

As yet economic theory has failed to cope with the complexity of the real world and our understanding of many macroeconomic phenomena, including the exchange rate, is limited.

Part IV
The Political Economy of World Financial Reform

11 The Interests of Developing Countries in World Financial Reform

1. INTRODUCTION

Previous chapters have taken a rather global view, implying that all countries have similar interests in the full range of reform proposals. This is far from the truth. Though all countries benefit from a stable and efficiently operating set of international financial arrangements, common interest often ends there. Individual countries and groups of countries have their own preferences, based on their private costs and benefits. If a dollar standard confers private benefits on the United States, it is hardly surprising if the US resists moves to strengthen the SDR, unless as a means of strengthening the demand for the dollar.

Rather than look at the position of all the significant country groups in international financial negotiations, this chapter concentrates on the special interests of developing countries. This seems appropriate, given the attention that has been focused on them, with calls for a new international economic order and the various proposals of the Brandt Commission.

The layout of the chapter is as follows. It starts by examining the extent to which developing countries may legitimately be regarded as a special case in international financial reform. It then goes on to examine various means by which special assistance might be offered to this group of countries through the international financial system. In the process the chapter draws on many of the ideas introduced and discussed earlier in the book.

One very important conclusion needs to be stressed at the outset, namely that the use of the collective phrase 'developing countries' implies a homogeneity of interests that rarely exists. During the 1970s and early 1980s this was perhaps particularly true if developing countries were defined to include OPEC, since many OPEC members were creditors in the system, whereas most other developing countries were debtors. However, important distinctions also exist between the higher- and middle-income developing countries, on the one hand, and the low-income and least-developed countries, on the other. The former have been the principal recipients of commercial credit and have been the countries in which debt problems have most visibly arisen. At the same time, and as data in Chapter 2 showed, their economic performance during the 1970s was in many ways stronger than that in many other groups of countries – certainly stronger than that in the low-income countries, which received relatively little commercial credit and became the principal clients of the IMF at the beginning of the 1980s.

Again, however, these sub-classifications conceal important differences between individual countries. Not all middle-income countries have encountered severe debt problems, while India's position in the international financial system, say, is very different from that of Bangladesh, even though both countries may appear in many lists of low-income countries.

In practice most of this chapter relates to the low-income countries, since reforms to help deal with the debt problems of the better-off developing countries were discussed in Chapter 8.

2. DEVELOPING COUNTRIES AS A SPECIAL CASE IN INTERNATIONAL FINANCIAL REFORM

Over the years there has been a growing feeling among members of the international community that developing countries encounter international financial problems different either in kind or in degree from those encountered by industrial countries. In recognition of this, a number of financing facilities have been introduced by the IMF primarily to help developing countries.[1] The Committee of Twenty took the view that developing countries required and warranted special treatment, and subsequently the Development Committee (formally the Joint Ministerial Committee of the Fund and World Bank on the Transfer of Real Resources to Developing Countries) has been charged with examining ways to encourage an additional flow of resources to developing countries.

The argument that developing countries are a special case is based on a number of points. Fundamentally, these relate to their vulnerability to balance of payments shocks, and to their ability to cope with disequilibria and the consequent adjustment costs. The decline in the terms of trade of developing countries was examined in Chapter 2. Their supposed balance of payments vulnerability rests heavily on the claim that export receipts are relatively unstable. The factual basis for this claim is not clear-cut, and differences exist both between countries and over time, but perhaps on balance the available evidence tends to support it. The ability of developing countries to cope with the related deficits depends on their access to financing and on their capacity to correct their balance of payments. Again, in this context there are marked differences between countries that, by convention, are grouped together. For those developing countries entering the post-1973 period with relatively large reserve holdings or regarded as being creditworthy by international commercial banks, financing offered a practical as well as theoretical short-term alternative. For others, in particular the low-income countries, the financing option has in effect not been available, and they have had to adjust.

The method of adjustment adopted has frequently been to contract import volume, and this, in turn, has had a deleterious effect on the growth of per capita gross national product (GNP). Adjustment through export expansion has been made more difficult by the low levels of demand and increasing protectionism in industrial countries. Furthermore, to the extent that more developing countries attempt to adjust in this manner, it tends to become a less feasible alternative.

For a number of reasons developing countries feel that post-war international monetary arrangements have discriminated against them: first, in terms of the distribution of the adjustment burden, which puts greater pressure on deficit countries than on surplus countries to adjust, especially deficit countries that have limited scope for financing; and second, in terms of the distribution of the seigniorage associated with the creation of international reserves, which has not gone to them but to richer countries. An important component of the new international economic order desired by many developing countries is that changes in the international monetary system be designed to direct a larger share of the benefits of its operation to developing countries. Whether this simultaneously implies a real sacrifice for industrial countries depends on whether the reforms improve the monetary system's efficiency. The importance of distinguishing clearly between efficiency and equity reaffirms itself throughout the discussion below.

3. MECHANISM FOR ASSISTING DEVELOPING COUNTRIES

3.1 The SDR link

The general arguments both in favour of the link and against it are well documented in the literature. Rather than presenting an overview of these, therefore, this section addresses itself to a more limited number of questions that are nevertheless both fundamental and topical in the light of the changes in the SDR described in Chapter 5. These are:

(i) What factors determine the benefits to developing countries from a link?
(ii) Is there a case for having a market-equivalent rate of interest on SDRs and does the existence of such an interest rate rule out the possibility that developing countries will gain from a link?
(iii) What form of link will developing countries favour, and is this form likely to prove attractive to industrial countries?

Before moving on to these questions, however, let us make a number of more general points. First, the link is a device intended to provide additional aid, redistributing the world's wealth in favour of developing countries. Second, the method by which the link attempts to obtain this result is by allocating all or part of the seigniorage associated with the creation of international reserves to developing countries. Third, there may be incidental, but probably relatively insignificant, benefits for industrial countries in terms of an increase in exports, output, and employment; not only will world wealth be redistributed but it may also increase. Fourth, although the claim that the link will be inflationary is theoretically correct, especially in conditions of world full employment, all quantitative studies agree that the size of this effect is likely to be small, even for surplus countries. Fifth, the link raises political as well as economic issues, as it poses questions relating to the democratic control of aid flows; many versions take the associated aid outside the control of individual governments and put it under the control of the Fund and other international financial agencies.

Advocacy of the link clearly depends primarily on equity considerations. The argument may be expressed as follows. Under international financial systems, profits are to be made from reserve creation, arising from the fact that the value of reserves exceeds their costs of production. A gold-exchange system is, therefore, not neutral in terms of the transfer of real resources; these flow from the rest of the world to gold-producing and gold-holding countries and to reserve currency countries. These arguments have led to the identification of the United States as the major beneficiary of the post-war international financial system. At the same time, both the strength and the weakness of the various link proposals are that the unrequited real resource flow would be directed away from the United States and toward developing countries. The strength lies in the equity of such a proposal. The weakness lies in the fact that the United States is likely to resist such a change. But what would be the resource flows implied by a link? An answer to this question may be provided by returning to the first question posed above.

3.1.1 Benefits to developing countries from a link

The total benefits to developing countries from a link depend, first, on the number of SDRs allocated to them and, second, on the benefits per SDR. From a user's point of view, the benefits vary positively with the social marginal productivity of real resources and inversely with the social discount rate, the interest rate on SDR net use, and the size of any reconstitution requirements. The benefits to users exceed the grant element associated with SDRs to the extent that the excess of the rate of return to real resources over the rate of discount exceeds the commercial interest rate. For countries holding 100 per cent of their cumulative SDR allocation, the benefit from an allocation of SDRs is essentially the liquidity yield on them. For countries making a net acquisition of SDRs while holding a given portfolio of foreign exchange, the marginal liquidity yield is reduced by the real resource cost of earning the additional SDRs. While a high rate of interest on SDRs favours countries acquiring them, a low rate of interest favours net users. Only a handful of developing countries have held their entire cumulative allocation of SDRs, and even fewer have actually acquired them. The vast majority have been net users, and for this reason have benefited in the past from the relatively low rate of interest on SDRs.

While there are a number of difficulties in imputing real resource flows from data on net use and acquisition, attempts to estimate the effect of the unlinked SDR scheme on real resource transfers strongly suggest that the initial flow of real resources has been toward developing countries, implying that an 'informal link' has operated. Since the potential permanent real resource inflow available to net users of SDRs rises as the reconstitution requirement diminishes and falls as the rate of interest of SDRs rises, it might be expected that developing countries have a somewhat ambivalent view on recent changes in regard to the SDR that have lowered the reconstitution requirement from 30 per cent to 15 per cent and then to zero, and at the same time raised the interest rate from 60 per cent of the combined market rate to 80 per cent, and, from 1981, to 100 per cent. In fact, in terms of short-run potential real resource inflows, developing countries have probably gained more from the abrogation of the reconstitution requirement than they have lost from the interest rate increase. However, in the medium to long term this situation will be reversed.

The benefits to developing countries from SDRs, however, are considerably greater than figures on resource flows suggest, since such flows fail to take into account either the marginal productivity of the resources received, which may be particularly high in the case of developmental imports, or the fact that significant benefits are derived from holding SDRs, as well as from spending them. Furthermore, developing countries may have benefited indirectly from SDR allocations to industrial countries through induced policy changes in the recipient countries, which may have resulted in an increased capacity for developing countries both to earn foreign exchange by exporting to industrial countries and to acquire it through increased investment in and aid to developing countries by industrial countries.

While the introduction of a formal link would increase the direct benefits to developing countries, it would reduce or remove this indirect benefit. The problem here is one of quantification. Certainly the indirect benefit to developing countries has not been immediately apparent following allocations of SDRs in the 1980s.

Also difficult to quantify is the extent to which conventional aid is likely to be seen by donors as being independent of the link. If aid donors regard the link as a substitute for other forms of aid, developing countries may lose from its introduction. Certainly if, as seems likely, the distribution of linked aid is different from that of conventional aid, the pattern of aid disbursement will change as a result of introducing the link and the change may well be regressive. However, the quantity of aid is not the whole story; a link may still be advantageous from the viewpoint of developing countries, even if it leads to a small net reduction in aid, if at the same time it raises the quality of aid in terms of raising the grant element and relaxing the associated tying arrangements. Because the increase in the rate of interest clearly emerges as having reduced the benefit of SDRs to developing country users, an important question is whether this increase was necessary and whether it was in their interests in other ways.

3.1.2 The case for a market-equivalent interest rate and its implications for the link

From the viewpoint of the efficiency of the international monetary system, there is a strong case for SDRs to carry a market-equivalent interest rate. This stems from the theory of the optimum quantity of money discussed in Chapter 5. Applied to SDRs, the argument runs as follows. The optimum stock of SDRs is reached when their marginal benefit in the form of the liquidity yield equals their marginal cost of production. As the latter is almost zero, SDRs should be created up to a point where the marginal liquidity yield is almost zero. The international community will benefit from having such an optimum stock of SDRs in terms of the balance of payments strategies permitted, which will involve more financing, a slower rate of adjustment, and a lower welfare cost in terms of lost output and unemployment. To encourage this optimum stock of SDRs to be held over the long run, however, the opportunity cost of holding SDRs needs to be reduced to practically zero. This reduction may be achieved by paying a rate of interest equivalent to the rate of return on other assets. Even though the 'basket' method of SDR valuation makes the capital value of SDRs more stable than that of the individual currencies comprising the basket, central banks will find SDRs an unattractive asset if the rate of interest they carry is significantly below that available on convertible currencies.

The motivation for raising the interest rate on SDRs has clearly been to encourage their acceptance as the principal reserve asset in the international financial system. Developing countries have therefore found themselves in a dilemma. To make the link an effective and significant source of aid, they want SDRs to be the principal source of reserve creation. To ensure this role, SDRs need to carry a commercial interest rate. But a commercial interest rate seems to lower the grant element on SDRs to zero and means that the seigniorage goes to holders of SDRs in proportion to their holdings, rather than to net users.

Some antagonists have, in any case, criticized the objective of non-neutrality embodied in the link, and as originally established, the SDR was intended to be neutral with respect to resource transfers. The real resource flows that have actually taken place were, therefore, not an intentional part of the SDR scheme.

Support for neutrality is based on two arguments: first, that the existing distribution of resources throughout the world is acceptable, or indeed optimal (largely a normative issue); second, that it is inappropriate to induce real resource transfers through international monetary reform. This argument is valid only to the extent that the inclusion of a link in SDR allocation imposes costs in terms of efficiency. Raising the interest rate to a commercial level would seem to defend the SDR's integrity, while by encouraging recipients to hold their allocations it would seem to nullify any inflationary repercussions. So where does this leave the developing countries?

If it is accepted that efficiency dictates a commercial interest rate, the question immediately arises as to whether this is completely inconsistent with any form of SDR link. Although a competitive SDR interest rate certainly reduces the benefits of the link to net users, it is invalid to conclude as a result that these benefits fall to zero.

First, most of the developing countries that are able to raise commercial credit must pay a rate above the combined market rate used for calculating the rate of interest on SDRs. Furthermore, the rate on SDRs represents a weighted average of rates across countries, and these may be subject to considerable disparity. To a certain extent, then, the grant element on SDRs depends on the currency in which commercial borrowing would otherwise have been undertaken.[2] These two factors combine to suggest that SDRs may continue to incorporate a significant grant element for developing countries, even with a so-called market-equivalent interest rate.

Second, some developing countries find it impossible to borrow even at commercial interest rates; these countries face an availability constraint. The allocation of SDRs to them, even at a commercial interest rate, will help to overcome this. Indeed, to the extent that capital market imperfections prevent resources from moving to where their marginal productivity is highest (in developing countries?), the link serves to raise international economic efficiency by encouraging world output to rise.

Third, from a theoretical point of view it is the interest rate on the marginal acquisition of SDRs that needs to be at a commercial level. In terms of efficiency there is no reason why the rate paid by developing country users should not be subsidized, thereby raising the grant element. The problem here is the practical one of how the subsidy would be financed. In principle, financing could be arranged by transfer of SDRs from industrial countries to developing countries, with the former retaining the interest obligations, or by allocation of additional SDRs to developing countries in perpetuity, or by a charge imposed by the Special Drawing Rights Department of the Fund at a lower rate for developing countries on their net use than the rate paid to countries acquiring SDRs.[3]

Finally, aside from the interest rate on them, SDRs are a form of unconditional credit; they have no fixed repayment schedule and require no statement of need by users. Developing countries, wary of borrowing from the Fund because of the conditionality associated with some types of Fund drawings and viewing commercial borrowing as also having some conditional characteristics, may find SDRs very attractive. Furthermore, since net users only have to pay interest and do not have to repay capital, in the short run payments on SDR net use therefore tend to be lower than they would be for an equivalent commercial loan. On the other hand, developing countries are concerned that an increasing interest rate on SDRs brings with it an increase in general Fund charges. There is also the possibility that a higher rate may induce a greater reluctance on the part of surplus countries to adjust by spending reserves. In each of these cases a higher interest rate on SDRs imposes costs on developing countries.

3.1.3 Different links and developing country preferences

Although it is usually described as 'the link', numerous proposals for a link share the basic idea of raising the proportion of any given SDR allocation to developing countries. One set of proposals suggests an 'inorganic link', through which developing countries would make voluntary contributions in the form of currencies or SDRs to development agencies or developing countries at the time of each SDR allocation. Some versions of this inorganic link imply that contributions could only be spent in the contributing country. The only difference between an inorganic link and conventional aid is that such a link would be related to the receipt of SDRs. Not surprisingly, then, developing countries may regard any form of inorganic link as inferior to an organic version. The only reason they might support its introduction is that they see it as better than nothing and as standing more chance of being accepted and implemented because it requires no change in the Fund's Articles of Agreement. An inorganic link might be a stepping-stone toward an organic link, which specifies a formal connection between the creation of SDRs and the provision of development financing and which requires amendments to the Articles of Agreement.

There are a number of variants of the organic link, as follows:

(a) an increase in the proportion of SDRs allocated directly to developing countries,
(b) a direct allocation of SDRs to development agencies, and
(c) an agreed contribution of SDRs to development agencies or developing countries by industrial countries.

Version (a) could be based on existing Fund quotas, or it could imply a change in the distribution of quotas in favour of developing countries that would also raise their access to Fund resources in general and their voting rights; or it could mean severing the connection between the distribution of SDRs and Fund quotas. It can be argued that quotas do not provide an appropriate basis on which to distribute linked SDRs. After all, quotas are supposed to reflect countries' demand for reserves to hold. A principal objective of the link is, however, that SDRs should be spent by developing country recipients. It might be more appropriate, therefore, to distribute SDRs on the basis of per capita income, reflecting the link's aim of redistributing wealth. Furthermore, the distribution formula could be amended to take more account of balance of payments instability and the costs of adjustment. On both of these criteria, a larger proportion of SDRs would go to developing countries.

Under version (b), development agencies could either exchange the SDRs allocated to them for currencies to be used to finance loans to developing countries or transfer the SDRs to the accounts of countries supplying developmental goods, allowing these recipients to pay exporters in domestic currency. From the point of view of developing countries, a drawback of this version, compared with version (a), is that the additional financing might be tied to projects or might be conditional on the acceptance of specified macroeconomic policy objectives in such a way that the quality of the aid is reduced. The development agencies could also, therefore, exert an important influence over the attitudes of developing countries toward version (b). For similar reasons, developing countries might not favour the intermediation of industrial countries that would be a part of version (c). Clearly, the only reason why any developing country is likely to favour some form of intermediation, as opposed to direct country allocation, is if it stands to receive more SDRs as a result. Since, for any given allocation of SDRs, more for some developing countries means less for others, it is clear that the precise form of link is potentially contentious issue among developing countries. While they are likely to show a uniform preference for an organic and untied version of the link, beyond that their interests may be expected to diverge.

Two further types of link that have been proposed and discussed within the Fund would integrate the link with the activities of the Fund. Version (d) would use SDRs to provide the financing for some form of subsidy account. Under this version, SDRs could either be directly allocated to such an account, or contributions could be made by initial recipients voluntarily or according to a prearranged formula. The account would then redirect the SDRs at its command to developing countries or only to low-income countries either as grants (in which case contributors would themselves have to retain the obligations associated with the SDRs contributed) or as a line of interest-bearing credit (in which case the developing countries receiving the SDRs would be asked to meet the related interest obligations). In this latter case there would be no 'subsidy' as such, although developing countries would still receive more SDRs than they would under a distribution based on quotas. In many ways this version differs little from versions (b) and (c). One significant difference, however, is that, as proposed, the SDRs would be used by developing countries to help meet Fund charges. In this way version (d) of the link is, to an extent, tied to Fund conditionality and may therefore be less attractive to developing countries, though clearly the idea of subsidized interest rates would appeal to them.

Under version (e), SDRs would either be directly allocated or contributed to a special account, which would use them to support stabilization programmes approved by the Fund. In effect, developing countries agreeing on a programme with the Fund would gain access to more resources than before. The SDRs could be used either to expand drawings under existing tranches and facilities or to finance a new Fund-lending facility. In one sense developing countries might find such a scheme attractive, since they would receive more financing for accepting a programme to which they had already agreed in order to secure a Fund standby arrangement or extended facility drawing. Version (e) would therefore provide an extra incentive for developing countries to turn to the Fund. However, there is little doubt that they would prefer a scheme of direct and unconditional allocation to one that posits the intermediation of the Fund, as the appropriateness of the Fund's conditionality for developing countries is in some debate. Given the market-equivalent interest rate on SDRs, creditworthy developing countries might be expected to prefer to borrow from the Euro-currency market because such borrowing is to some extent independent of Fund conditionality. Version (e) would become more attractive to developing countries if the SDRs allocated to them by the special account did not have to be repaid and if the interest rate on their use of the SDRs was subsidized by, for instance, contributors retaining all or part of the related obligations.

On balance, even with a market-equivalent interest rate on SDRs, there still seems to be considerable scope for introducing a link that would be of significant advantage to developing countries – and perhaps, in particular, to low-income countries that do not find it easy to obtain financing from private capital markets. However, one way in which developing countries might make a link more palatable to industrial countries is to point out the contribution it could make to solving the problem of recycling. If recycling is at a sub-optimal level, the world economy as a whole pays the cost in terms of lost output and employment. A link will be of much greater benefit to developing countries, however, if the SDR's relative importance in the international financial system can be increased.

3.2 A substitution account

As revealed in Chapter 5, the long-term objective of a substitution account is to improve the structural operation of the international monetary system by replacing reserve currencies, and perhaps also gold, with SDRs.

It might be anticipated that developing countries would be strongly in favour of such an account, since they would benefit both from increased exchange rate stability and from the possibility of adapting an SDR system in order to include a link. Clearly, the establishment of a link will be of little benefit to developing countries unless the creation of SDRs occurs at frequent intervals and in substantial amounts. From the viewpoint of the developing countries, what is needed is a system in which the incremental demand for reserves is met by an additional supply of SDRs. The link and the proposed substitution account therefore seem to be complementary. While a link establishes a structural connection between the creation of SDRs and the provision of financial flows to developing countries, a substitution account attempts to ensure some structural connection between reserve growth and SDR creation. Both these connections are needed if reserve growth is to lead to more financing for developing countries.

It is not surprising, then, that the reservations of developing countries during discussions about the establishment of a substitution account have related primarily to the specifics of the actual account proposed rather than to the general principle of substitution. Criticisms of a substitution account by developing countries have related to the following factors:

(a) its effect on the SDR,
(b) its effect on the process of international adjustment and the distribution of the adjustment burden,
(c) its effect on exchange rate instability and the management of global liquidity,
(d) its effect on developing countries as holders of reserves, and
(e) its financial arrangements.

3.2.1 Effect on the SDR

The concern of developing countries in this context has two dimensions: first, that the issuance by a substitution account of a high-yielding SDR-denominated asset may damage the prospects that the SDR will become the international monetary system's principal reserve asset; and second, that the existence of a competitive rate of interest on assets issued by the account will raise the rate of interest on SDRs and thereby the charges on the use of Fund resources in general. Indeed, this second concern has been presented as perhaps the major deterrent to the support of a substitution account by the developing countries. However, given the increase in the rate of interest on SDRs, this is no longer a valid objection. The attention of developing countries should perhaps now be more appropriately focused on ways in which an SDR system based on competitive interest rates may be used or adapted to direct financial flows to them and on ways in which the concessionary element of such flows may be raised for the low-income countries. One method would charge reserve centres a higher rate of interest on the account's holdings of their currency than is paid to depositors, using the differential for development financing.[4]

3.2.2 Effect on international adjustment

In principle, a substitution account provides an opportunity for encouraging reserve currency countries to adjust their balance of payments. This may be achieved by requiring such countries, particularly the United States, to amortize the account's holding of their currencies over time by buying back previously issued liabilities-with SDRs that have been either allocated to them or earned through the net exportation of real resources. Amortization was a constituent element of versions of the substitution account discussed by the Committee of Twenty, but it was abandoned in later versions, which as a result were seen by developing countries as having the prime objective of supporting the US dollar. As noted earlier, it is a central part of the criticism by developing countries of the post-war international financial system that there have been asymmetrical pressures on countries to adjust, with the non-reserve currency deficit countries carrying a relatively large proportion of the burden.

Amortization of reserve currencies also provides an opportunity to introduce a version of the link that does not rely on net additions to international reserves, or that permits the additional financial flow to developing countries to exceed any increase in the quantity of international reserves – something that would be impossible under the more conventional versions of the link. This opportunity results from the fact that amortization implies a fall in the quantity of international reserves, as dollars held outside the United States, where they are counted as reserves, are returned to the United States, where they are not so counted. Indeed, without this compensating increase in linked SDRs, developing countries as a group could easily lose from the world deflationary impact of balance of payments correction in the United States. Individually, developing countries might still lose, even with a compensating link, if the distribution formula for SDRs differs from the pattern of US imports among developing countries. From the point of view of the world demand for their exports, developing countries might therefore be expected to prefer redistribution of the adjustment burden to take the form of expansionary policies in surplus countries rather than deflationary policies in the United States. In view of this, it is only by moving toward an asset settlement system based on SDRs, and away from a liability system that relies on deficits in the United States for additional reserves, that developing countries will be able to gain a larger share of the benefits from reserve creation. Furthermore, developing countries see the gold-exchange system as imparting an inflationary bias to the world economy because the creation of reserves is uncontrolled.

3.2.3 Effect on exchange rate stability and global liquidity management

The concern of developing countries is that a substitution account will do little to help stabilize exchange rates through a reduction in the incidence of currency switching, since it will convert only the relatively involatile currency holdings of central banks, and not the more volatile privately held balances.

With regard to the management of global liquidity, it has been argued that the account will create reserves simply as a reflex to the reserves already created by individual national authorities and will do nothing to induce the more democratic control of reserve creation from which developing countries stand a chance of benefiting. In a narrow sense this is true but, as implied earlier, the consolidation of reserve currencies that a substitution account would accomplish may be seen as a first step toward an SDR system based on asset settlement and could therefore eventually lead to the better management of global liquidity.

3.2.4 Developing countries as holders of reserves

Concern has been expressed that developing countries could lose from the introduction of a substitution account in their role as holders of reserves. This could be brought about if a market in SDR-denominated assets failed to develop, if such assets had a low degree of usefulness, if they carried a low rate of interest relative to that available in the Euro-currency market, where a number of developing countries have placed reserves, or if the possible sterilization of reserves forced developing countries to turn to the Euro-currency market for funds at a time when it was both difficult and expensive to borrow from that market. The conclusion is that developing countries might prefer to hold their reserves in the form of dollars rather than in SDR-denominated assets.

Of course if participation in the account were to be voluntary, there would be no reason for developing countries to convert dollars into SDRs unless they considered this to be to their own advantage. On the other hand, voluntary participation may be less effective for bringing about a move toward establishing the SDR as the principal reserve asset, and developing countries may thus benefit from a higher degree of compulsion. With a compulsory substitution account, developing countries would simply have to regard the loss of freedom with respect to reserve management as a price they have to pay. The question, then, is not so much a matter of whether there are costs but rather whether these exceed the benefits. For the majority of developing countries this is unlikely to be the case, although it may well be, at least initially, for those richer developing countries with significant reserve holdings and Euro-currency deposits that would be bypassed as recipients of SDRs in some versions of the link. To argue that developing countries as a group benefit more from the free operation of the Euro-currency market and from a largely unmanaged international financial system seems to ignore the position of a large number of them, in particular the low-income countries, which have few dealings with the private market. Again, however, it seems that developing countries will not have an unambiguous view.

3.2.5 Financial arrangements of the account

Although the prime purpose of a substitution account is to change the composition of reserves, its financial arrangements could (as explained in Chapter 5) also exert an influence over the total quantity of reserves – and this could be significant for developing countries. Assuming, for example, that currencies deposited with the account are to be invested in the issuing country and that interest is to be paid to the account in the same currency, and assuming further that interest is to be paid on SDRs issued by the account in the form of SDRs, the total quantity of reserves would rise at a rate equivalent to the interest on the SDRs, expressed as a fraction of total reserves. If, on the other hand, interest on the account's holdings of currencies is to be paid in SDRs, this would reduce the total quantity of reserves, compared with a system where interest is paid in the issuer's own currency. Whether total reserves would actually fall would depend on the rate of interest paid to the account by reserve centres compared with that paid by the account to recipients of SDRs. A profit for the account implies a reduction in total reserves, a loss implies an increase in total reserves, and breaking even implies no change in total reserves.

A more specific concern of developing countries in the discussions about a substitution account in early 1980 was over the proposal that the Fund's gold should be used to provide backing for it and to guarantee its financial viability. Developing countries, not surprisingly, viewed this suggestion as being inconsistent with the whole concept of the Trust Fund and saw it as implying a 'reverse link'. In conjunction with their view that the version of the account then being discussed made the United States the principal beneficiary, the use of the Fund's gold to support the account rather than to provide concessional assistance for the poorer developing countries was particularly unacceptable.

Since the general objectives of a substitution account, as presented at the beginning of this section, are to the advantage of developing countries and since the account could be organized so as to be of direct benefit to developing countries in terms of generating additional financial inflows, it is not in their interests to resist all attempts to introduce such an account but to argue for a version of the account that directs at least a share of the direct benefits to them.

3.3 Gold

The mechanics of a substitution account could, in principle, be applied equally well to gold as to reserve currencies. Furthermore, substitution of gold would also be consistent with objectives of the Second Amendment to the Fund's Articles to reduce the role of monetary gold and enhance the role of the SDR. The implications for the total quantity of reserves would depend initially on the SDR price paid for gold deposits relative to the price at which gold is valued for calculating reserves. Assuming that reserve gold is valued at its market price, the activities of a gold substitution account would only reduce total reserves and thereby create the opportunity for additional SDR allocations if a price below the market value was paid for gold deposits. The acquisition and holding of gold by the Fund would, however, be inconsistent with the declared objective of reducing the monetary role of gold. In the longer run, therefore, the account's stock of gold would have to be disposed of by gradually selling it for industrial and artistic use. Profits accruing to the account could then, in principle and at least in part, be directed toward developing countries, with depositing countries also perhaps receiving a secondary payment.

A central problem with all reforms that try to use the operation of the international monetary system for the benefit of developing countries is that changes that are technically feasible may not be acceptable in practice to industrial countries, whose compliance under existing institutional arrangements is necessary for their activation. The potential conflict between what is equitable and what is acceptable is highlighted by what has happened with respect to gold during the 1970s. Events in this sphere of international finance have also clearly shown how the stated intentions of the Fund and the aspirations of its developing member countries may be frustrated in what are largely unforeseen ways.

Since the Jamaican Accord of 1976, a stated objective of international monetary reform has been to reduce the monetary role of gold – an objective that developing countries have seen as in their own interests. In an attempt to help realize this objective, the Fund abandoned the official price of gold and undertook to dispose of a third of its gold stock. It was agreed that 25 million ounces of gold would be sold back to Fund members in proportion to their quotas at a price of SDR 35 an ounce and that a further 25 million ounces would be sold at a series of public auctions over a period of four years, with the profits going to a Trust Fund that would make disbursements on concessional terms to eligible developing countries, essentially the poorer developing countries. Thus, developing countries made an apparently significant advance, inasmuch as an element of international monetary reform became structurally related to the provision of additional financial assistance to them.

There is no doubt that the Trust Fund has provided eligible countries with both an absolutely and relatively important source of low-conditionality financing. However, neither can there be doubt that developing countries have actually lost as a result of the abandonment of the official gold price and the dramatic increase in the market price of gold that this change probably facilitated. Furthermore, to the extent that concern over the future stability and form of the international monetary system has caused the demand for gold and therefore its price to rise, the failure to restore confidence in the system and to find credible solutions to international financial problems has acted against the interests of developing countries. Inasmuch as the instabilities of the 1970s were a reflection of the rise in the price of oil, non-oil developing countries were affected by this phenomenon twice over.

The general move toward revaluing reserve gold at its market price has meant that countries have experienced an increase in their reserves in proportion to their gold holdings. Such revaluation has generated both a wealth effect, in the form of potential resource transfers, and a liquidity effect. As regards the wealth effect, the prime beneficiaries have been the gold-holding and gold-producing countries. It has been estimated that 90 per cent of reserve asset gold is held by industrial countries, with five of them holding more gold individually than all the non-oil developing countries together. It has also been estimated that the net gain for industrial countries from gold revaluation during the 1970s was well in excess of $400 billion, compared with under $30 billion for non-oil developing countries. The inequitable distribution of the gains from the sale of gold by the Fund is further emphasized if they are calculated on a per capita basis, and if allowance is made for the fact that a large proportion of the gold that developing countries hold as a group is held by India and Afghanistan.

The liquidity effect of the revaluation of gold has been to prevent any *de facto* demonetization of gold. On the contrary, with gold valued at its market price, it reasserted itself as the principal reserve asset and as the major source of reserve growth during the 1970s. Far from there being a move toward the greater control of reserves, as envisaged in the Second Amendment of the Fund's Articles, the aggregate value of reserves depends to a very significant degree on the vagaries of the gold price, which at best is likely to be only loosely related to the requirements of the system for international liquidity. Some insight into the significance of these changes for developing countries may be gained by calculating how much more their reserves would have risen if the aggregate reserve growth during the 1970s had been brought about through the creation of SDRs. The answer seems to be about $100 billion. Reserve growth through gold revaluation, as opposed to SDR creation, is clearly to the relative advantage of industrial countries (and, in particular, the major gold-holders among them) and to the relative disadvantage of developing countries.

The neutrality of reserve growth, so much a theme of the case against the link, has not been achieved in recent years, and the potential resource transfer has been in favour of the wealthiest industrial countries. Developing countries may therefore express legitimate interest in proposals designed to redirect this potential resource transfer. Technically there are a number of ways for achieving this. One, as outlined above, would be through a gold substitution account. A second would be to impose some form of tax on the windfall profits of gold-holders – as global fiscal policy may in principle be a more appropriate instrument for achieving a redistribution of wealth than international monetary policy. However, neither of these proposals seems to meet the necessary condition of acceptability to industrial countries. Of greater relevance, therefore, might be the proposal to use the remaining stock of gold held by the Fund to provide financing for developing countries. This general notion itself incorporates a number of possibilities, and developing countries may disagree among themselves over the most appropriate arrangements by which the transfer would be achieved.

The financing could, for example, be used to enable the Fund to expand its activities, or to widen them by introducing new lending facilities or by changing the conditions under which resources are lent. Alternatively, it could be used to subsidise interest payments or to provide some kind of guarantee fund to support commercial lending to developing countries. Each of these uses implies that the financing would be related to Fund conditionality, and thus these uses might not be favoured by potential recipients. As regards the provision of subsidies, the views of individual developing countries would no doubt depend on whether they would be eligible for them or not. Low-income countries might prefer this variant to a guarantee fund that they might feel would not be of special benefit to them unless the guarantees were to be offered only on their commercial borrowing. At the same time, countries that had previously had access to private financing without a guarantee might also be apprehensive about the effects that a guarantee system would have on their relative creditworthiness.

The financing could, of course, be channelled directly and unconditionally to developing countries according to some distribution formula. Again, the views of individual developing countries would depend heavily on the formula adopted – whether, for example, it was related to Fund quotas or to some other measure of need. Another option would be to distribute the financing through international development agencies, such as the World Bank or regional development banks, or through a new world development fund. Again, the attitudes of individual countries would depend on their potential access to such institutions. Countries that preferrred programme aid rather than project aid or that did not feel able to meet commercial interest rates might, for example, be opposed to distribution through the World Bank.

However, there is another problem. If the Fund sold its stock of gold, a further appreciation in the price of gold could again confer greater benefits on the purchasers of gold – almost certainly the industrial countries – than on the developing countries. This implies either that some form of international capital gains tax would be needed or that the Fund should use its stock of gold only as collateral for raising loans from private capital markets. In this case the low-income and less creditworthy countries may feel that they would be excluded from the additional commercial financing that would result.

3.4 Fund conditionality

Many of the proposals discussed in this chapter would lead to an extension of the activities of the Fund, although reforms of the Fund could also be undertaken independently. To the extent that the reforms provide the Fund with additional resources to lend to developing countries, one criticism of the Fund that will be tempered is that the quantity of finance received does not warrant the degree of Fund influence that is exerted. However, attitudes of developing countries toward such reform will depend significantly on their view as to the appropriateness of Fund conditionality. This question is taken up in the next chapter.

While some modifications in Fund conditionality are probably in the interests of developing countries, the issues are more complex than is often implied. Furthermore, it should not be assumed that developing countries have no influence over their own interests with respect to conditionality. First, as the Fund maintains, the imposition of strict conditions may reflect a late request to the Fund for assistance. While the Fund may help to break the vicious circle between strict conditionality and late requests by modifying conditionality, developing countries may also help significantly by turning to the Fund before their economic problems reach crisis proportions, when there is little alternative to a strict stabilization programme.

Moreover, it is not sufficient for developing countries merely to argue that Fund conditionality is inappropriate; what is needed is an articulation of the available alternatives. The evidence drawn from developing countries that have rejected Fund-type stabilization programmes in favour of alternative strategies is far from uniformly optimistic. Where it turns out that the Fund does actually know best, developing countries may damage their own interests by ignoring the Fund's advice. In these circumstances less strict conditionality may permit developing countries to postpone necessary adjustment and thereby cause their basic economic situation to deteriorate more than necessary. In this sense, strict conditionality may be in the interests of developing countries.

3.5 A commodity-backed international currency

Providing commodity backing for an international currency is an idea of surprising resilience. One such scheme was presented in a background paper for the Arusha Conference on the International Monetary System and the New International Order. Significantly, there was no direct mention of the scheme in the Conference's final statement, the so-called Arusha Initiative, in which it is simply stated that 'decisions need to be taken to make the (SDR) the principal reserve asset in international payments and to ensure that the role of national currencies in international settlements is effectively reduced. For that purpose the SDR should be made more attractive'. However, in order to 'acquire the attributes of an international currency', the background paper maintains that the SDR needs 'solid backing, redeemability and more automatic forms of issue limitation'. To this end, it suggests that SDRs be issued against the deposit of warehouse receipts of commodities constituting one or more commodity units. A commodity unit would be made up of a basket of basic storable commodities, of which the relative amounts would reflect their relative importance in international trade. The value of SDRs would be defined in terms of the commodity unit, and a world central bank would fix the buying and selling prices for the commodity units, denominated in SDRs, with a margin of, say, 5 per cent between them. In addition to the backed issue of SDRs, there would be an additional fiduciary issue of SDRs linked to development financing.

The principal benefit from the introduction of a commodity-backed currency is its supposed ability to 'address the three problems that are hindering the viability and proper functioning of the international economy: inadequate growth of output and employment, persistent rise in prices, and instability of primary exports'. Further analysis suggests, however, that a commodity-backed SDR is neither necessary nor sufficient to ensure the realization of these goals.

With respect to primary product price instability, although the price of the bundle of commodities would tend to be stabilized, this would not necessarily be the case for all the individual commodities comprising the composite unit. Indeed, in circumstances where not all primary product prices move in the same direction, as might be the case if price instabilities are primarily caused by supply-side changes or if the increasing prices of some commodities in the bundle have to be counterbalanced by offsetting falls in the prices of other commodities in order to stabilize the price of the bundle, then the scheme could raise the price instability for individual commodities. Furthermore, even if prices were to be stabilized, it does not follow that export earnings would also always be stabilized. Again, while the price of the bundle would be stabilized in terms of new SDRs, this does not automatically mean that the purchasing power of primary producers would be stabilized in terms of manufactured goods, since the domestic currency price of manufactures might rise or the exchange rate between new SDRs and the national currencies of producers of manufactured goods might depreciate.

Flexibility in exchange rates between national currencies and the new SDR could also disrupt the scheme's potentially advantageous effects on world inflation. Furthermore, in this connection the scheme would at the outset only provide backing for a proportion of international money, and would not therefore exert precise control over international credit creation because other components would remain uncontrolled. Indeed the Arusha proposal does not suggest tying the fiduciary issue of SDRs to commodities in any way.

As for the effects on world output and employment, the principal benefit of a commodity-backed SDR would appear to be its automatic counter-cyclical impact on the world's supply of international reserves. However, even this may be overstated. First, considerable slippage might result from the inconstancy in the quantities of other reserve assets. Second, the automaticity could operate in a perverse fashion; the effect of a major increase in the price of oil, for example (assuming that oil is included in the composite unit), would be to reduce the quantity of SDRs in what would tend to be an already deflationary environment.

In view of the uncertainties of the benefits from a commodity-backed SDR and the certain and significant storage, administrative, and negotiating costs, there seems to be a strong case for developing countries to pursue a policy that puts emphasis on modifying the existing unbacked SDR. In principle, such modifications could equally well achieve the greater central control of international liquidity and the pattern of resource transfers advocated by commodity-backing supporters. If industrial countries are not prepared to accept changes in the existing SDR scheme that would direct more resources to developing countries as a group, they seem unlikely to support a scheme that would do this automatically. Furthermore, actions have already been taken to make the SDR a more attractive reserve asset, and it is yet to be established that commodity backing is needed to accomplish this.

If the prime purpose of a commodity-backed SDR is to stabilize primary product prices, there are arguments for supporting a system of individual commodity buffer stocks in preference to a commodity-backed currency, which, at best, would only have an incidental effect on price stability. Buffer stocks are subject to a range of well recognized theoretical and practical difficulties. Not least among these is the problem of financing. Perhaps a more rewarding approach for developing countries would therefore be to investigate the possibility of using unbacked SDRs to finance commodity stabilization schemes. In prospect, such an arrangement would offer the possibility not only of stabilizing primary product prices but also of increasing the relative importance of SDRs in the international financial system and of providing some degree of monetary stabilization.

3.6 Financial arrangements among developing countries

Various financial arrangements among developing countries could comprise reserve pooling, clearance or payments unions, or even the establishment of an exclusively 'southern' currency. The basis of such plans is an attempt to make more efficient use of scarce hard currencies and to promote more trade among developing countries through the provision of additional credit. Although in many ways exclusive financial arrangements of this type may be appealing to developing countries frustrated by the lack of progress in their negotiations with the north and by the slow growth of export markets in developed countries, they are subject to numerous practical (though not necessarily insuperable) problems. Not least among these is how to deal with persistent creditors and debtors. Furthermore, such schemes may be of rather more appeal to some developing countries than to others, depending on the pattern of their trading relations. Inasmuch as the expenditure of one developing country is effectively tied to the output of other developing countries, schemes of this nature seem to represent a second-best solution for developing countries as a group by comparison with an equivalent allocation of SDRs.

4. SOME CONCLUDING REMARKS

This chapter has focused on a number of specific proposals for international monetary reform and examined them in terms of their impact on developing countries. It has been noted throughout, however, that the interests of developing countries may be far from uniform. During the 1970s a significant number of middle-income and higher-income developing countries apparently suffered little from the breakdown of the international monetary system and the associated move to the market place. They were able to attract commercial credit and to maintain growth and development. Aside from easing their debt problems, these countries may have relatively little motivation for reform, and will be concerned that any move back towards a more centrally organized set of international financial arrangements will confer few benefits on them and may indeed be to their absolute disadvantage. From the point of view of their own self-interest, they may be wary of reforms that incorporate the intermediation of international financial and development institutions, guarantees, and the like. These interests may be largely shared by oil-exporting developing countries that have found it convenient to place their unspent revenues on the Euro-currency market.

It is the remaining developing countries that have a vested interest in restoring the greater degree of central control that would come, in particular, from the establishment of the SDR as the principal reserve asset and from the related reforms. The strategic importance of the Euro-currency market in recycling has worked against their interests in two ways. Not only have they been deemed uncreditworthy by commercial banks and therefore been unable to gain access to private finance, but also and certainly up until about 1982 an impression was created in some influential circles that financing problems of developing countries could be left to the market, which provides an automatic and responsive mechanism as well as the necessary discipline and pressure for adjustment. The private market was seen as a preferable substitute for official intervention, and as a result the perceived need for international financial reform was reduced.

Ignored so far in this chapter, though discussed briefly in Chapter 10, has been the question of exchange rate flexibility. Developing countries, in general, have been rather sceptical about floating rates because of a number of areas of concern, including increased uncertainty and the inadequacy of forward cover, the implications for commodity price stability and the relative prices of developing country imports and exports, and the implications for reserve and debt management. Of more direct relevance in the context of this chapter is the fact that floating exchange rates represent a move away from a centrally managed financial system and, in principle, reduce the need for additional reserve assets.

The negotiating strategy for developing countries as far as international financial reform is concerned has two dimensions. The first is to agree among themselves on a package of proposals. The second is to identify proposals that are not only to their advantage but also acceptable to industrial countries. An additional problem is that industrial countries will not necessarily have an unambiguous view. Industrial countries may, however, be expected to become generally more receptive to proposals of the kind discussed here if and when their preoccupation shifts away from inflation and toward unemployment.

Finally, to return to a point made earlier, there is a mutuality of interests between developing and industrial countries in having a well functioning international financial system that encourages the growth of world trade and output. Developing countries lose from international instability and recession. Thus, it could be rather narrow-minded of them to resist all reforms that do not appear to maximize their own direct benefits. However, this is also a reason why developing countries are likely to remain in a relatively weak bargaining position.

12 International Financial Institutions: the Role of the IMF

1. INTRODUCTION

In the preceding chapters a number of references have been made to the activities of various international financial institutions. This chapter takes up some of these references. It also draws on some of the other themes discussed in previous chapters. In some sense, then, the chapter presents a set of conclusions to the book, though readers should feel free to disagree with them.

Space constrains a full investigation into all the institutions in international finance and the chapter focuses on the activities of the IMF, although this brings with it some brief discussion of the World Bank and the private international banks. Neglected, however, are governments, the regional development banks and the various European institutions.

Drawing on material already covered, the chapter attempts to show how changing circumstances have affected the Fund's traditional sphere of influence. It moves on to examine where the Fund might have a role to play in world finance, then examines a range of reforms that might be needed in order to activate this role, and some of the implications of these reforms.

2. BACKGROUND: THE CHANGING POSITION OF THE FUND

2.1 The loss of the Fund's traditional sphere of influence

Since 1973 the Fund has lost a significant proportion of its former influence. Its duties had consisted of overseeing what was an essentially fixed exchange rate system, providing short-term finance to assist countries facing temporary balance of payments difficulties, encouraging the development of a liberal system of international trade and payments, and exercising a measure of control, though a small one, over the quantity of international liquidity.

However, the period since 1973 has disrupted many of these activities. There has, for instance, been the move to flexible exchange rates, with the Fund generally having very little influence over the direction or size of exchange rate movements, even though it has made efforts to provide a degree of surveillance over these and to come up with an acceptable set of guidelines according to which government intervention in foreign exchange markets may be carried out. Furthermore, there has been a massive increase in the size of balance of payments disequilibria, with most of the associated 'recycling' of international finance, certainly up until 1982, taking place through the private international banks rather than the Fund. Not only has the size of the disequilibria increased but their nature has also changed. Many have been caused by changes in the terms of trade between primary goods and manufactures. Where these changes are secular rather than cyclical, the associated balance of payments deficits can hardly be described as 'temporary'. However, the policies that are most appropriate to bringing about a durable strengthening in the balance of payments in such circumstances may not induce sufficient short-term improvement. Temporary financial assistance of the traditional Fund type may then be inappropriate to the payments disequilibria that have been encountered in the 1970s and 1980s.

As well as the move to generalized floating and the changed size and nature of payments imbalances, the Fund has also been faced with a period of growing protectionism as countries have tried to ameliorate the effects of recession on their external accounts and to offset the implications of increased competition from the newly industrializing countries (NICs) for their traditional industries and thereby employment. Furthermore, changes in the quantity of international reserves have had very little to do with the Fund but much more to do with the macroeconomic policies pursued in the United States and other reserve currency countries, the operation of the Euro-currency market, and fluctuations in the price of gold.

In more general terms the Fund, established to administer the Bretton Woods system, has found that the breakdown of that system has left it with apparently little to administer. Although it has made attempts to modify its activities in the light of events, things have happened so fast and on such a scale that the Fund has found it difficult to respond either quickly enough or on a large enough scale.

2.2 The performance of the world economy and the new set of international financial arrangements

As established in Chapter 2, there are few if any grounds for arguing that the performance of the world economy has been satisfactory since 1973. Inflation has been rapid, unemployment high, economic growth slow, and balance of payments disequilibria large.

Similarly, the move away from an international financial system based on the official sector towards what is in effect a non-system based on the private sector has, after an initial period of limited success, encountered significant problems. Fears have been expressed over the instability of private bank lending, the overexposure of banks to developing countries, the debt problems faced by many of the countries to which the banks lent heavily, and the general fragility of the international banking system.

Significantly, it has been in this context that the role of the IMF as a principal and unique international financial institution has been partially restored by vetting the adjustment programmes of the major debtor countries.

2.3 The range of alternative roles

In endeavouring to identify a role for the Fund, one has a wide range of ideas from which to choose. By analogy, should it be a banker, a teacher, a policeman, a social worker, a missionary, or a doctor? By function, should it be an adjustment institution, or should it also provide significant amounts of finance? In terms of its clients, should it try to deal exclusively with the industrial countries and the NICs or should it provide finance to the poorer developing countries?

3. PRINCIPAL ELEMENTS OF AN INTERNATIONAL FINANCIAL SYSTEM AND THE SCOPE FOR THE FUND

The principal elements in any set of international financial arrangements relate to adjustment, liquidity and financing, the degree of central management, and the degree of confidence in the arrangements.

3.1 Adjustment

When looking at adjustment from the viewpoint of the Fund, there are two levels of aggregation that may usefully be identified. The first is with respect to individual countries and the second with respect to the world as a whole.

3.1.1 In individual countries

Both in principle and in practice it is within individual countries that the influence of the Fund is, and is likely to remain, most potent. This potency derives from the fact that drawings from the Fund that are in any way substantial are only permitted after a detailed macroeconomic programme has begun to be implemented. However, it is not just the availability of Fund resources that rests on IMF programmes; private international banks also take them into account in reaching their own lending decisions. The Fund, then, possesses an important instrument through which it may exert an impact on adjustment in countries which turn to it for financial assistance.

Of course not all countries turn to the Fund. Those in payments surplus, those whose currency doubles as an international reserve asset, or those with large reserves or access to private capital, will either be ineligible to draw resources from the Fund (in the case of surplus countries) or may choose not to do so in order to avoid the conditions that would be attached to such loans. The end result is that there are significant asymmetries in the system, with only a sub-set of countries being subject to the adjustment discipline enforced by the Fund.

Towards the end of the 1970s and at the beginning of the 1980s the outcome of this asymmetry was that the principal borrowers from the Fund were the poorest countries of the world, which were in deficit but which had no alternative sources of finance available to them. By 1982, however, other richer developing countries that had previously had fairly unimpeded access to private credit were beginning to turn to the Fund as their debt problems deepened and as the private banks showed more reluctance to lend to them.

Given the central importance of Fund conditionality as a means of influencing adjustment policy in individual countries and the often heated debate about it, it is perhaps worthwhile spending a little longer making a closer examination.

Critics of the Fund argue that the conditions it advocates reveal it to be a doctrinaire monetarist institution which places almost exclusive reliance on credit control as a means of strengthening the balance of payments, ignoring the structural nature of many deficits. They go on to argue that it places too much emphasis on short-run payments correction, under-estimating the adverse effects on growth and development. In part the short-run perspective adopted by the Fund is seen as reflecting a view that deficits are in the main caused by internal economic mismanagement, and in particular by the over-expansion of domestic demand. Critics further maintain that the Fund is inflexible and inadaptable, making use of a fairly standard programme of policies and showing little appreciation of the economic, institutional, political and social constraints under which policy is pursued in individual countries. At the same time, however, they also argue that the Fund shows political favouritism to countries pursuing market-related policies, making softer demands on these countries than on other countries which prefer planning to the market. Indeed there is a group of critics which argues that the Fund has been too soft in general and that its conditions have been inadequate to ensure that the necessary adjustment will be achieved.

Defenders of the Fund, and the Fund itself, reject these criticisms. They argue that the Fund is eclectic both in terms of its underlying theoretical analysis and, more importantly, in practice. They reject the idea that structural problems are ignored, pointing to the Extended Fund Facility (EFF) as evidence of an awareness of such problems and a willingness to help remedy them. Furthermore, they argue that the Fund provides long-term assistance by means of negotiating a *series* of short-term arrangements.

While maintaining that over-expansionary domestic demand policies are indeed the most common cause of payments difficulties and that outward-looking and market-related policies are the most effective way of strengthening the balance of payments, defenders also reject the idea that the Fund is unadaptable and inflexible. They argue that considerable flexibility is offered through the range of facilities under which members may draw – including the Compensatory Financing Facility (CFF), under which compensation is made for temporary shortfalls in export receipts resulting from adverse movements in the terms of trade – and that even elements which appear to be standard in Fund programmes, such as the control of credit creation, may be used in a flexible way by varying the amount of credit expansion permitted. In this and in other ways the Fund claims that economic, institutional, political and social constraints are taken into account. Again the Fund rejects the criticism of favouritism, pointing to the satisfactory working relations that have been maintained with a number of socialist regimes. Its frequent unpopularity with governments the Fund attributes not so much to differing ideologies as to the fact that the Fund forces governments to face up to the unpleasant facts of economic life and to curtail over-ambitious plans.

It is not easy to draw firm conclusions on these issues, since much of the relevant material is confidential. However, some tentative conclusions do seem valid from the available evidence. First, while an examination of Fund programmes shows that some form of credit control is almost always included, this does not necessarily prove that there is a monetarist ethic in the Fund. Rather, and as noted in Chapter 9, credit ceilings are used because they are seen by the Fund as an expedient method of monitoring the progress of programmes and as a policy variable over which the domestic authorities have some measure of control. Furthermore, the interventionist nature of the Fund, the use of devaluation as a means of changing relative prices, the concern shown over the state of the current account, the support for incomes policies in certain circumstances, and the Fund's preoccupation with the short run, are all inconsistent with the pure monetarist position described in Chapter 9.

Second, the Fund does seem to have concentrated on demand side variables both as the causes of payments deficits and as the means through which they may be reduced or eliminated. The focus of its attention has been on correcting payments deficits *per se* rather than on correcting them while doing minimum damage to the other policy objectives which governments might be expected to have. Even the Extended Fund Facility, which is supposed to be directed towards structural or supply-side factors has in practice included conventional demand side conditionality.

Third, while there is undoubtedly scope for the Fund to be flexible in its dealings with members and while the Fund has undeniably demonstrated a measure of flexibility, this has been strictly constrained. Having said this, we must add that the differing geo-political importance of members turning to the Fund, and their differing ability to lobby and influence the Executive Board, is reflected by a lack of uniformity in the treatment meted out by the Fund. However, while the Fund does favour using the market mechanism, it is simplistic to argue that it is anti-socialist.

Finally, although it is difficult to evaluate the impact of Fund programmes since, as discussed in Chapter 9, there is no generally accepted methodology by which this may be done, there is considerable evidence to suggest that they do not have a great deal of impact one way or another on the principal macroeconomic variables, such as the balance of payments, inflation, and economic growth. While such evidence confirms that there is room for improving IMF conditionality, it also suggests that the most vehemently outspoken critics of the Fund have overstated their case.

3.1.2 Global adjustment

As for the second aspect of the adjustment issue, the global dimension of many economic problems has been aptly illustrated by events during the 1970s and 1980s. The world as a whole has experienced accelerating and then decelerating inflation, rising unemployment and falling rates of economic growth. This is hardly surprising, since countries are closely linked through trade and capital flows. But if the problems are global, are not the policies relevant to dealing with them also likely to be global? This argues for a global view of the adjustment problem which allows for the complex interrelations that exist between countries.

Although the idea of world macroeconomic management may seem naive, given the practical problems and difficulties that national governments encounter in managing their own economic affairs, this does not detract from its relevance and desirability; indeed many of the difficulties that individual countries encounter may spring from the lack of such a global perspective. The Fund is at present one of the few institutions through which such global macroeconomic management might be achieved.

In practice the Fund has concentrated on its dealings with individual countries in the absence of any well defined global strategy. The result is that inconsistencies may arise between what might seem appropriate, and indeed feasible, in particular countries, and what is appropriate for the world economy. For example, the advocacy of export expansion in individual countries might be thwarted by the reluctance of surplus countries to expand demand and to desist from increasing the degree of protectionism; or the recommendation of deflationary policies designed to strengthen one country's balance of payments may weaken the payments position of other countries and exacerbate world recession.

Even with the constraints imposed by what is realistic, there is in principle some scope for the Fund to act in a globally counter cyclical way through varying the emission of SDRs and modifying its lending policies. In practice, Fund activities in both these areas have on occasions been pro-cyclical. SDRs were created in the early 1970s when there was a large increase in international liquidity from other sources, and conditionality was tightened up in mid-1981, with greater emphasis being placed on the short-term deflation of demand, at a time when the world was moving into deeper recession.

3.2 Liquidity

The Fund can make an impact on the quantity, composition and distribution of international liquidity both through its Special Drawing Rights Account and its General Account.

3.2.1 SDRs

The actual and potential role of SDRs was reviewed in Chapter 5. It was discovered that establishing the SDR as the principal reserve asset in the international financial system would have benefits in terms of offering greater scope for controlling the quantity of reserves, of modifying the distribution of seigniorage associated with reserve creation, and of reducing the degree of international financial and exchange rate instability associated with holders switching the composition of their reserves.

Although various steps catalogued in Chapter 5 have been taken to strengthen the SDR, it still remains a quantitatively relatively unimportant asset. If the significance of SDRs could be increased by making them more attractive and useful, this would clearly enhance the role of the Fund as the producer of SDRs. The scope for international financial management by the Fund would then be very much greater.

However, the objective of these changes has not been attained.

Reserve growth has not in the main or even significantly come about through the creation of SDRs, and the system has moved more in the direction of multiple currency reserves rather than SDRs.

3.2.2 The General Account

There are three main issues to consider here: the quantity of resources available, the balance between high and low conditionality resources, and the nature of high conditionality. The last of these has already been discussed in the earlier section on adjustment; and indeed the question of the balance between low and high conditionality finance is also important in the context of adjustment, since in the case of low conditionality finance there is no requirement on countries to negotiate a detailed programme of policies with quantified performance criteria. Such finance may be deemed appropriate either in circumstances where deficits are self-correcting and self-financing in the longer term or where, even when caused by external factors which are unlikely to be temporary, there is a strong presumption that the countries concerned will take appropriate action to strengthen their balance of payments without the need for Fund pressure to be exerted. The external causation of payments deficits need not on its own, then, be sufficient justification for low conditionality finance. Even so, the marked increase in the proportion of Fund finance in the General Account available only at high conditionality that occurred at the end of the 1970s and the beginning of the 1980s remains difficult to defend on the basis of any equivalent increase in the need for adjustment.

Apart from the distribution between low and high conditionality finance, the total volume of General Account resources has failed to keep pace with almost any proxy of the need for such resources. For instance, the size of Fund quotas expressed in relation to world trade fell by more than 66 per cent between 1960 and 1981. As a result, and as discussed in Chapter 6, the Fund has in general been a relatively insignificant source of finance.

Whether one looks at the SDR Account or the General Account one must conclude that the Fund has little significance as far as international liquidity is concerned. However, this observation, relating to what has happened in practice, contrasts sharply with the influence that could, in principle, be exerted by the Fund.

Even in practice the above conclusion may be somewhat misleading, given doubts about just how important international liquidity is within an international financial system based on flexible exchange rates. There is also the arguement that while the Fund is a relatively unimportant direct source of finance, its activities have an important catalytic effect on both private commercial flows and official aid. To the extent that this is true, it is easy to under-estimate the role of the Fund in the liquidity element of the international financial system.

3.3 The degree of central management

It is quite possible in principle to conceive of an international financial system within which the Fund exercises an important degree of central management, co-ordinating the macroeconomic policies of member countries, including their exchange rate policies, and pursuing a range of internationally agreed policies relating, for example, to SDR creation, debt relief and aid. The reality is rather different. Although flexible exchange rates create the impression that there is no need for such policy co-ordination, since different macroeconomic policies in different countries are in principle made consistent through variations in exchange rates, in practice, and as noted in Chapter 10, flexible exchange rates have failed to insulate economies from one another and have had a number of undesirable features. Furthermore, the move towards the market place that took place in the 1970s automatically meant that the degree to which the international financial system was centrally managed was reduced. One implication has been that the size and pattern of international financial flows has become more unstable and uncertain. As discussed in Chapter 6, private banks out to make profits are under an incentive to lend when prospects look good and pull out when they look bad. As a result, their activities tend to be pro-cyclical rather than counter-cyclical. If, for this reason, reliance on the banks leads to international economic inefficiency, and if, in addition, the distribution of commercial finance is inequitable, a case may be made out for the failure of the market system and for a greater degree of central management of the system under the auspices of the Fund.

3.4 Confidence

The existing set of international financial arrangements cannot be described as one in which there is a great deal of confidence, and there are frequent alarms over impending international financial collapse, even if most of these are unfounded. The lack of confidence applies both to the non-system itself and to the financial status of a range of individual countries.

Here again there is scope for the Fund to make a significant contribution. The restoration of confidence that might be associated with a greater degree of Fund participation in both international adjustment and financing issues would be of considerable benefit to the world economy. The above review of the various elements of any international financial system reveals that in principle there is a large and important role that the Fund could play. Equally clearly, it is a role that the Fund has not been playing since the breakdown of the Bretton Woods system.

4. A ROLE FOR THE FUND

This section attempts to define more precisely a role for the Fund and to examine the means by which it might be activated.

To begin with, it is helpful to recall that the Fund was originally established to encourage international co-operation to cope with recession and protectionism on a world scale and to discourage individual countries from pursuing policies that would beggar their neighbours and eventually themselves. This rationale for the Fund seems as appropriate in the 1980s as it was in the 1940s. Indeed Article 1 of the Fund's original Articles of Agreement describes its purposes in a way that would be widely accepted as very relevant to the world economy now. These purposes are:

(i) To promote international monetary co-operation through a permanent institution which provides the machinery for consultation and collaboration on international monetary problems.

(ii) To facilitate the expansion and balanced growth of international trade, and to contribute thereby to the promotion and maintenance of high levels of employment and real income and to the development of the productive resources of all members as primary objectives of economic policy.

(iii) To promote exchange stability, to maintain orderly exchange arrangements among members, and to avoid competitive exchange depreciation.

(iv) To assist in the establishment of a multilateral system of payments in respect of current transactions between members and in the elimination of foreign exchange restrictions which hamper the growth of world trade.

(v) To give confidence to members by making the general resources of the Fund temporarily available to them under adequate safeguards, thus providing them with the opportunity to correct maladjustments in their balance of payments without resorting to measures destructive of national or international prosperity.

(vi) In accordance with the above, to shorten the duration and lessen the degree of disequilibrium in the international balance of payments of members.

While there can surely be little to criticise in this statement of objectives, the fact of the matter is that they are not being realized. Few commentators would argue that the performance of the world economy since 1973 has been consistent with the 'maintenance of high levels of employment and real income . . . as primary objectives of economic policy', or with balance of payments correction that has not resorted to 'measures destructive of national or international prosperity'. Indeed, as noted earlier, there is some evidence to suggest that in practical terms Fund policies have, on occasion, mitigated against achieving its own objectives as described in the Articles. There is then a case for reform, not so much to change the underlying purposes of the Fund but rather to ensure that these are more nearly realized.

5. A PROGRAMME FOR REFORM

5.1 Enhancement of the Fund's resources

With greater resources the Fund would not only be able to offer more support to countries encountering difficulties in gaining access to commercial finance, but it would also be able to take on a larger share of global recycling in general and there would accordingly be a move back towards the official sector and away from the private sector as a principal avenue through which balance of payments financing takes place. Additional resources for the Fund could be raised in a number of ways. Perhaps the most straightforward way would be to raise quotas. However, given the seemingly constant negotiations that go on over Fund quotas, there is an argument for changing the mechanism through which quota increases come about and for linking them to some index of the world's need for Fund resources; after all, there is already a formula upon which individual countries' quotas are at least approximately based. Quota changes could, for example, be based on a formula which takes into account the value of world trade, the size of payments deficits, the availability of alternative sources of finance, and the macroeconomic performance of the world economy. Alternative ways of raising resources include further sales of the Fund's remaining stock of gold, additional creation of SDRs, or direct borrowing from private capital markets. However, not only does an extended role for the Fund require extra financial resources, it also requires additional staff. It is often forgotten that, by comparison with many international institutions, the Fund is relatively small in terms of the number of people it employs.

5.2 Enhancing the Fund's contribution to adjustment

There are two dimensions to this. The first is directed towards increasing the Fund's effectiveness in its dealings with individual countries, and is based on a modification of the nature, though not the strictness, of conditionality. Less reliance might be placed on the control of credit as the principal means of strengthening the balance of payments, and more emphasis placed on measures such as exchange rate changes or changes in taxes and subsidies, which have the effect of switching real resources into the traded goods sector. The aim would be to improve the balance of payments more by raising real output and less by deflating domestic demand. The focus of attention would be on using policies that are cost–effective in the sense of achieving a given improvement in the payments position while having the minimum adverse effect on output and employment.

This is certainly not to argue that the rate of credit should be ignored, since it is clearly important to keep aggregate monetary demand under control. The idea would be to encourage the Fund to become more flexible in the kind of programmes it supports, according to the circumstances of individual countries.

The second dimension of adjustment relates to global adjustment. The Fund could form a view on the global size and pattern of payments disequilibria, and on the size of sustainable financial flows and on what general policies are appropriate globally. It could then try to ensure that its own policies were consistent with this view. At the very least it could avoid making policy changes that were globally pro-cyclical.

Within this global view the Fund needs to give further thought to ways in which pressure may be brought to bear on surplus countries to adjust their economies, since, as shown in Chapter 10, the expectation that the introduction of flexible exchange rates would eliminate the adjustment asymmetry has not been justified. Various policies are available, such as charges on or the effective freezing of excess reserves, the withholding of future SDR allocations, or a revamped version of the scarce currency clause. What is clear is that for as long as some countries effectively refuse to accept a reduction in their surpluses, it is impossible for other countries, as a group, to be successful in reducing their deficits. Attempts by the latter group of countries to do so, and the induced reactions in the former group, will merely impose a deflationary bias on the world economy.

In the context of global adjustment the Fund should also continue to investigate ways in which the exchange rate system might be modified to provide both flexibility and stability. Evidence clearly suggests that the old Bretton Woods system of the not-very-often adjustable peg was insufficiently flexible but that the system that has replaced it has been insufficiently stable and too exposed to destabilizing speculation. Some regime which lies between these two extremes, such as some version of managed floating or sliding parity, would seem worthy of close scrutiny.

5.3 Enhancement of the role of SDRs

The full potential of SDRs has yet to be realized, and it is important that the Fund should examine why many of its aspirations for the SDR have been thwarted. As discussed in Chapter 5, potential reforms in this area relate to the quality and usefulness of the SDR as a reserve asset, unit of account, and possibly also medium of exchange; the quantity of SDRs created, with again a case existing for some form of indexing to proxies for the need for reserves; the distribution of SDRs and seigniorage associated with their creation; and the means by which the move from a gold and reserve currency system to an SDR system may be most efficiently achieved.

5.4 Modification of existing facilities

Within the context of the modifications to Fund conditionality discussed earlier, the significance of the Extended Fund Facility could be increased. However, there is also a strong case for further modifying the Compensatory Financing Facility so that it affords more compensation against externally generated fluctuations in the terms of trade. The logic of such compensation suggests that there is little reason to discriminate beween export shortfalls and import excesses except to the extent that it is probably more difficult in practice to explain the causes of import excesses and to identify what proportion may be due to expansionary domestic demand policies. However, recent modifications to the CFF which allow for excess payments on imported cereals imply that the Fund has accepted the logic of generalizing the CFF to cover both the export and import components of terms of trade instability.

Given that, as revealed in Chapter 9, terms of trade movements have been an increasingly significant cause of payments deficits, it is also a matter of concern that drawings under the CFF have, for protracted periods, accounted for a falling share of the total use of Fund credit and that only a small percentage of the deterioration in many countries' terms of trade has been compensated for by the CFF. There is a case for increasing the size of the CFF relative to other Fund tranches and facilities. This would raise the proportion of low conditionality finance available from the Fund and would automatically tend to increase the extent to which Fund finance is provided in a counter-cyclical fashion, since drawings under the CFF tend to rise during a world recession.

5.5 Extending schemes for interest rate subsidization

The Fund has already used subsidies to reduce the rate of interest paid by poor countries (somehow defined) on drawings under the Oil Facility and the Supplementary Financing Facility. These schemes could be extended to cover all drawings on the Fund, thereby enabling it to make a greater contribution to the flow of aid. However, Fund aid of this type has a number of significant advantages over more conventional types of aid, not least because it is tied to Fund programmes.

5.6 Depoliticising the Fund

The existing structure of the Fund means that many decisions taken by the executive directors may be influenced by political factors.

There can be little doubt that on a number of occasions loans to particular countries have been affected by the politics of the situation, though not always in a consistent fashion. Granting a greater measure of operational discretion to the Fund's staff might allow it to depoliticise some decisions and to provide a larger measure of continuity.

Furthermore, although changing the representation and voting rights of country groupings within the Fund might have few discernible real effects, measures to reduce the apparent domination of the Fund by industrial countries could contribute to creating a more balanced environment in which the developing countries see themselves as having greater influence and therefore become more committed to the institution. At the same time it would clearly be unwise to take such organizational reforms too far and risk losing the support of industrial countries, whose support of the Fund is absolutely vital to its effectiveness.

This programme of reforms in effect answers many of the questions that have been raised concerning the role and functions of the Fund. To the question 'do we need the IMF?, the answer is an unequivocal 'yes'. But the Fund needs to be reformed in order to become more relevant and effective. To the question, 'should it be an adjustment or financing institution?', the answer is 'both'. In some countries the Fund might be expected to provide little finance but to play an important role, in conjunction with the private international banks, by vetting and validating adjustment programmes. Yet in other countries the banks may be unwilling to lend, and in these circumstances the Fund may be a very important or even almost exclusive source of finance; indeed it may be the lender of first and only resort rather than simply the lender of last resort. In terms of its functions therefore the Fund has to accept that it may have significantly different roles to play in different countries.

To the question, 'should it be a monetary and balance of payments institution or a development agency?, it should be recognized that no clear distinction can be drawn between balance of payments and development issues. Balance of payments policies have implications for development and vice versa. Balance of payments policies should be selected on the twin bases of effectiveness and cost–effectiveness.

6. THE IMPLICATIONS OF REFORM

Two of the principal implications of the reforms discussed above are for the Fund's relations with the World Bank and the private international banks.

6.1 The Fund and the World Bank

As far as the former is concerned the conventional division of labour between the two institutions has blurred over recent years, and would change further if the reforms discussed above were implemented, with the Fund lending more longer-term finance related to structural deficiencies. Traditionally, the Fund has been thought of as a balance of payments related institution concentrating on the macroeconomic management of demand primarily through domestic financial policy. The orientation of the Fund has been towards short-term programme support. The World Bank, on the other hand, is seen as a long-term development institution which, through a mainly microeconomic approach, works on real output and aggregate supply. Most of its support goes to specific projects rather than to programmes.

However, where payments deficits have been caused by structural problems which require long-term solutions, and where development is constrained by the balance of payments, the distinction between payments problems and development problems loses much of its relevance. What has been observed is that the Fund at the end of the 1970s and the beginning of the 1980s moved in the direction of longer-term lending, showing some recognition of development problems, while the Bank started providing structural adjustment loans in support of programmes designed to strengthen the underlying balance of payments.

However, this evolution of the two institutions occurred in an *ad hoc* fashion and it is relevant to ask whether their responsibilities need to be formally redefined.

At the very least through close consultation it should be ensured that their activities do not conflict. More radically it has been suggested by some commentators that they should merge. In between these two extremes there is a range of other proposals; one, for instance, is that countries facing structural payments problems should be encouraged, or indeed required, to apply simultaneously for both an EFF loan from the Fund and a structural adjustment loan from the Bank. Fund staff would then concentrate on the demand side of a jointly recommended package of policies and Bank staff on the supply side. The institutions would in effect be exploiting their areas of traditional expertise but a balanced programme comprising both demand and supply elements would be the outcome.

It is, of course, the relevance of the final programme that is ultimately the most important thing; the institutional question is simply which set of arrangements is most likely to come up with a relevant cost-effective programme, and which set is likely to be most efficient in terms of avoiding the unnecessary duplication of functions. It may well be that closer co-operation, with mutual representation in country missions, is the most realistic option in these terms.

6.2 The Fund and the private banks

The Fund's relations with the private international banks have been highlighted by events in the 1970s as initially the banks moved into balance of payments financing and then backtracked as debt problems arose, usually leaving the Fund to sort out the consequences.

A number of questions arise from the experience of the 1970s and 1980s. Should there be a more tightly defined specialization in terms of function or country dealt with? What is the significance of the catalytic effect of Fund programmes on private lending? Should the Fund make more information available to the banks and would this improve the banks' decision-making? Should the Fund be prepared to guarantee, rediscount, or refinance private loans? Should there be closer co-ordination of lending policies and, if so, how should this be achieved?

While there is scope for more systematic co-operation between the Fund, the private banks, and indeed central banks, and for more co-ordination between Fund programmes and the lending policies of the banks, and while there is a basic community of interest in avoiding serious international financial instability, co-operation is constrained by their different institutional objectives.

7. THE POLITICAL ECONOMY OF REFORM

While one important issue relates to the nature of desirable reforms, another relates to the means by which the reforms are most likely to be achieved? Although there is a view that the Bretton Woods institutions should be scrapped and a new start made, there is a strong case for resisting this option. Not only would it be difficult to get the necessary degree of agreement, but also the reforms mentioned above suggest that in many ways only relatively minor reforms are required in order to increase substantially the beneficial contribution that may be made by the existing institutions.

Since it is in the nature of international financial reform that it usually takes place in a piecemeal fashion, it is probably unrealistic in most circumstances to hanker after reform on a grand scale. However, it is important to have a grand strategy, so that individual reforms fit into it rather than conflict with it. It is this all-embracing view that has been largely lost since the breakdown of the Bretton Woods system. The time is ripe for a reassessement of where we stand and of what type of international financial arrangements will best serve the world economy into the future.

Notes and References

2. WORLD ECONOMIC PERFORMANCE: FACTS, THEORIES AND CONTROVERSIES

1. P is profits, Y is national income and K is the stock of capital, P/Y is the profit share, P/K the profit rate and

$$P/K = \frac{P/Y}{K/Y}$$

It follows that P/K will fall if P/Y falls provided only that K/Y does not fall by as much as P/Y.
2. In terms of a simple *IS–LM* model the rise in the price of oil may have exerted a globally demand deflationary effect by adversely affecting entreprenurial expectations and by raising the global average propensity to save. Both these effects would have shifted the global *IS* schedule to the left. In addition, the uncertainty caused by the rising price of oil as well as its upward impact on the global price level may have increased the nominal demand for money at the global level and have shifted the global LM schedule to the left. In combination, and with other things remaining constant, these effects would account for falling income and rising unemployment. The predicted impact on interest rates depends on whether *IS* shifts further or less to the left than does *LM*. The analysis may be illustrated simply by the diagrams (below).

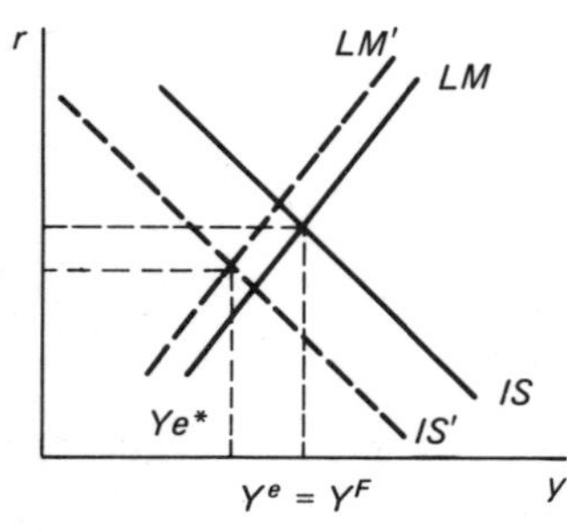

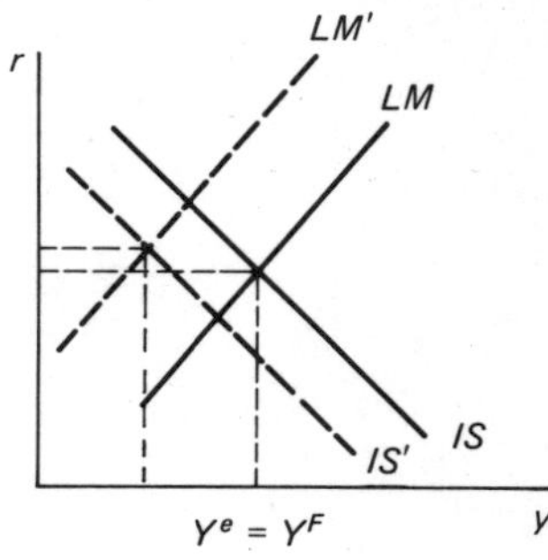

3. THE WORLD'S FINANCIAL SYSTEM IN PERSPECTIVE

1. The United Nations Monetary and Financial Conference.
2. For historical reasons three countries, the United States, the United

Kingdom and Canada, had an unusually large influence in the negotiations at Bretton Woods. Germany, Italy and Japan were enemy countries and were therefore not represented. France was still under German occupation and its government in exile played only a marginal role. Most of the developing countries of Africa and Asia were still colonies and their interests were presumed to be taken care of by the relevant colonial power. LDCs actually represented included Egypt, Ethiopia, Liberia and India. The Soviet Union was brought into the deliberations only towards the end. Although the war was not over, there were unmistakable signs that only the United States and Canada from among the major trading nations of the pre-war world showed promise of emerging from the war with minimum economic damage. Much of Continental Europe had been devastated, as had Japan. Under these circumstances, it was inevitable that the United States would play the dominant role. The war had not only shattered US isolation, it had acted as a spur to productive capacity and technology. The US trade surplus for the period 1946–9 was US $32 billion and she held over 70 per cent of the world's gold reserves.

3. It was understood that the proposed system could not come into full operation until the economic disruption caused by the war had been largely overcome. Provision was therefore made for transitional arrangements to cover the early post-war period. Through the Marshall Plan the US made capital available for the reconstruction of Europe and Japan. In its early years the Fund concentrated on validating devaluations, the most important of which clustered in 1949, and on making loans to Latin America.
4. The Articles of Agreement of the IMF incorporated a 'scarce currency clause' by which members of the IMF were entitled to undertake policies designed to reduce the surpluses of those countries whose currencies were declared scarce in the Fund. By definition, countries with persistent surpluses would find that there was excess demand for their currency and that their currency was therefore scarce. In fact the scarce currency clause was never invoked.
5. International Monetary Fund Committee on Reform of the International Monetary System and Related Issues.
6. *International Monetary Reform: Documents of the Committee of Twenty*, IMF, Washington, 1974.
7. Interim Committee of the Board of Governors of the IMF on the International Monetary System.
8. Joint Ministerial Committee of the Board of Governors of the Bank and the Fund on the Transfer of Real Resources to Developing Countries.
9. The nature of the relation between the oil price rise and floating exchange rates is simply that the oil price generated balance of payments disequilibria of such a size and of such a volatile nature that discrete changes in otherwise fixed exchange rates were incapable of coping with the situation.
10. At the same time, however, the world recession itself, in part caused by the rise in the price of oil, served to reduce the demand for international reserves.
11. See the IMF 'Guidelines for the Management of Floating Exchange

Rates', press release issued by the IMF, 13 June 1974, reprinted in B. Tew, *The Evolution of the International Monetary System 1945–77*, Appendix B.

5. INTERNATIONAL RESERVES: SUPPLY, DEMAND AND ADEQUACY

1. There may be certain circumstances where even substantial holders of gold may act to reduce the price of gold. The US has, for example, sold gold in an attempt to defend the dollar.
2. Although it might be imagined that countries would be anxious to revalue their stock of gold, they have been concerned about the inflationary consequences of doing so. Valuing gold at the market price has other implications, investigated later in this chapter.
3. The reasons for this are investigated in Chapter 6.
4. The explanation usually adopted takes the form of an expectations model of inflation. But there is no unanimity of opinion on such models.
5. Some economists hold the view that SDRs will never prove fully acceptable while they are unbacked. Proposals are then put forward for backing new allocations of SDRs with a basket of primary commodities, the view being taken that this will help to stabilize the world economy. A brief review of such proposals is made in Chapter 11.

6. SHORT-TERM CAPITAL MARKETS, THE PRIVATE BANKS, AND THE IMF

1. It is generally believed that the first Euro-currency transaction was conducted by the Soviet-controlled Moscow Narodny Bank in the early 1950s, with this bank holding dollar-denominated deposits with European banks.
2. They are called *Euro* dollars because the main market is found in Europe, with London being the most important centre. However there are other offshore markets in the Middle East, Asia and The Caribbean.
3. The rate of interest banks operating in the Euromarkets charge each other is the London Interbank Offer Rate (LIBOR). They will normally pay rather below this rate to ultimate lenders and charge something over it – the so called 'spread' – to ultimate borrowers.
4. By the end of 1981 OPEC accounted for nearly 20 per cent of deposits on to the Euro-currency market. The strong preference for Euro-currency deposits is reflected by the fact that OPEC asset holdings of Euro-currencies represented an average of about 33 per cent of their total surplus during 1974–81.
5. Since a higher rate of interest is less likely to deter high risk borrowers who do not anticipate repaying the loan than low risk borrowers who do, a rise in interest rates will raise the average riskiness of the banks'

portfolio. Some borrowers may form the view that the international financial community would not allow them to default, in which case their demand for loans will be fairly inelastic with respect to the rate of interest. In fact a rise in interest rates may have a contradictory impact on the demand for loans, since it will make fewer projects profitable and reduce demand but it will also raise the cost of servicing existing debt and therefore increase the demand for loans. With an upward sloping demand schedule the interest rate becomes unstable.

6. Regression analysis has related borrowing to various proxies for demand and supply factors and has found the demand proxies to be the significant ones. Thus it has been found that borrowing tends to rise as the ratio of reserves to imports falls and as the ratio of debt service to exports rises. The credit rationing approach instead suggests that these relations will have the opposite signs. Similarly, it has been found that the investment rate has a very significant positive impact on borrowing, and this has been taken as further evidence for the demand side explanation. It is rather too early to say that this evidence allows us to draw firm conclusions on the issues raised, since alternative explanations exist for the relations discovered and too little evidence has yet been examined. Banks may, for instance, look to the investment rate as an indicator of creditworthiness, in which case the strong relation may be used in support of the supply approach. Furthermore, other studies using different methodologies and covering different time periods have reached different conclusions.
7. Spreads also seem to vary over time inversely with the level of interest rates, going down as nominal interest rates go up and vice versa. One reason for this might be that higher rates entice banks into more international as against domestic lending and it is this extra competition which bids down spreads.
8. Econometric work that has tried to model the behavioural decision to default has suggested that a significant number of countries have been close to a point where defaulting would be quite rational. Aware of such an incentive, it is suggested that banks ration credit to ensure that the amount of outstanding debt is always just below the point at which a country would opt for default. However, such work may be criticized in particular for the ways in which costs are measured. By, for instance, ignoring trade credit and assuming that loans are used exclusively to finance consumption, it probably under-estimates the cost of default. Certainly the revealed preference of borrowers to avoid default is consistent with the under-estimation of costs in such studies.

7. FOREIGN AID AND THE PRIVATE BOND MARKET

1. In most statistical sources and certainly in the DAC sources used in this chapter the word 'aid' or 'assistance' refers only to flows which qualify as official development assistance (ODA), i.e., grants or loans:

– undertaken by the official sector;

- with promotion of economic development and welfare as main objectives;
- on concessional financial terms (if a loan, at least 25 per cent grant element).

In addition to financial flows, technical co-operation is included in aid. It comprises grants (and a very small volume of loans) to nationals of developing countries receiving education or training at home or abroad, and to defray the costs of teachers, administrators, advisers and similar personnel serving in developing countries.

2. Just how significant the impact of untying would be on donors' export performance in developing countries depends clearly on how effective the tying has been and on how successfully the donor then marketed its exports.

8. DEBT

1. Given that a proportion of future domestic saving pays the interest on external borrowing, the rate of economic growth at this stage will clearly tend to be lower than it would have been without such payments. Yet by enabling countries to overcome financial constraints on growth and allowing their economies to 'take-off', borrowing may still give them a higher standard of living, even when they are repaying loans, than if they had not borrowed in the first place. It all depends on how productively the borrowed resources are used. If borrowing leads to an increase in income and this in turn leads to an increase in savings, after allowing for the saving that goes as interest payments, growth will clearly rise as a result of borrowing.
2. What happens to debt as a proportion of national income depends basically on the relative sizes of the rate of interest and rate of growth of income. Given conditions where both indebtedness and income are increasing, the debt ratio will tend to rise if the rate of interest exceeds the rate of income growth.
3. Although we have discussed the debt ratios using exports as the denominator, the size of debt service payments or interest payments can also be judged against the size of the GDP. While this measure can provide additional insights, it does suffer from the fact that, in the short run at least, not all sources of national income can be used to service debt. Furthermore, there is the question of what exchange rate to use in order to convert domestic currency GDP into GDP expressed in the currency in which debt is measured. Changing the exchange rate can change the apparent size of the debt problem.
4. Technically a distinction needs to be made between rescheduling and refinancing. The latter can be defined as negotiating a new loan of equal or greater amount than the debt due and then repaying it with the proceeds of the new loan. In a sense the distinction is more than simply technical, since the source of refinancing can be other than the original source of the loan, whereas in the case of rescheduling it is the same.

5. The IMF has opened two subsidy accounts in relation to the Oil Facility and the Supplementary Financing Facility. However, these have been exclusively directed towards assisting the least developed countries. Chapter 11 discusses further the possibility of extending the use of subsidies for this purpose.
6. Another group of proposals for alleviating the debt problem focus on the over-lending of banks as its cause. They therefore advocate a greater degree of regulatory supervision, and measures to reduce the book value of old debt in banks' balance sheets. Of course while it may be true that banks overlent in the 1970s the problem in the 1980s may be more that of 'underlending' in response to the newly perceived default risk. The more general problem seems to relate to the intrinsic instability of bank lending.

10. EXCHANGE RATES: SYSTEMS AND POLICIES

1. There is an argument that macroeconomic problems are not *caused* by the exchange rate mechanism and that solution do not lie therein. Instead exchange rate disequilibria reflect inappropriate monetary and fiscal policies. Attention should therefore be directed at these. With appropriate (co-ordinated) macroeconomic policy any exchange rate regime will be satisfactory.
2. Of course if such trade-offs do not exist and unemployment settles at its 'natural' rate, then the unification of inflation rates implied by exchange rate union will involve no long-term unemployment cost. There may, however, still be adjustment costs as well as costs in terms of having to accept a particular unified rate of inflation that would not otherwise be chosen.

11. THE INTERESTS OF DEVELOPING COUNTRIES IN WORLD FINANCIAL REFORM

1. The list includes the Compensatory Financing Facility in 1963, the Buffer Stock Financing Facility in 1969, and the Extended Fund Facility in 1974. A Trust Fund and various subsidy accounts have also been established to assist poor countries.
2. Care has to be exercised here, however, since to an extent the interest rate dispersion reflects the likelihood and expected direction of exchange rate variation in a particular currency.
3. However, this would still leave the problem of dealing with a deficit in the Special Drawing Rights Department of the Fund.
4. The Brazilian and Iranian representatives during the Committee of Twenty meetings proposed onlending to developing countries by the substitution account of the currencies deposited with it. The Brazilian scheme further incorporated the idea that currency loans should be used only to finance imports from the issuers of those currencies, thus neutralizing the effects that an untied scheme might have on reserve growth and inflation.

Further Reading

1. INTRODUCTION

There are a large number of textbooks that present an analytical framework for international financial economics. Personal preferences vary but they include Victor Argy, *The Postwar International Money Crisis: An Analysis* (London: George Allen and Unwin, 1981); Richard E Caves and Ronald W Jones, *World Trade and Payments: An Introduction,* 3rd ed. (Boston: Little, Brown and Company, 1981); Rudiger Dornbusch, *Open Economy Macroeconomics* (New York: Basic Books, 1980 – more advanced); Chris Milner and David Greenaway, *An Introduction to International Economics* (London: Longmans, 1979); and John Williamson, *The Open Economy and the World Economy: A Textbook in International Economics* (New York: Basic Books, 1983).

Useful sources of data on international financial issues are *International Financial Statistics,* published monthly by the IMF; *World Economic Outlook,* published annually by the IMF; and the *World Development Report,* published annually by the World Bank in conjunction with Oxford University Press. Further sources of data as well of information on institutional changes are the IMF's *Annual Report; IMF Survey,* published about twice per month; and *Finance and Development,* published quarterly jointly by the IMF and the World Bank.

2. WORLD ECONIMIC PERFORMANCE: FACTS, THEORIES AND CONTROVERSIES

For a clear and concise discussion of the issues behind assessing macroeconomic performance see Donal Dovovan, 'Measuring Macroeconomic Performance', *Finance and Development,* June 1983. A typically monetarist explanation of world economic performance may be found in Michael Parkin, 'Oil Push Inflation?', *Banca Nazionale del Lavoro Quarterly Review,* June 1980. A good example of the structural, or more precisely sectoral, explanation as applied to the United Kingdom is Robert Bacon and Walter Eltis, *Britain's Economic Problem: Too Few Producers,* second edition (London: Macmillan, 1978). J. Eatwell, J. Llewellyn and R. Tarling, 'Money Wage Inflation in Industrial Countries', *Review of Economic Studies,* October 1974, provides a clear statement of the productivity spill-over, cost push interpretation of the global acceleration in inflation, while Nicholas Kaldor's, 'Inflation and Recession in the World Economy', *Economic*

Journal, December 1976, is perhaps the standard reference on the terms of trade explanation. Equally standard as providing a framework within which the macroeconomic effects of oil price changes may be analysed is Max Corden's, *Inflation, Exchange Rates and the World Economy* (Oxford University Press, 1977), particularly Part 3, 'International Adjustment to the Oil Price Rise'. Michael Beenstock, *The World Economy in Transition* (London: George Allen and Unwin, 1983) provides a provocative explanation of events, resting heavily on the emergence of the NICs, while Louis Turner and Neil McMullen and others, *The Newly Industrialising Countries: Trade and Adjustment* (London, Royal Institute of International Affairs with George Allen and Unwin, 1982) see the global macroeconomic consequences of the NICs as being less central. George Zis, 'Exchange Rate Fluctuations: 1973–82', *National Westminster Bank Quarterly Review,* August 1983, highlights the importance of exchange rate uncertainty in increasing the rate of inflation and level of enmployment. A more thorough review of the global policy options is provided in Graham Bird, 'Beyond the Brandt Report: A Strategy for World Economic Development', *Millennium: Journal of International Studies,* Spring 1980. Meanwhile Chapter 17 on 'Global Macroeconomics', in John Williamson's *The Open Economy and the World Economy* (New York: Basic Books, 1983) provides a review of events in the world economy since the beginning of the 1970s. The statistical sections of this chapter may be conveniently updated from the most recent *World Economic Outlook,* published by the IMF.

3. THE WORLD'S FINANCIAL SYSTEM IN PERSPECTIVE

Most textbooks on international financial economics contain chapters or sections which trace out the evolution of the system. John Williamson in Chapter 15, 'International Monetary Arrangements', of his book *The Open Economy and the World Economy* (New York: Basic Books, 1983) provides a particular succinct treatment. A longer and more detailed account is provided by Victor Argy in *The Postwar International Money Crisis* (London: George Allen and Unwin, 1981). A standard reference on the subject still remains Brian Tew's, *The Evolution of the International Monetary System, 1945–77* (London: Hutchinson, 1977). John Williamson also gives a considered account of the attempt at 'grand design' reform in *The Failure of World Monetary Reform, 1971–74* (London, Nelson, 1977). Other useful references which deal with some aspect of international financial history include, W. M. Scammell, *International Monetary Policy: Bretton Woods and After* (London: Macmillan, 1975); L. B. Yeager, *International Monetary Relations, Theory, History, Policy,* second edition (New York: Harper and Row, 1976; Benjamin J. Cohen, *Organising the World's Money* (New York: Basic Books, 1977); J. Dreyer, G. Harberler and T. D. Willett (eds), *The International Monetary System: A Time of Turbulence* (Washington DC: American Enterprise Institute, 1982). The official IMF histories provide an important primary source of information and documentation. See J. K. Horsefield, *The International Monetary Fund 1945–65* (Washington DC:

IMF, 1969, 3 volumes); and Margaret G. de Vries, *The International Monetary Fund, 1966–71* (Washington DC: IMF, 1976, 2 volumes).

Given the unavoidable lag in publication and the rapid speed at which international financial events sometimes take place, students should bring the material in this chapter up to date by consulting the *IMF Annual Reports, IMF Survey and Finance and Development;* for further details of these publications see the Further Reading for Chapter 1.

5. INTERNATIONAL RESERVES: SUPPLY, DEMAND AND ADEQUACY

Readers should begin by updating the empirical parts of this chapter by consulting *International Financial Statistics*. A useful and relatively brief, though now somewhat dated, survey of some of the issues discussed here may be found in John Williamson, 'Surveys in Applied Economics: International Liquidity', *Economic Journal,* September 1973. From the quite large literature dealing with the demand for reserves, Graham Bird, *The International Monetary System and the Less Developed Countries,* second edition (London: Macmillan, 1982). Chapter 5 runs through the basic theories and attempts to differentiate between the demand in industrial and developing countries. Robert H Heller and Mohsin Khan, 'The Demand for International Reserves Under Fixed and Flexible Exchange Rates, *IMF Staff Papers,* December 1978, analyses the implications of different exchange rate regimes. J. A. H. de Beaufort Wijnholds provides a thorough review of the demand for reserves and the methods for assessing reserve adequacy in his book, *The Need for International Reserves and Credit Facilities* (Leiden: Martinus Nijhoff Social Sciences Division, 1977). A very detailed examination of many issues raised by this chapter, and in particular the role of and reforms to the SDR are contained in George M von Furstenberg (ed.), *International Money and Credit: The Policy Roles* (Washington DC: IMF, 1983). From amongst the many relevant and interesting papers contained in this volume, that by Richard E Cumby, 'SDRs and Plans for Reform of the International Monetary System: A Survey', Chapter 10, is perhaps particularly useful for non-specialist students. For an analysis of whether there should be new allocations of SDRs, see John Williamson, *A New SDR Allocation',* Policy Analyses in International Economics, No. 7 (Washington DC: March 1984). A clear, concise analytical and empirical investigation of multiple reserve currencies may be found in C. Fred Bergsten and John Williamson, *The Multiple Reserve Currency System* (Institute for International Economics, forthcoming).

Amongst the other issues raised by this chapter Nicholas Kaldor, 'Inflation and Recession in the World Economy', *Economic Journal,* December 1976, argues the case for commodity backing for international reserves; and Mohsin Khan, 'Inflation and International Reserves: A Time Series Analysis', *IMF Staff Papers,* December 1979, looks at the relation between reserves and inflation.

6. SHORT-TERM CAPITAL MARKETS, THE PRIVATE BANKS, AND THE IMF

There are numerous texts and articles which deal with aspects of the Euro-currency market. A thorough analysis is provided by George McKenzie in his book *The Economics of the Eurocurrency System* (London: Macmillan, 1976). Other standard textbooks include G. L. Bell, *The Euro Dollar Market and the International Financial System* (London: Macmillan, 1973); E. W. Clendenning, *The Euro Dollar Market* (Oxford: Clarendon Press, 1970); and P. Einzig and B. S. Quinn, *The Euro Dollar System* (London: Macmillan, 1977). A short and clear evaluation is provided both by R. I. McKinnon, *The Eurocurrency Market,* Essays in International Finance, No. 125 (Princeton, 1977); and by David T. Llewellyn, *International Financial Integration* (London: Macmillan, 1980), Chapter 9, 'Euro-currency Markets and their Control'.

An authoritative and comprehensive examination of international banking has been made by Benjamin J. Cohen (with F. Basagni), *Banks and the Balance of Payments: Private Lending in the International Adjustment Process* (Montclair, NJ: Allenheld Osmun, 1981). An excellent, though at the time of writing unpublished, analytical and econometric review of international lending and borrowing is James Riedel's, 'Determinants of LDC Borrowing in International Financial Markets: Theory and Empirical Evidence,' a paper presented to the SSRC International Economics Study Group, LSE, 1983. An interesting though not uncontroversial analysis of the risk of default has been made by Jonathan Eaton and Mark Gersovitz, 'Debt with Potential Repudiation: Theoretical and Empirical Analysis', *Review of Economic Studies,* April 1981. The determinants of creditworthiness are econometrically estimated by I. Kapur, 'An Analysis of the Supply of Eurocurrency Finance to Developing Countries', *Oxford Bulletin of Economics and Statistics,* August 1977. A detailed analysis of many aspects of the IMF's association with developing countries (its principal clients), including the volume, type, and direction of its lending and the 'catalytic effect', is made in Tony Killick, Graham Bird, Jennifer Sharpley and Mary Sutton, *The Quest for Economic Stabilisation: The IMF and the Third World* (London: Overseas Development Institute with Heinemann, 1984).

The empirical sections of the chapter may be updated from *International Financial Statistics, IMF Annual Reports* and *World Financial Markets.*

7. FOREIGN AID AND THE PRIVATE BOND MARKET

The statistical sections of this chapter are rather cursory. Fortunately, additional data may easily be collected from *World Financial Markets* for private capital flows and from *Development Co-operation* for aid flows. These sources also permit the statistics to be updated.

Almost all textbooks on development economics have at least one chapter dealing with foreign aid; see, for example, Salvatare Schiavo-Campos and Hans Singer, *Perspectives of Economic Development* (Houghton Mifflin,

1970), and Hans Singer and Javed Ansari, *Rich and Poor Countries,* third edition (London: George Allen and Unwin, 1982). For a critical assessment of aid, see Peter Bauer and Basil Yamey, 'The Political Economy of Aid', *Lloyds Bank Review,* October 1981, and Dudley Seers, 'Time for a Second Look at the Third World', *Development Policy Review,* May 1983. Paul Mosley, 'The Quality of Overseas Aid', *ODI Review,* No. 2, 1982, provides a concise discussion of the importance of the quality and not just the quantity of aid. A statistical analysis of the distribution of aid has been made by P. D. Henderson, 'The Distribution of Official Development Assistance Commitments by Recipient Countries and by Sources', *Oxford Bulletin of Economics and Statistics,* February 1971, while useful statistical analyses of the effects of aid may be found in V. Bornschier, C. Chase Dunn, and R. Rubinson, 'Cross National Evidence of the Effects of Foreign Investment and Aid on Economic Growth and Inequality: A Survey of Findings and a Reanalysis', *American Journal of Sociology,* 1978, and G. V. Papanek, 'The Effects of Aid and Other Resource Transfers on Savings and Growth in Less Developed Countries', *Economic Journal,* September 1971. Danny Leipziger provides an interesting discussion of the merits of lending as opposed to giving in, 'Lending versus Giving – the Economics of Foreign Assistance', *World Development,* April 1983, while the implications of untying aid are investigated by A. G. Coverdale and J. M. Healey, 'The Real Resource Cost of Untying Bi-lateral Aid', *Oxford Bulletin of Economics and Statistics,* May 1981.

8. DEBT

There is a great deal of statistical information available on debt. The problem is not that of being unable to find enough data but rather that of avoiding getting bogged down in detail. Another problem is that data from different sources may not always coincide. Useful sources include the World Bank's *World Debt Tables* and *World Development Report,* the DAC's *Development Co-operation,* and the IMF's *World Economic Outlook.* Morgan Guaranty's *World Financial Markets* also quite frequently carries useful summary statistics on debt, as does the *IMF Survey* and *Finance and Development,* published jointly by the IMF and the World Bank.

A problem with something as topical as debt is that books can quickly become out of date. With this in mind, two useful volumes are George Abbott's *International Indebtedness and the Developing Countries* (London: Croom Helm, 1979), and Pierre Dhonte's *Clockwork Debt* (Lexington Books, 1980). A brief but still comprehensive treatment of the principal issues is Brahram Nowzad, Richard Williams and others, *External Indebtedness of Developing Countries,* IMF Occasional Paper, No 3, 1981. D. C. McDonald, 'Debt Capacity and Developing Country Borrowing: A Survey of the Literature', *IMF Staff Papers,* December 1982, provides a further useful review of the principal issues. The journal *World Development* ran a special issue in February 1979 dealing with LDCs' debt problems, and it contains a range of papers on various aspects of the subject. For a briefer and more easily readable edited collection of useful articles by Irving S. Friedman, William R

Cline and others see 'Managing International Debt', *Economic Impact*, No. 46, 1984/2. For a comprehensive critical review of various proposals for debt relief see William Cline's, *International Debt and the Stability of the World Economy*, Policy Analyses in International Economics, No. 4, (Washington DC: Institute for International Economies, September 1983). A cogent argument for an extra substantial allocation of SDRs in order to alleviate the debt problem is made by John Williamson, *A New SDR Allocation?* Policy Analyses in International Economics, No. 7 (Washington DC: Institute of International Economics, March 1984).

9. THE NEED FOR AND MEANS OF BALANCE OF PAYMENTS ADJUSTMENT

All textbooks on international finance contain a discussion of many of the issues raised in this chapter. In addition to those books already mentioned, Benjamin Cohen's *Balance of Payments Policy* (London: Penguin Books, 1969) remains a very clear introduction to the subject. For a more advanced treatment, see Robert M. Stern, *The Balance of Payments: Theory and Economic Policy* (London: Macmillan, 1973). A comprehensive and clear analysis of the various approaches to the balance of payments is to be found in A. P. Thirlwall's, *Balance of Payments Theory and the United Kingdom Experience* (London: Macmillan, 1980).

A useful and reasonably brief survey of the monetary approach is M. Kreinin's and L. H. Officer's *The Monetary Approach to the Balance of Payments: A Survey*, Studies in International Finance, No. 43 (Princeton, 1978), while a collection of some of the earlier important contributions to this line of analysis can be found in Jacob A. Frenkel and Harry G. Johnson, *The Monetary Approach to the Balance of Payments* (London: George Allen and Unwin, 1976). and in the IMF's, *The Monetary Approach to the Balance of Payments* (Washington DC: IMF, 1977). For a more critical analysis of the monetary approach, see Thirlwall, *op. cit.*, and D. A. Currie, 'Some Criticisms of the Monetary Analysis of Balance of Payments Correction', *Economic Journal,* September 1976. Thirlwall also provides a compelling explanation of Britain's balance of payments problems in terms of structural factors.

A largely successful attempt to synthesize the various approaches to the balance of payments is contained in John Williamson's *The Open Economy and the World Economy* (New York: Basic Books, 1983). Another seminal contribution towards synthesis in J. A. Frenkel, T. Gylfason and J. F. Helliwell, 'A Synthesis of Monetary and Keynesian Approaches to Short-run Balance of Payments Theory', *Economic Journal,* September 1980.

Mohsin Khan and Malcolm Knight, 'Sources of Payments Problems in LDCs', *Finance and Development,* December 1983, report the results of an econometric investigation into the sources of payments deficits since 1973, upon which the remarks in Section 3.5 of this chapter are based.

Again most textbooks review the range of balance of payments policies. One examination of these from the viewpoint of developing countries which also draws on the available empirical evidence is Graham Bird, 'Balance of

Payments Policy in Developing Countries', in Tony Killick, Graham Bird, Jennifer Sharpley and Mary Sutton, *The Quest for Economic Stabilisation: The IMF and the Third World* (London: Overseas Development Institute with Heinemann Educational Books, 1984). This book also contains a detailed investigation of the IMF's adjustment role. On this latter topic, also see John Williamson (ed.), *IMF Conditionality* (Washington DC: Institute for International Economics, 1982). For an interesting discussion of some aspects of global interdependence, see Michael Stewart, *Controlling the Economic Future* (Brighton: Wheatsheaf Books, 1983), and 'The Realities of Economic Interdependence', *Finance and Development,* March 1984.

10. EXCHANGE RATES: SYSTEMS AND POLICIES

Given the volume of material that now exists on exchange rates, the stage has been reached where surveys of the literature are beginning to appear. A good and concise, though quite demanding, survey is Anne O. Krueger's *Exchange Rate Determination* (Cambridge University Press, 1983). Other useful reviews are J. R. Shafer and B. E. Loopesko, 'Floating Exchange Rates after 10 years', *Brookings Papers in Economic Activity,* No. 1, 1983; Rudiger Dornbusch, 'Exchange Rate Economics: Where Do We Stand?', *Brookings Papers in Economic Activity,* No. 1, 1980; and Morris Goldstein, *Have Flexible Exchange Rates Handicapped Macroeconomic Policy?* Special Papers in International Economics, No. 14 (Princeton, 1980).

Useful collections of articles are J. Frenkel and H. G. Johnson, *The Economics of Exchange Rates* (London: Addison-Wesley, 1978), and 'Proceedings of a Conference on Exchange Rates Regimes and Policy Interdependence', *IMF Staff Papers,* March 1983.

An attempt to synthesize some of the approaches to exchange rate determination may be found in T. Gylfason and J. Helliwell, 'A Synthesis of Keynesian, Monetary and Portfolio Approaches to Flexible Exchange Rates' *Economic Journal,* December 1983.

The case for a managed rate system is clearly articulated in John Williamson's *The Exchange Rate System,* Institute for International Economics, Policy Analyses in International Economics, No. 5, September 1983. Williamson has also provided, 'A Survey of the Literature on the Optimal Peg', *Journal of Development Economics,* August 1982. Surveys of optimum currency areas include Y. Ishiyama, 'The Theory of Optimum Currency Areas: A Survey', *IMF Staff Papers,* July 1975; E. Tower, and T. D. Willett, *The Theory of Optimum Currency Areas and Exchange Rate Flexibility,* Special Papers in International Economics, No. 11 (Princeton 1976); and Peter Robson, *The Economics of International Integration,* Chapter 6.

11. THE INTERESTS OF DEVELOPING COUNTRIES IN WORLD FINANCIAL REFORM

A scene-setting review of the case for modifying the international financial system to give greater assistance to developing countries may be found in the two Brandt Reports, *North–South: A Programme for Survival* (London: Pan Books, 1980), and *Common Crisis, North–South: Co-operation for World Recovery* (London: Pan Books, 1983). A fuller discussion of many of the issues raised in this chapter is undertaken in Graham Bird, *The International Monetary System and the Less Developed Countries,* second edition (London: Macmillan, 1982), which in particular includes a fairly extensive investigation into the SDR-link and commodity reserve currencies.

A more detailed empirical examination of the substitution account from the viewpoint of developing countries is Graham Bird's, 'Reserve Currency Consolidation, Gold Policy, and Financial Flows: Mechanisms for an Aid Augmented Substitution Account', *World Development,* July 1981. The same issue of this journal also carries a compelling argument for using gold to assist developing countries in David A. Brodsky and Gary P. Sampson, 'Implications of the Effective Revaluation of Reserve Account Gold: the Case for a Gold Account for Development', *World Development,* July 1981.

IMF conditionality and its reform is the principal topic discussed in Tony Killick, Graham Bird, Jennifer Sharpley and Mary Sutton, *The Quest for Economic Stabilisation: the IMF and the Third World* (London: Overseas Development Institute with Heinemann Educational Books, 1984).

The case for commodity backing may be found in Justinian F. Rweyemamu, 'Restructuring the International Monetary System', *Development Dialogue,* No. 2, 1980, and in various publications by Nicholas Kaldor; see, for example, his 'Inflation and Recession in the World Economy', *Economic Journal,* December 1976. For an excellent review of commodity backing, see Frances Stewart and Arjun Sengupta's *International Financial Co-operation: A Framework for Change* (London: Pinter, 1982), which also makes out the case for an exclusively southern currency.

12. INTERNATIONAL FINANCIAL INSTITUTIONS: THE ROLE OF THE IMF

Since this chapter draws on discussions in earlier chapters, much of the further reading recommended for these chapters is again relevant here.

For a review of the debate over IMF conditionality, see Graham Bird, 'Relationships, Resource Uses, and the Conditionality Debate', in Tony Killick *et al., The Quest for Economic Stabilisation: the IMF and the Third World* (London: Overseas Development Institute with Heinemann Educational Books, 1984). This book also contains a very much more detailed analysis of IMF conditionality and of proposed reforms. For a clear and concise statement of the Fund's own views, see Bahram Nowzad's *The IMF and its Critics,* Essays in International Finance, No. 146 (Princeton: December 1981). A further discussion of ways in which various Fund facilities such as the CFF and EFF might be reformed may be found in Graham Bird's *The International Monetary System and the Less Developed Countries,* second edition (London: Macmillan, 1982).

A useful examination of the appropriate specialization of the Fund and the

World Bank is contained in John Williamson (ed.), *IMF Conditionality* (Washington DC: Institute for International Economics, 1983), while a much more detailed discussion of the relation between the Fund and the private banks exists in Graham Bird's 'The Banks and the IMF – Division of Labour', *Lloyds Bank Review,* October 1983. Readers should bear in mind that things can change between a book being written and its being published. However, by consulting *Finance and Development, IMF Survey* and *IMF Annual Reports,* they should have few problems in updating the institutional content of this chapter.

Author Index

Subject Index

LIBRARY OF DAVIDSON COLLEGE

Books on regular loan may be checked out for **two weeks.** Books must be presented at the Circulation Desk in order to be renewed.

A fine is charged after date due.

Special books are subject to special regulations at the discretion of the library staff.

MAR. -9 1987